Everett H. Emerson

English Puritanism
from John Hooper to
John Milton

1 9 6 8

Duke University Press

Durham, N.C.

Printed in the United States of America
by Kingsport Press, Inc., Kingsport, Tenn.

For

The Folger Shakespeare Library,
its Director and Staff

Preface

The study that follows seeks to serve several purposes. First, it offers a brief history of English Puritanism from its beginnings to 1641, when its victories transformed and disintegrated it, if indeed it ever had any integration. The history is based on a fresh study of important primary sources and incorporates the findings of modern specialized research in English political, economic, social, religious, and literary history. Second, this history is supplemented by a consideration of the careers of twenty Puritan leaders and spokesmen, from John Hooper in the reign of King Edward VI to John Milton on the eve of the Puritan Revolution. Third, it provides significant samples from the writings of each Puritan whose life and works have been surveyed. Many who are interested in Puritanism have had little or no opportunity to know writings by these men, for their works, with few exceptions, are to be found only in a small number of research libraries. Thus the study attempts to achieve a measure of both breadth and depth.

The new image of the Puritan which is emerging from modern studies is a much more attractive one than the old. The Puritan is now conceived as both more humane and more intellectual, and indeed most Puritan leaders from Walter Travers in the 1570's and '80's to Thomas Gataker in the 1620's and '30's were in fact both humane and intellectual. We are now closer to the truth than we were when the Puritan was thought to be an old, dour, know-nothing killjoy. But the idea that there is such a thing as "the Puritan" is itself of questionable value. Doubtless in the first fifty years of the Massachusetts Bay Colony a kind of intellectual and psychosocial homogeneity did exist among the leaders, but in pre-Civil War England one can clearly discern three things: the establishment of traditions among those dissatisfied with the Church, through the influence of great personalities such as Thomas Cartwright, Laurence Chaderton, and William Perkins on their contemporaries and students; a tendency for Puritanism to be identified with bourgeois values, especially in the 1620's and '30's; and a strong identification with Calvinism as the opponents of Puritanism began to attack it.

In this book are represented some of the varieties of Puritanism as they are to be found in the ninety-year period from 1550 to 1641. During all these years, except for Queen Mary's reign, Puritan reformers were an important force, but a force whose nature was constantly changing. Puritanism is not easy to understand because little except its negative characteristic remained constant: only its desire to purify the Church of England from within. What the desired purity was, never was determined.

The Puritans whose careers are discussed and whose writings are to be found here were controversialists, propagandists, theologians, moralists, preachers, satirists, and philosophers. The book focuses on individual men in the conviction, stated above, that synthetic discussions are apt to be misleading. All those chosen are important for their writings or their activities or both. All of them attacked the established Church, and nearly all met trouble with the authorities for their Puritanism. Others of course were important: Dod, Baynes, Sibbes, Gouge, the two Goodwins, to name a few. But it has seemed best to consider only twenty men with care instead of looking at others more casually.

The writings reprinted here were chosen because of their historical, religious, and literary interest. The selections reflect frequent Puritan concerns: piety, the corruptions of episcopacy and Roman Catholicism, predestination, problems of conscience, the need for a stricter morality and a different church polity, the place of religion in the family, the process of salvation, the spiritual life. Many of these selections speak to the human condition, speak to man now though centuries have passed since they first appeared. I address this volume to whoever is interested in the history, literature, and religion of sixteenth- and seventeenth-century England, and to those who want to know more about the context of our earliest American literature, that of the New England Puritans. Because some of these Puritans still have something to say, I offer their writings in modernized form. I have used modern spelling and punctuation and have broken up some interminable sentences and paragraphs. But in removing what are for most readers impediments, I do not believe that I have essentially altered what was said or the way in which it was said. All dates are in new style.

Any choice of selections is likely to offend many readers. To provide only a portion of a sermon delivered at a time when the preparation and organization of a sermon was a carefully cultivated art may seem very improper. But many published sermons, such as the one of Chaderton's excerpted here, are very long, and some, such as the one of Hooker's presented in part, seem to have been combined with others on the same text when prepared for publication. If only complete or fully unified writings were offered, this volume would be more than twice its present size.

In the preparation of this book I was aided by the Lehigh University Institute of Research, the Folger Shakespeare Library, and Florida Presbyterian College, all of which provided me with grants-in-aid.

To the Folger I am in many ways indebted, for there I had access to a rich mine of primary and secondary materials under the best of all possible conditions. I am grateful to the Folger staff, especially to Dr. Louis B. Wright and Miss Dorothy Mason. I also acknowledge with thanks the cordial helpfulness of the staffs of the libraries of Harvard University, Princeton Theological Seminary, Union Theological Seminary, Amherst College, the University of Massachusetts, Yale University, and Lehigh University. Among the many who have offered helpful advice are John Shawcross of Rutgers University, Barbara Lewalski of Brown University, Frederick R. White, E. Ashby Johnson, and William C. Wilbur of Florida Presbyterian College, Craig R. Thompson of Haverford College, L. J. Trinterud of San Francisco Theological Seminary, A. J. Carlson of Austin College, William Haller of the Folger Library, Larzer Ziff of the University of California, Berkeley, Lawrence Sasek of Louisiana State University, Winthrop S. Hudson of the Colgate-Rochester Theological Seminary, and Charles George of the University of Pittsburgh. Mr. George's article in the *Journal of Modern History* for 1953 was very influential on my thinking. I have been much helped by the members of my graduate seminar on Puritanism at the University of Massachusetts and the readers of the Duke University Press. My greatest debt is to my wife Katherine.

For permission to use the copies in their possession as bases for texts reproduced here, I am grateful to the Folger Shakespeare Library (writings by Bastwick, Cartwright, Chaderton, Dent, Gilby, Hieron, Hooker, Hooper, Martin Marprelate, Perkins, Smith, and Travers), Union Theological Seminary Library (Gataker), Princeton Theological Seminary Library (Dering, Preston, Whately), Yale University Library (Udall), Harvard University Library (Milton, Greenham), and Henry E. Huntington Library (Stock).

Table of Contents

English Puritanism from John Hooper to John Milton

English Puritanism, 1550–1641

Puritanism may be considered to extend back to the days of St. Paul, but one usually thinks of it as a peculiarly English—and, by extension, American—phenomenon. It arose from the special circumstances of the English Reformation, special in that in both the break with Rome and the Elizabethan Settlement religious and political considerations were thoroughly mixed. From the point of view of the twentieth century, such a mixture seems inevitable, and its consequences appear to many students of the period to have been fortunate indeed, since they include the stability which lies behind the golden age of Elizabethan literature. But for many idealists of the sixteenth and seventeenth centuries, the consequences were disastrous, for they included the incomplete reformation of the Church of England. Those so dissatisfied that they actively sought its further purification or refused to abide by the laws of the Church which they considered only partially reformed—these men were the Puritans.

If Puritanism is to be defined as a reforming movement within the already partially reformed Church of England, John Wycliffe and his Lollard followers should not be included in the ranks of the Puritans. It is perhaps not appropriate or desirable to include among the proto-Puritans such reformers of the period of Henry VIII as William Tyndale and Thomas Bilney; religion in Henry's reign was such a changing thing that today's Puritan might be tomorrow's contented conformist. Bilney, who died a martyr in 1531, would have been conformed in Edward's day.

The beginnings of Puritanism

We shall wait until the accession of Edward VI in 1547 to find our first Puritans. The factors that led to their existence then are important for an understanding of Tudor Puritanism in general. The first factor is the least tangible: the English tradition of nonconformity. Although Wycliffe and Tyndale are not properly labeled Puritans, their reformist example was influential. The Lollards, who denied transubstantiation and looked to the Bible for doctrine, kept a kind of Protestantism alive into the 1530's and 1540's, as is demonstrated by the forced abjuration of 218 Lollards between 1527 and 1532 in the London diocese alone. Bilney had preached to East Anglian Lollard communities, and Lollard precedents can be found for most specimens of heresy in Henry's day. Late Lollardry blended easily with early Protestantism; in communities where Lollardry had flourished between 1558, Puritanism developed afterwards.

A second factor is more readily analyzed: the influence of exile on English Protestants. In 1539 the reactionary Statute of Six Articles caused many radical Protestants to flee to the Continent. In Edward's reign the government repealed the unpopular heresy acts and permitted the growth of Protestantism. The Communion service was to be said in English, and a general confession was authorized as a substitute for private confession. But the returned exiles, notably Miles Coverdale, John Rogers, John Bale, and John Hooper, were all well imbued with the ideals of the Continental Reformed churches and were far from happy with the moderate Protestantism being promoted by Thomas Cranmer, Archbishop of Canterbury, and his aide Bishop Nicholas Ridley, neither of whom had seen the Continental churches. (The career of one of these exiles, John Hooper, is discussed below, pp. 47 ff.)

A third factor was the influence of Continental reformers and Reformed congregations within England. The defeat of the German Protestant forces at Mühlberg and the Interim Agreement that followed caused many Protestants to look to England for a new home. Several who came were prominent leaders. The famous theologian Peter Martyr, who had been divinity professor at Strasbourg, came to England and occupied a similar position at Oxford. Martin Bucer, another Continental theologian, occupied the chair of divinity at Cambridge. Though Cranmer invited Lutherans as well as Reformed, only the latter came, and Lutheran influence waned. The Continental Reformed approach to worship could itself be observed in Edwardian England, when a notable church for foreigners, ministered to by John à Lasco, was established in London.

Another factor which encouraged Puritanism was that the middle-of-the-road Protestants, such as Cranmer and Ridley, were inclined to identify themselves with the State. The Erastian tendency toward expediency, a mark of this group (whom I shall call conservatives for lack of a better name), had little appeal for the zealous Protestant, whose mark was his unwillingness to compromise.

Despite the caution of the leaders, the reign of Edward VI was marked by a fairly rapid movement of the Church toward a more Protestant position. The first Book of Common Prayer (1549) prescribed some of the traditional vestments: the cope, vestment, tunicle, and alb for the priest; rochet, surplice, and hood for the bishop. These were objected to by Bucer and others whom one is entitled to call Puritans, and by 1550 even Ridley and Cranmer were eager to have all vestments abolished. The second Book of Common Prayer (1552) ordered a somewhat cautious step towards the Puritan position: neither alb, vestment, nor cope was to be used; the bishop was to wear a rochet; the priest or deacon, only a surplice. The moderation of the change was doubtless dictated by a desire not to offend the conservatives too much. But in the meantime Cranmer and Ridley had forced the Puritan Hooper to wear vestments at his consecration as bishop, after a stubborn resistance that led even to his confinement.

The most radical Puritan accomplishment of Edward's reign is unique in that it was the result of the Crown's intervention on behalf of the Puritans. After the second Prayer Book had been passed by Parliament, John Knox, the vigorous Scottish reformer, preached a strong sermon before the King against kneeling to receive the Communion. Subsequently, against Cranmer's will, the King and Council added the "black rubric" that "no adoration was done or ought to be done, either unto the Sacramental bread or wine there bodily received, or unto any real and essential presence there being of Christ's natural flesh and blood." Cranmer's view of the matter again illustrates the conservative-Puritan opposition. He wrote that the Puritans say, ". . . it is not commanded in the Scripture to kneel, and whatsoever is not commanded in the Scripture is against the Scripture, and utterly unlawful and ungodly." Cranmer believed that "this saying is a subversion of all order as well in religion as in common policy." He went so far as to say, ". . . whosoever teacheth any such doctrine . . . I will set my foot by his, to be tried by fire, that his doctrine is untrue; and not only untrue, but also seditious and perilous to be heard of any subjects, as a thing breaking their bridle of obedience and loosing from the bond of all princes' laws." The words could well have been Archbishop Whitgift's or Archbishop Laud's: the identification of Puritanism and sedition in the minds of conservatives became more specific only at a later date. (After the breach with Rome, attacks on the Church were in a real sense attacks on the State, for the Crown was the head of the Church.)

The events of the last days of Edward and the reign of Mary suggest the direction in which the Church might well have gone in Elizabeth's day. Edward himself showed much sympathy with the Puritan position, and had he come to maturity, he would doubtless have established something resembling the Continental churches. After Edward's death the conservatives were discredited by Cranmer's part in the plot to put Lady Jane Grey on the throne; Hooper favored Mary. When it became clear that Mary was to undertake a policy of persecution, the Puritans stood firm. Hooper and Rogers could have fled, but Rogers instead as proto-martyr set an example for Ridley, and Hooper's horrible slow burning was not soon forgotten.

The development of the reformed Church of England during Mary's reign had many important consequences in the history of Puritanism. The Protestants who fled to the Continent had two allegiances. Some, under Knox, felt that they were now free to establish among themselves a system of discipline and a service of worship of a type which had not been permitted in England. Others, under Richard Cox, wanted their religion to be English, not international. A famous dispute between these parties took place at Frankfort; the Knox group was finally defeated and left.

About a fourth of the Marian exiles lived in Geneva, where a prayer book was prepared which declared that the Marian persecution was God's judgment on the incomplete Edwardian reformation. Among those to use this book were Lever, Pilkington, Sampson, Humphrey, and Coverdale, Puritan notables in Elizabeth's day. But even those who continued to think of themselves as members of the Church of England—Sandys, Cox, Jewel, Grindal—began to adopt a more simple service as time went on. All four of these later became bishops.

The Elizabethan Settlement

When Mary died and Elizabeth acceded to the throne, all indications were that the Church of England would become more Protestant than it had been at the death of Edward. Those who returned from abroad found many churches without ministers because of deprivations, especially in London, where few clerics who had deserted Protestantism now deserted Catholicism. With few clergy available, some Puritans found themselves serving as many as four churches. (The number of qualified ministers remained low until late in Elizabeth's reign: the closing of the monasteries had lessened the number of university students, and many of those who were graduated, especially at Oxford, were attached to the Roman Church. At Cambridge only twenty-eight men commenced B.A. in 1568; in 1583 the number was up to 277.)

Though Elizabeth was clearly Protestant, she was thoroughly unpredictable, especially in the determination of church policy. It was Elizabeth who rejected the proposals of a committee called to revise the Edwardian Prayer Book—a committee which included none of the decidedly radical Puritans but which did include four men who had not left England in Mary's time. Even such a committee went beyond the second Edwardian Prayer Book in recommending stricter discipline and an optional posture in receiving the elements of Holy Communion. But the Queen's ways were more conservative and the new Prayer Book made room for the doctrine of the Real Presence of Christ in the Sacrament. The vestment rule went back even further: the minister shall use "such ornaments as were in use by authority of Parliament in the second year of the reign of Edward VI." As it turned out, however, it was easier to make prayer books and rules than it was to enforce their observance.

The views at this time of those later to be the leaders of conformity are well illustrated by a letter from John Jewel to Peter Martyr (then at Zurich) late in the 1550's. He writes of debate concerning the "scenic apparatus of divine worship": "Those very things which you and I have so often laughed at are now seriously and solemnly entertained by certain persons, (for *we* are not consulted,) as if the Christian religion could not exist without something tawdry." Sandys, another conservative-to-be, referred in 1560 to copes as "popish vestments."

What Elizabeth sought is now clear, though it was not evident to her contemporaries. She wanted to keep as many within the Church of England as possible for reason of State. Her use of cross and candles in her own chapel might cause even such conservatives as Cox to refuse to officiate there, but to the Continental Roman Catholic powers, the use of the cross and candles held out hope that Elizabeth might one day come back to their Church.

The predicament which Elizabeth faced is well described in the advice given her by Armagil Waad, a former public official with Protestant leanings. Since "the Queen [is] poor, the realm exhausted . . . division among ourselves; wars with France and Scotland; the French King bestriding the realm, having one foot in Calais and the other in Scotland; steadfast enmity but no steadfast friendship abroad," the best policy is to

proceed to the reformation having respect to quiet at home, the affairs you have in hand with foreign princes, the greatness of the Pope, and how dangerous it is to make alteration in religion, specially in the beginning of a prince's reign. Glasses with small necks, if you pour into them any liquor suddenly or violently, will not be so filled, but refuse to receive that same that you would pour into them. Howbeit, if you instil water into them by a little and little, they are soon replenished.

When Elizabeth made appointments to key church positions, she neglected completely the Genevan group of former exiles. Her choice for Archbishop of Canterbury was Matthew Parker, her former tutor, who had lived quietly in England in Mary's time. Parker, a lover of quiet decency and order, had till now been a relatively obscure figure. William May, whose background was similar to Parker's, became Archbishop of York. Of the exiles, Jewel, Sandys, Pilkington, Grindal, and Parkhurst were among those named bishops. Though all were moderate Puritans at first, and winked at nonconformity, all in time came to identify themselves with the standing order, even if they never fully lost their sympathy for their former brethren. Their attitude is explained by Grindal, who wrote to the Continental reformer Bullinger in the midst of a dispute about conformity in 1567.

We, who are now bishops, on our first return, and before we entered on our ministry, contended long and earnestly for the removal of those things that have occasioned the present dispute; but as we were unable to prevail, either with the Queen or the Parliament, we judged it best, after a consultation on the subject, not to desert our churches for the sake of a few ceremonies, and those not unlawful in themselves, especially since the pure doctrine of the Gospel remained in all its integrity and freedom. . . .

It was just a matter of time, he thought. Bishops Horne and Grindal describe their attitude as toleration of the undesirable (sign of the cross in baptism, kneeling at the Lord's Supper, and other matters) "until the Lord shall give us better times." Perhaps, thought some, better times would come with the next ruler. Edward's and Mary's reigns had been short; perhaps Elizabeth's would be too. And a likely successor, Henry Hastings, was decidedly Puritan in his sympathies.

Besides her recognition of the importance of a middle course, Elizabeth was offended with the Genevan party, those most opposed to compromise, because of the teachings of their leaders, John Knox and Christopher Goodman. In Mary's reign these men had taught that a woman could not serve as ruler and that monarchy is by nature elective. (The later fortunes of the Genevan group can be followed through the life and letters of one of them, Thomas Wood.)

The fact that the Elizabethan Church was as Protestant as it was resulted from the Queen's forced dependence at the beginning of her reign on Protestant divines, like Grindal and Jewel, who had been on the Continent, for Elizabeth found the bishops who remained in office from Mary's reign unwilling to permit any change. And it seems likely that the Elizabethan Settlement would have been even more conservative had not peace with Catholic France permitted Elizabeth to give in somewhat to Protestant pressure in Parliament. Perhaps her resentment of this pressure was responsible for Elizabeth's unwillingness to make later concessions to Protestant desires. The Elizabethan compromise seems to have been largely a compromise between the cautious Protestant Elizabeth and the moderate Protestant clerical leaders. Even the non-Geneva Protestants maintained that they accepted this compromise only temporarily.

The earliest indication of forthright Puritan rejection of the settlement seems to be Thomas Sampson's unwillingness to serve as Bishop of Norwich. Another notable Puritan, Thomas Lever, was (for a year) unwilling to accept a regular living under the settlement.

The history of Puritanism during the eighty years from 1560 to 1640 consists largely of efforts to change the settlement of 1559, efforts made through every available channel. In 1559 the Convocation, the Assembly of the Clergy, had been dominated of course by Roman Catholics, since the Elizabethan Acts of Supremacy and Uniformity, separating the Church of England from Rome and making it Protestant again, had yet to be passed. But the Convocation of 1563 was a different matter. Many decidedly Puritan proposals were made, and a set of six articles, more moderate than most, failed by only one vote to pass the lower house of Convocation. These would have abrogated saints' days, omitted the sign of the cross in baptism, abolished organs, left kneeling at Communion to the discretion of the diocesan bishop, required the surplice only, and caused the minister to face the people in prayer. The reason for the defeat of these articles and even of some which Archbishop Parker favored is not entirely clear, though it has been noted that several who accepted Mary's religious position opposed the measures; it seems likely that pressure from court was a factor. But, more important, those former exiles who had agreed to accept for a time the ceremonies which Elizabeth required had no clear and united policy, though they were already less sympathetic with the more militant Protestants.

Although it was this Convocation which drew up and adopted the Thirty-nine Articles—fully acceptable in doctrine to the evangelical, radical wing—the Puritans did not after this time have any faith in Convocation as an instrument of reform. A nonconformist later described the Puritan view of the matter: "The clergy investigate and resolve, but in this case they establish and fix nothing unless the Queen and the Archbishop approve."

The same situation was soon found to prevail in Parliament, though the House of Commons was less pliant than Convocation to the Queen's pressure. After being occupied with the problem of the succession in 1563, the House of Commons heard in 1566 proposals that were later to be identified with Puritanism: limitation of nonresidence among the clergy, improvement in the quality of the ministry, and elimination of corruption in the presentation of clerical livings. The first bill passed gave statutory confirmation to the Thirty-nine Articles, but the Queen instructed the Lord Keeper that the bill was not to proceed. Elizabeth's view was that no bill concerning religion was to be introduced without her knowledge and assent. Though the House of Commons delayed a government bill to show its disapproval of her action, no effective reforms were made in Parliament in this decade.

The controversy over vestments

Not only was Elizabeth capable of denying the initiative in religious matters to others, she could also take it herself. In 1561 the Queen made a progress through Essex and Suffolk, where she observed that few or none of the clergy wore the surplice, for Bishop Parkhurst was far from strict in commanding the wearing of vestments. A letter of complaint from the Queen's Secretary, Cecil, soon was in Parker's hands.

But the nonconformist position was as yet by no means defensive: for it was common for those who refused the vestments to attack those who did wear them, even from the latters' pulpits if opportunity permitted. Peter Martyr advised Thomas Sampson in 1559 that he might wear vestments rather than be deprived but urged that at any rate Sampson should preach against them. One minister boasted of having preached seven or eight sermons against vestments. The division of the Church on this issue of course delighted the Roman Catholics, who somehow managed to persuade many that the requirement of vestments was an indication that the old doctrines were to be restored.

Matters were brought to a head when Parker decided to try to settle the matter by means of a conference with leading representatives of the nonconformists, whom he called "Precisians," Sampson,

Dean of Christ Church, Oxford, and Laurence Humphrey, President of Magdalen College, Oxford. All three agreed that vestments were by nature indifferent, but the Oxford heads held that because they had been consecrated to idolatry, they were not to be worn. Later it was suggested by the opponents of vestments that if what was indifferent were commanded, it ceased to be indifferent. As the argument continued, Parker sought the advice of his episcopal colleagues, only to find considerable difference of opinion among them.

In January 1565 the Queen once more took the initiative. In a very revealing letter to Parker she charged that in the province of Canterbury he had permitted variety "not only in opinions but in external ceremonies and rites." The former she expressed no further concern with; but the latter should, she commanded, be eliminated by the action of Parker and the other members of the commission for ecclesiastical causes, the body later to be called the High Commission. (The Supremacy Act had given the Crown visitational and corrective jurisdiction in spiritual matters, to be exercised by a commission appointed by the Crown.)

Parker's first step was to write to Grindal, Bishop of London, relaying the gist of the Queen's letter, and ordering him to instruct the other bishops to see that the laws were obeyed and to report disturbances to Parker. By early May 1565, Parker, with Grindal, Cox, and others of the High Commission, prepared a draft of ordinances for the establishment of conformity. The Queen felt herself free to edit the ordinances, but made it plain that she would not herself authorize them. Parker, though forced to action by the Queen, was obliged to act on his own authority, despite his protests to the Queen. The effect of the Queen's strategy was that the nonconformists blamed not her but Parker and the bishops for the troubles they came to experience. (The Queen may have been motivated by a desire to avoid offending the country gentry, who possessed the bulk of the power of nominating the parish clergy.)

The peculiar tone of the "Advertisements," as Parker called them when they were published in 1566, can be shown by quotation of a part of them:

. . . by diligent conference and communication . . . and at last by assent of the persons before said [Parker and some of the other bishops] these orders and rules ensuing have been thought meet and convenient to be used and followed; nor yet prescribing these rules as laws equivalent with the eternal Word of God, as of necessity to bind the consciences of her [the Queen's] subjects in the nature of them considered in themselves, or as they should add any efficacy in more holiness to the virtue of public prayer, and to sacraments; but as temporal orders mere ecclesiastical, without any vain superstition, and as rules in some part of discipline concerning decency, distinction, and order for the time.

The rules themselves were as mild as the passage quoted, but they did require the surplice, and they did suggest that there was to be no further reform in the Church.

In the meantime Parker had continued to press Sampson and Humphrey to conform on the issue of vestments and also the use of wafer bread in administering the Communion—the nonconformists insisted on common bread. In the midst of his efforts with his two troublesome Puritans, Parker found that they had been appointed to preach at Paul's Cross outside St. Paul's Cathedral, in Lent. Preaching at Paul's Cross was an honor. After investigation, Parker found that the arrangements had been made by Robert Dudley, later Earl of Leicester, one of four members of the Queen's Council who from time to time intervened in behalf of the Puritans. (The others were Cecil himself, Sir Francis Knollys, and Sir Francis Walsingham.) In April Parker moved to have both men deprived, and in time Sampson was forced to leave Christ Church, the first deprivation for Puritanism in Elizabeth's reign. For some reason Humphrey was not suspended, and Sampson later had several preferments, including a prebend at St. Paul's Cathedral.

Humphrey's eloquent defense of himself in a letter to the High Commission explains the Puritan position:

Religion requireth naked Christ to be preached, professed, and glorified, that *graviora legis* by the faithful feeding pastors should be furthered; and after that go by order tending to the edification, and not destruction advanced. . . . But alas, a man qualified with inward gifts for lack of outward shows is punished, and a man outwardly conformable, inwardly clean unfurnished, is let alone, yea exalted. The painful preacher for his labor is beaten, the unpreaching prelate, offending in greater, escapeth scot-free. . . . Is not this Pharisee?

Although Humphrey and Sampson were Oxford men, Cambridge

was already more inclined than Oxford to nonconformity. When Parker indicated that vestments were to be worn at Cambridge, many leading men there including heads of colleges protested to Cecil, the Chancellor of the University. Among these, ironically was John Whitgift, later the Puritans' leading opponent; Matthew Hutton, later Archbishop of York, was another. Cecil was unwilling to listen, and in time the University was reduced to order.

In March 1566 Parker decided to take further steps towards requiring conformity. About one hundred and ten of the clergy from London and Southwark were called to Lambeth, where Parker asked them to sign their assent to the Thirty-nine Articles, the wearing of the prescribed vestments, and the rubrics of the Book of Common Prayer. Thirty-seven refused, and Parker felt that this number included the best men. They were suspended and warned that failure to subscribe in three months would mean deprivation. Parker's chaplains served in the churches of the nonconformist ministers, but there was great quarreling between the substitutes and the people, who frequently favored those suspended.

The warfare soon spread to the press. Robert Crowley, who had begun his propaganda efforts in Edward's reign with the publication of *The Vision of Piers Plowman*, wrote with the assistance of others who likewise had been deprived *A Brief Discourse Against the Outward Apparel and Ministering Garments of the Popish Church*. (The work has been called the first Puritan manifesto.) Parker promptly replied. Bishop Grindal of London arranged the publication of a letter from the important Continental Protestant Heinrich Bullinger, in which he supported the Bishop's position. One result of the dispute was an increasing sense of separation from each other felt by both parties. In time Parker's program to exact conformity was carried out, despite the Archbishop's generosity and the refusal of Bishops Parkhurst, Sandys, and Pilkington to deprive nonconformists.

The Queen continued to demonstrate her political astuteness in her dealings with religious matters. In 1564 and 1565 Elizabeth was trying to placate the Roman Catholics and even went so far as to reprimand the Dean of St. Paul's when he preached against images. But the successes of the Scottish Protestants soon caused Elizabeth to exert less pressure on the Puritans—too late for a few, who had withdrawn from the Church to separatism, disappointed in their efforts at reform from within.

Presbyterian Puritanism

The year 1569 is a landmark in the growth of Puritanism, for in that year many Puritans turned to presbyterianism, in part doubtless because they now thought of the bishops as their opponents. The occasion of the shift to presbyterianism was the election of Thomas Cartwright as Lady Margaret Professor of Divinity at Cambridge and his subsequent series of lectures on the first two chapters of the Acts of the Apostles. He found occasion to deal in these lectures with questions of ecclesiastical policy. Cartwright taught that congregations should have a voice in the elections of ministers, who should be capable of teaching. (Many ministers of the time were not.) Seeing presbyterianism, church government by elders or presbyters, as the polity of the apostolic church, he proclaimed it to be the model for all time and condemned all other types of church government. He taught that the title of archbishop should be done away with and that bishops should have only spiritual functions.

The lectures drew many hearers and a considerable number of sympathizers. Attacked by Grindal (now Archbishop of York) and others, Cartwright was defended by thirty-three members of the University. Finally the heads of the college, under the leadership of John Whitgift, silenced him in the summer of 1570, and in December he was deprived under new statutes of the University. Soon he found his way to Geneva, where he studied the working of the presbyterian system in practice. (Cartwright's life and writings are discussed below, pp. 66 ff).

The split between the bishops and the Puritans was widening, and Cartwright's lectures had converted more to Puritanism than had any force since the exile. Furthermore, it changed the character of the reform movement: now the Puritans were no longer concerned merely with the elimination of minor details. They sought to establish a complete program. (Of course some Puritans never accepted the need for such sweeping changes.)

The presbyterian program in its simplest form would have required that each parish choose its own minister; each minister would have a congregation, and all ministers would be equal. Each congregation would be governed by a group of elders from its own number: the session. The sessions would unite to form governing bodies called classes, presbyteries, synods, or assemblies, and these bodies would have the power of excommunication when it was approved by the congregation concerned. An alternative to presbyterianism and episcopalianism, congregationalism, was favored by some Puritans but did not really become a competitor until the 1630's. Its fundamental characteristic is that it recognized no power beyond the congregation; each congregation is independent.

Among those identified with Cartwright and presbyterianism at this time were Edward Dering (discussed below, pp. 55 ff.), Thomas Lever (a leader of the Marian exiles), and John Foxe. Author of the immensely influential *Book of Martyrs* (properly *Acts and Monuments*), Foxe found that his scruples about vestments kept him from preferment after the exile. His extreme Protestant views colored his conception of church history and thus popularized Puritanism, for six editions of the English translation of his book were published during Elizabeth's reign, the first in 1563. Copies were to be found in many churches.

From Cartwright's time on, Cambridge was the headquarters of Puritanism. (Oxford had for a time inclined towards Puritanism through the preaching of Sampson and Humphrey. The Earl of Leicester, who favored the Puritans, was able to help them in his position as Chancellor of Oxford University.) Many Puritan leaders are identified with Cambridge: Chaderton, Perkins, Preston, Hooker, Cotton, to name just a few. At the Westminster Assembly, after the triumph of Puritanism, sixty-two clergymen represented Cambridge to thirty-four for Oxford.

The Admonition *controversy*

Puritans continued to seek changes in the Church through Parliament. In the House of Commons of 1571 sat a number of Puritans, notably Peter Wentworth, Anthony Cope of Harwell, and Tristram Pistor. They introduced a complete Puritan program embodying all of the pre-presbyterian Puritan demands: the elimination of vestments, confirmation, giving of a ring in marriage, kneeling at communion, and private baptism. But all that was obtained was a bill which limited subscription to "the Articles of Religion which only concern the confession of the true Christian faith and the doctrine of the sacraments." Subscription to the ceremonial articles was not required. In this Parliament the Queen once again showed herself opposed to further reform of the Church and was directly responsible for the failure of the Puritan campaign; the bishops themselves were also revealed to be opposed to the desires of their Puritan brethren.

In 1572 another bill was introduced in Parliament. It would have limited the Act of Uniformity to Roman Catholics and would have permitted the clergy, with the consent of the bishop of the diocese, to use the form of service of the French and Dutch congregations in England. Even though the bill was soon much watered down, the Queen once more took steps to see that changes in religion were not even discussed.

The Puritans could not expect to get anywhere by attacking the Queen, but they were not reluctant to attack Parliament. Before this session was over, Thomas Willcocks and John Field published *An Admonition to Parliament*. Written in a lively, vigorous style and providing a full statement of the Puritan—now presbyterian—policy, it had an explosive effect and led to an extended debate. The *Admonition* declared that Parliament must eliminate the pomp and idleness of the bishops and their claim to be the exclusive source of ordinations; it asked for the establishment of congregational choice in the selection of a minister; it sought the substitution of sitting for kneeling, and the revivification of excommunication. (A common Puritan complaint was that the Church did little to punish sin.) Significantly, it renewed the argument which Cranmer had singled out for attack: that nothing should be done in the Church without express warrant from the Word of God.

The new Puritan position of Cartwright and the *Admonition*, a thoroughly radical one, was soon understood to be such by the bishops. Matthew Hutton, Dean of York, explained to Cecil that to start with,

it was but a cap, a surplice, and a tippet; now it is grown to bishops, archbishops, and cathedral churches, to the overthrow of established order, and to the Queen's authority in causes ecclesiastical. These reformers would take the supreme authority in ecclesiastical matters from the prince, and give it unto themselves with the grave seigniory in every parish.

The *Admonition* was answered in 1572, the year of its publication, by Whitgift, who now became the Puritans' chief opponent. Whitgift's *Answer to a Certain Libel Entitled An Admonition to the Parliament* was in time answered by Thomas Cartwright, in his *Reply to An Answer* (1573), a work which had several printings. (A portion is published below.) Whitgift's *Defense of the Answer* appeared in 1574, and Cartwright's two parts of *The Second Reply* were published in 1575 and 1577. In the latter year the Queen commanded the suppression of the *Admonition*, Cartwright's replies, and other related works. The dispute itself is too complicated for discussion here, though it should be noted that Cartwright's system is at variance with the Tudor view of the State, for to Cartwright, the magistrate is not the head of the Church, but only a member, and the Church is autonomous.

The ministry and economics

The chief obstacle to the establishment of the presbyterian system was the lack of a learned ministry. As early as 1559 the Queen's injunction commanded, "Because through lack of preachers in many places of the Queen's realm and dominion the people continue in ignorance and blindness, all parsons, vicars, and curates shall read in their churches every Sunday one of the homilies. . . ." The first book of homilies was published in 1547, and a second in 1563, supplementing with twenty sermons the twelve of the first. These were to be used by all ministers who did not have a license to preach. A small proportion of the churches had a licensed preacher because the livings of many churches were inadequate to maintain an educated clergyman; the income of many was less than ten pounds a year.

The Puritan solution to the shortage of preachers was the establishment of "prophesyings," meetings of ministers for the study of the Bible. They began in Norwich, where Parkhurst was bishop, in 1564 and became common throughout England. But in 1574 they were stopped by the Queen's command in Norwich, and in 1576 the Queen commanded Grindal, Archbishop of Canterbury after Parker's death, to suppress the prophesyings everywhere. His refusal and his subsequent sequestration by Elizabeth are famous. Elizabeth bypassed Grindal and ordered the bishops to stop the public exercise by those "pretending to a more purity." But in many areas prophesying continued, under other names.

In his letter to Elizabeth explaining his position Grindal complained that

this Church of England hath been by appropriations . . . spoiled of the livings, which at the first were appointed to the offices of preaching and teaching. . . . So as at this day, in opinion, where one church is able to yield sufficient living for a learned preacher, there be at least seven unable to do the same.

In 1603 close to four thousand of the slightly more than nine thousand ecclesiastical livings in England were in the hands of impropriators; that is, the revenue went not into the hands of the parson but largely to the Crown, the nobility, bishops, university colleges, and cathedral deans and chapters. An especially unattractive Elizabethan bishop, William Hughes of St. Asaph's, held an archdeaconry and sixteen livings, and leased lands to his wife, children, sisters, and cousins. A more typical bishop was Bancroft, who held six livings. The large number of episcopal impropriations has caused Christopher Hill to suggest that they "must have helped— to say no more—many a minister to ask himself whether the New Testament really did authorize prelatical bishops." Puritanism, for some ministers, was, according to Hill, "a knife and fork question." Though the Bishop of Carlisle reported in 1599 that in his diocese no vicar or curate had an income of more than seven pounds, yet the clergy as a whole was severely taxed. Constituting only about 2 per cent of the population, they paid in the reigns of Elizabeth and James about 25 per cent of the principal direct tax.

The Puritan demands for a learned ministry were on at least two occasions—the petition to Parliament in 1584 and the Millenary Petition of 1604 (to be discussed later)—accompanied by practical suggestions for economic reform. Two examples may be noted: prebends of cathedrals should be reserved for preaching ministers; and lay impropriations should be taxed 1/6 or 1/7 of their real value, the proceeds to maintain preaching ministers. The adoption of such suggestions might have improved the situation in one nine-county area where there was a ratio of one resident preaching minister per four churches, and where the clergy included tailors, fishmongers, grocers, and painters, many of whom continued in their first vocation while serving as ministers. Lord Burghley refers to how the Bishop of Lichfield and Coventry made "seventy ministers in one day for money, some tailors, some shoemakers, and other craftsmen." Most of them he knew to be "not worthy to keep horses."

Puritan losses and gains

The accidents of history often had profound consequences for Puritanism. Thus the more active Puritans were dealt a severe blow in 1573 when a half-mad Puritan, intending to kill Sir Christopher Hatton (thought to be a crypto-Catholic), instead wounded Sir John Hawkins. The event thoroughly discredited the Puritans and caused the government to take steps to enforce conformity. Dering was silenced, Field and Willcocks kept in confinement, and a warrant issued for Cartwright's arrest. But by 1575 the invasion of England by Roman Catholic seminary priests made it seem desirable for the government to leave the less troublesome Puritans alone for a time.

Before his powers were taken from him, Grindal tried to execute certain reforms. The only Marian exile to serve as Archbishop of Canterbury, Grindal felt an obligation to his past. He had accepted a bishopric at Elizabeth's accession on the grounds that reform was possible from within. He now sought to bring about the reforms he envisioned by the creation of new canons. He wanted to control pluralities, eliminate baptism by midwives (a practice which implied the Roman Catholic view of baptism), and improve the quality of the clergy. But Grindal was stopped by the Queen's intervention from effecting these and other reforms. Elizabeth could not see that they were necessary because of her rage against the Puritans.

Despite the Queen, Puritan practices were used here and there. At Bury the Genevan form of worship was followed, magistrates exercised jurisidction usually reserved for ecclesiastical courts, and the Bishop of Norwich's authority was flouted with some success. Other towns were well established Puritan centers. At Ashby-de-la-Zouch, the Puritanism of Henry Hastings, Earl of Huntington, had an enduring effect. Hastings patronized Anthony Gilby, who wrote *A Pleasant Dialogue Between a Soldier of Barwick and an English Chaplain* (1581), a highly effective piece of anti-episcopal propaganda. (Gilby is discussed below, pp. 93 ff.) After Gilby, the famous Puritan Arthur Hildersam served as minister for nearly forty years at Ashby, though he was silenced four times. At nearby Leicester was established a lectureship that brought Lever, Sampson, and Gilby there.

The career of another influential figure also illustrates the continuity of Puritanism. John Dod, minister at Hanwell, Oxfordshire, from 1585 to 1604, was a prominent personage in the Puritan movement in the last part of Elizabeth's reign. After a long period during which he was silenced, he preached again in Charles's reign at Fawsley, Northamptonshire. Here he was intimate with Sir John Eliot, Pym, and Hampden. And to him John Preston came that he might die in his presence, as had Job Throckmorton twenty-seven years earlier. Dod was co-editor of Cartwright's posthumous works. (Both Preston and Throckmorton are discussed below, pp. 236 ff. and pp. 133 ff.)

Nonconformists would have suffered much more severely in Elizabeth's reign had it not been for the influence of members of the Queen's Council. The Council forced Aylmer, Bishop of London, to accept William Charke as preacher at Lincoln's Inn, though Charke had been expelled from his fellowship at Peterhouse for nonconformity. Charke's influence at Lincoln's Inn and Gray's Inn, and Walter Travers's influence at the Inner Temple caused the lawyers to be more sympathetic with Puritanism. The union of the lawyers and the Puritans was a contributing factor in the dispute which lead to the Civil War.

Aylmer's power was limited also in his work as head of the High Commission, which exercised much of the power of the Church. The hindrance was the Queen's adviser Cecil, now Lord Burghley, who wrote Elizabeth about 1583 that "the bishops, in these dangerous times, take a very ill and unadvised cause, in driving them [the Puritans] from their cures." For, he said, though they are over squeamish and nice in their opinions, and more scrupulous than they need; yet, with their careful catechising and diligent preaching, they bring forth that fruit which your most excellent majesty is to desire and wish, namely the lessening and diminishing the papistical numbers . . . and, for those objections, what they would do if they got a full and entire authority in the Church; methinks they are *inter remota et incerta mala*, and therefore, *vicina et certa* to be considered.

Whitgift as archbishop

A new period of persecution began in 1583 with the advent of John Whitgift to the see of Canterbury. Whitgift, unlike Grindal, had experienced only the Church of the Elizabethan compromise, and he thoroughly identified himself with it. Whitgift's chief complaint with the state of affairs when he came into power was that he did not have power enough. He took steps to increase the dignity of his office by maintaining an army of retainers and living in state like a rich nobleman, none of which helped his reputation with the Puritans.

Whitgift's first instrument for attacking nonconformity was the so-called Articles of 1583. Though some desirable changes were made in the rules concerning the quality of those to be ordained, most of the rules were intended to eliminate nonconformity. No one was to preach except those who said the service and administered the sacraments according to the Book of Common Prayer and signed a statement that nothing in the Book of Common Prayer is contrary to the Word of God and that *all* of the Articles of Religion were "agreeable to the Word of God." Formerly, as noted above, the law required only acceptance of the articles concerned with faith and doctrine.

Whitgift made the tactical error of reactivating the ecclesiastical courts, an action which brought down upon him the jealous wrath of the common lawyers and contributed to their alignment with the Puritans. Because of the dubious legality of many of the clerical regulations, the Puritans, who now had expert legal assistance, were in a good position to defend themselves against suspension. Whitgift thereupon abandoned the practice of suspension for non-subscription and instead made use, through the High Commission, of the *ex officio mero* oath, which required those called to answer any questions which might be asked. Failure to agree to the oath resulted in imprisonment for contempt. Silence was accepted as confession. With this weapon, forty-five ministers were suspended in one day in Suffolk.

In time a compromise was effected between Whitgift and the bishops on the one hand the Puritans on the other. Walsingham arranged a conference between Bishops Sandys, Cooper, and Whitgift and the Puritans Travers and Sparke in the presence of Burghley, Lord Grey, and Leicester. There it was agreed that Walsingham would assist the authorities in preserving order in the Church provided Whitgift would limit his suspensions to those who would not promise to use the Book of Common Prayer. Though new ministers were required to approve the book as altogether scriptural, most ministers previously suspended were restored. In some ways a Puritan victory, the agreement was so used by Whitgift as to bring new prestige to the Establishment.

Whitgift gradually brought about a profound change in the Church, striking to his contemporaries. In 1590 George Cranmer wrote to Richard Hooker that before Whitgift became Archbishop,

the greatest part of the learned in the land were either eagerly affected or favorably inclined that way [towards Puritanism]. The books then written for the most part savored of the disciplinary style; it sounded everywhere in pulpits, and in the common phrase of men's speech; the contrary part began to fear that they had taken a wrong course; many which impugned the doctrine yet so impugned it, not as being the better form of government, but as not so convenient for our State, in regard of dangerous innovations likely to grow. . . .

Cranmer felt that it was thanks to Whitgift that the Puritan ascendancy over episcopacy had been reversed.

The organization and collapse of presbyterianism

For a good while Puritans had reason to believe that a victory for them was in the offing. The prophesying movement had borne fruit and throughout England a presbyterian church structure was being quietly erected. John Field and Thomas Willcocks, authors of *An Admonition to Parliament* (1572), had as early as 1570 established a brotherhood of London presbyterians. These presbyterian Puritans came from a younger and more rebellious generation than such earlier Puritans as Thomas Sampson. They sought to organize Puritan congregations into a formal presbyterian organization. But by 1575 the threat of the Counter-Reformation for a time created a spirit of unity among English Protestants, and presbyterianism was neglected. Under Whitgift's vigorous attack, Puritans once again turned to presbyterianism, this time more openly. William Fulke's *Brief and Plain Declaration Concerning . . . Discipline and Reformation* (1584), Walter Travers's *Ecclesiasticae Disciplinae . . . Explicatio*, and Travers's "Disciplina Synodica" provided the platform, and Field was again the organizer and also the historian. Many now joined the cause who had always been Puritans but had hitherto deliberately avoided identifying themselves with the hard core of the party, Cartwright, Travers, and Field, Cambridge dons William Perkins and Laurence Chaderton (both discussed below, pp. 154 ff. and 102 ff.), the famous Essex preacher George Gifford, and John Dod. But even now, these men, like both earlier and later Puritans, were convinced that in England there should be one Church. They were far from being separatists.

Outward indications of the vigorous intentions of the presbyterian Puritans first appeared as early as the Parliamentary session of 1584–85. At that time the Puritans made a great effort to influence Parliament by concentrating influential Puritans, clergy and laity, in London and preparing a survey of the state of the ministry throughout England. Apparently efforts were also made to elect to Parliament those favorable to Puritanism.

Even though the establishment of the presbyterian discipline was only barely under way, to some hasty idealists the time seemed ripe to replace episcopacy. At the Parliament bills were submitted to replace the Elizabethan Prayer Book with a Genevan model and to substitute presbyterianism for episcopacy. This extremist move obstructed even modest Puritan reforms, which were stopped repeatedly by the Queen and Whitgift. Whitgift's treatment of the House was full of contempt.

Sir John Neale has called Whitgift "a sinister figure, whose prac-

tices were a menace to the emergent liberalism of English life."
P. M. Dawley considers him to be thoroughly identified with the
Anglican tradition, a man of "integrity of mind and devotion of
spirit." But the two agree as to Whitgift's tremendous influence
on the course of English history. For before Whitgift the presbyterian Puritans had been, in Neale's words, "able to shake Crown,
Church, Council, and Parliament." Even the determined Elizabeth
might not have been able to keep the Puritans down without Whitgift, who considered Puritanism the Church's great enemy. The
sympathies of the House of Commons suggest that Elizabethan
England was decidedly pro-Puritan, but Whitgift learned a lesson
from the Puritans and by using borough patronage established in
the end of Elizabeth's reign a solid if small pro-Establishment party.

The collapse of the presbyterian movement came about from
causes in addition to Whitgift's determination. In 1588 Field died,
and soon after Richard Bancroft, Whitgift's chaplain, in a sermon
at Paul's Cross, exposed Puritan plans to establish presbyterianism.
Using some of Field's papers, he made a more complete exposure
in 1593 in *Dangerous Positions and Proceedings Published and
Practiced in the Land of Britain* and *A Survey of the Pretended
Holy Discipline*.

The many frustrations which the Elizabethan Puritans had suffered weakened the cause of those who sought reform within the
Church, and the 1580's and 1590's saw a considerable increase in
separatism. Henry Barrow, John Greenwood, and John Penry, leaders in the movement, all were executed in 1593, but the impatient
continued to be attracted to the ideal of "pure religion" even if
they had to leave the Church to have it.

The minor successes and major defeats of Puritanism during the
age of Elizabeth should not blind one to the fact that before the
development of an Anglican school of piety—identified with Lancelot Andrewes, George Herbert, and Jeremy Taylor—many of the
most devout members of the Church of England were Puritan in
sentiment. As A. G. Dickens puts it, ". . . the vast majority of
Elizabethan Englishmen who cared deeply about religion were
either Roman Catholics or Anglican Puritans. Until 1600 or later
that spirituality within the Anglican Church which could reason-
ably be described as non-Puritan remained rather exiguous."

Some important Puritan books

Ironically, an important cause of the collapse of English presbyterianism was a Puritan success. The seven tracts written mostly under the pseudonym of Martin Marprelate and published in 1588 and 1589 are violent attacks, mostly personal, on the bishops and their deputies. Though they were answered—solemnly by Bishop Cooper in *An Admonition to the People of England* and scurrilously by the literary wits John Lyly, Thomas Nashe, and Gabriel Harvey—the Marprelate tracts were a popular success. But they shocked sober-minded Puritans like Cartwright; and sober-minded statesmen, however sympathetic they had been to Puritanism, now vigorously persecuted the movement. Puritanism to many now meant anarchism, and the organization all but collapsed. (A discussion of the Marprelate affair follows, pp. 133 ff.)

A book that was to have been a fundamental blow in a Puritan propaganda campaign was belatedly published in 1593. Entitled *A Part of a Register*, it seems mild indeed after Martin Marprelate's attacks, but it is of interest to the student of Puritanism because it demonstrates the sense of continuity and of belonging to a tradition felt by many Puritans. The work tells of the persecution of Puritans great and small from Dering to Udall.

To all but men of great faith, the Puritan cause seemed lost by 1593. But there were some Puritans with such faith, many believing that Elizabeth's successor-to-be, James Stuart, would make England presbyterian like Scotland. Time would reveal that these hopes were ill-founded. As early as 1590 Elizabeth warned James that there were some who would have no kings but a presbytery. For a time James seemed to favor presbyterianism. Thus in 1592 he said that the presbyterian church in Scotland was "the sincerest kirk in the world," and he favored the Puritans John Udall, Thomas Cartwright, and Robert Waldegrave. But soon he sought greater power. He wanted to master the religious situation in Scotland. Finally he forced episcopacy on the church there.

During the 1590's Puritan energies found a new outlet and also a new concern with theology. When Archbishop Whitgift called in all copies of Nicholas Bownd's *Sabbatum Veteris et Novi*

Testamentum, a new issue arose between Puritan and episcopalian over the proper observance of the Sabbath. This dispute was to assume real importance in the seventeenth century.

Puritanism and Calvinism

A more meaningful dispute, one concerned with basic theology, was foreshadowed in the 1590's. Almost every Anglican divine who expressed theological opinions in Elizabeth's reign was a predestinarian, and most were Calvinists. But in 1595 William Barrett, fellow of Gonville and Caius College and a candidate for the B.D. degree, preached a Latin sermon containing liberal theological views: he questioned the absoluteness of predestination. Barrett was immediately labeled a heretic by Cambridge officials. A dispute followed, finally settled when Whitgift and other officials drew up the Lambeth Articles, which are thoroughly Calvinistic. Whitgift was very near the truth in saying that they were "uniformly professed in this Church of England"; at any rate, they were up to the time he set them forth. His plan was to publish them for general use, but at this point the matter came to the attention of the Queen. Her view, as always, was that to define is possibly to exclude. No fuller definitions were in order, she felt, and without them shifts in theological opinion could be made more easily. The theological embarrassments which the Queen prevented will be obvious to one who reads the revisions of the Westminster Confession.

Despite the Queen's views, Whitgift had the power to send the Articles down to the University, and he instructed the authorities to see that nothing contrary to them was taught. The Vice-Chancellor, as resident head, informed Barrett that he must prepare a recantation. But while the proceedings were still under way Lord Burghley objected and the case was dropped. But this dispute gave a new emphasis to theology, and Burghley's action promoted departure from strict Calvinism. A group of four prominent University men, two professors and two heads of colleges, indicated their sympathy with the liberal principles, now that to do so was clearly safe. Among these men was Lancelot Andrewes the great preacher, soon to be a leader of the liberal wing.

Now for the first time an organized anti-Calvinist group existed, and at Cambridge, the very headquarters of Puritanism. Soon the Puritans, whose activities had been mostly concerned with efforts to remove the remnants of "popery," all but abandoned their attack in order to shift to the defense of their fundamental principles of predestinarian Calvinism.

Even more important for the century that followed was Richard Hooker's *Of the Laws of Ecclesiastical Polity*, the first four books of which were published in 1593. Hooker's testimony to the value of human reason, profoundly contrary to Calvin's thought, adumbrates a basic difference between the episcopalian and the Puritan in the days of Laud. Hooker and his followers identified episcopal church government with the law of reason; Puritans became identified as Calvinists and Biblists. The staunchest defenders of Calvinism and Puritanism did not—perhaps could not—reply to Hooker. But except for Whitgift, the leading defenders of Calvin's views were Puritans: William Perkins and Willliam Whitaker, Regius Professor of Divinity at Cambridge.

King James and Puritanism

Although Puritanism had passed through many stages during the long reign of Elizabeth, the more moderate Puritans in 1603 were hoping for the same reforms that many had sought in 1560. On the accession of James the desire for reform found a voice in the Millenary Petition, so called because supposedly a thousand ministers supported it. It sought to eliminate the cross in baptism, confirmation, the surplice, the ring in marriage, profanation of the Lord's Day, and bowing at the name of Jesus. It asked for the use of only the canonical Scriptures in the lessons prescribed for reading in church services and for a less strict requirement concerning rest on holy days, the elimination of the *ex-officio* oath and of excommunication by lay officials, limitation of subscription to the articles of religion and royal supremacy, improvement of the ministry, and limitation of nonresidency.

James expressed willingness to listen to the Puritan demands, much to Whitgift's sorrow. The Puritans were filled with hope. Their hour, it seemed, had come at last. England was in tumult.

But hopes and fears began to die when James issued a proclamation declaring that he believed the Church of England to be near to the condition of the primitive church and did not intend to alter the church polity. He made it plain, however, that he was quite willing to listen to Puritan requests.

A conference was planned; it has come to be called the Hampton Court Conference. Among the Puritans there was much discussion of who should represent the reform party. The choice probably would have been Cartwright, but he died in 1603. Travers, the author of the organizational manual, was an obvious candidate. But those finally chosen were moderate Puritans not prominently identified with presbyterianism. They were Laurence Chaderton, head of Emmanuel College, Cambridge; John Reynolds, head of Corpus Christi College, Oxford; John Knewstubs, fellow of St. John's College, Cambridge; and Thomas Sparke, rector of Bletchley, Buckinghamshire.

What is remembered most about the conference is James's declaration that he would make the Puritans conform, or, said he, "I will harry them out of the land." But M. H. Curtis recently has shown that the Hampton Court Conference was not, in itself, the defeat for the Puritans it has generally been conceived to be, for James's own ecclesiastical policy agreed in part with that of the Puritans. Like them he wished to improve the ministry of the Church. Like them he wanted to modify the jurisdictional powers of the Church's chancellors, vicars-general, and other authorities. Like them he sought the unity of the Church, though not a unity based on radical revision of its structure.

On the first day of the Conference the King met with episcopal authorities (Whitgift and eight other bishops) and members of the Council. James put the bishops on the defensive by asking them to tell him what needed reforming. The bishops, unwilling to admit the existence of defects, were obliged to recognize certain difficulties in the Book of Common Prayer.

On the second day, James and his Council met with the Puritans, Bishops Bancroft and Bilson and several deans; on the third day a plenary session was held. James's position was moderate. He did indeed tell the Puritans to obey the bishops, but he also told the bishops to be considerate to the Puritans and treat them "more

gently than ever they had before." He showed anger only when
Reynolds favored modifying the hierarchy to permit a compromise
between episcopacy and presbyterianism.

On the final day James ordered sweeping changes, all thoroughly
in line with Puritan wishes. Of the more than ten changes, four
may be mentioned as typical: the administration of private baptism
by women and laymen was to be abolished; chancellors, officials,
and commissaries were to lose the power of excommunication;
parish livings were to be improved to encourage a more learned
ministry; and the abuses of nonresidency and pluralities were to
be corrected. These decisions might have had the effect of strength-
ening the moderate Puritans. But it rested with the episcopal party's
members on the ecclesiastical committees to bring about the changes,
and they saw to it that nothing was done except for slight mod-
ifications in the Book of Common Prayer, which were almost
compensated for, in the Puritan view, by the new "errors and
inconveniences . . . added in the new book."

Archbishop Bancroft and Puritanism

In Elizabeth's reign only the more militant Puritans were presbyterians. But the bishops' reluctance to follow the king's wishes
in time persuaded moderate Puritans that episcopacy itself, not
merely errors which episcopacy permitted, was its real enemy.
They continued to try for changes. In 1604 they petitioned Convocation for toleration of nonconformity. Even one of the bishops
spoke for it. But Bancroft, president of Convocation since Whitgift's recent death, demanded conformity.

As we have seen, regulations governing conformity were constantly changing in the late sixteenth century. The Church had
no real constitution; only fragments in the form of canons, tem-
porary forms and orders, statutes, and injunctions. The definition
of the Church was deliberately kept vague to permit as many as
possible to hold membership conscientiously. But Bancroft, who
now succeeded Whitgift as Archbishop, believed that the Church
could not be strong unless the Puritans were excluded from it.

In 1604 Convocation made an elaborate set of canons, a real
constitution for the Church. One of these defined a member of

the Church as one who, among other things, believes that the rites and ceremonies of the Church can be used with a good conscience and that government of the Church by bishops and archbishops is agreeable to the Word of God. Excommunication was the penalty set forth for lack of such belief. The canons also censured those who maintained that the form of worship used in the Church of England was corrupt, and even those who affirmed that the synod which drew them up was improper. Although the House of Commons drew up bills which declared the key canons void, and the Puritans argued that many of the canons were illegal because opposed to statute law, nothing was done to modify them.

James permitted a period of probation for the Puritans during which the bishops would deal with the recalcitrant, especially the learned and the mild, but when leniency had little effect the Privy Council ordered bishops to proceed to deprivation. The Puritans were labeled those who "under a pretended zeal of reformation" really acted from "a factitious desire of innovation."

Puritan lecturers, clergymen without benefices whose income came directly from their auditors, were easily deprived because they held office by benefit of license from the bishop. But those who held livings were advised by the common lawyers to take the position that a clergyman had the same right to his house and church that any other subject had to his home. Bancroft consulted with the Lord Chief Justice and the Attorney General and proceeded to deprivations.

One of the most revealing incidents of the time took place when the Archbishop of York, no friend to the Puritans, protested that the Roman Catholics, not the Puritans, were the troublemakers in his area. He was advised that he was mistaken; the King opposed the Puritans because they were presbyterians and the King believed that his own position as monarch depended on the maintenance of episcopacy. His expression "no bishop, no king" appears to have represented a sincere belief.

The universities were crucial for the continuity of Puritanism. Therefore the King forbade anyone to be admitted to a degree unless he swore his adherence to episcopacy and his rejection of presbyterianism. A thorough investigation was made into religious affairs at Cambridge. There Emmanuel College, a Puritan strong-hold, agreed to conform, and Chaderton, its head, reported that he had no Puritan recusants in the college. But Puritanism was not yet shut out of Cambridge, not even in 1616 when all candidates for degrees were required to signify their acceptance of the King's supremacy, the Prayer Book, and the Thirty-nine Articles.

The King was now flooded with petitions which favored the nonconformists threatened with suppression. Many pamphlets de-fended the Puritans. At least one was forthrightly presbyterian. Another was a famous defense of congregationalism, William Brad-shaw's *English Puritanism* (1608). Those who replied to the Puri-tan pamphlets often found that the hierarchy admired this form of piety; it was a great help in finding preferment.

Despite all the furor, only about ninety were deprived at this time. Some, however, were prominent, notably Arthur Hildersam and John Dod. Others not so well known refused to conform but were allowed to remain at their posts. Some Puritans, believing that ceremonies though inexpedient were indifferent, conformed. Among the laity nonconformity manifested itself in an unwilling-ness to receive the Holy Communion.

Puritan memories apparently were short, for once again the Puritans turned to Parliament for protection. They succeeded in obtaining a majority sympathetic to their position, but when the House of Commons discussed religion, the King sent instructions for the House to consult with Convocation. Consult with the bishops the House of Commons would, but only with the bishops as members of the other House of Parliament. To this proposal the bishops would not agree. The Commons then proceeded on its own and passed a bill affecting the educational standards of the clergy. The House of Lords failed to act on the measure. Petitions to the King and more efforts at conference likewise got nowhere.

The defeat of Puritanism in the 1590's, the dashing of the hope that James would make changes of the sort the Puritans sought, the new canons, and the continued vigilance of Bancroft, now Arch-bishop of Canterbury, led to a gradual but radical change in the nature of Puritanism, and the change in time led to an increase in the strength of Puritanism. With no hope that a basic reform could be brought about in the Church, Puritan ministers decided to cultivate their gardens; they poured their energies into preaching. As their good fortune would have it, this shift in tactics took place just at the time when Puritanism had much to offer the rising commercial and industrial classes. Puritan insistence that the Sabbath be kept holy and that the old system of holy days, inherited from the Middle Ages, be dispensed with offered a work cycle highly desirable to the new classes. Puritanism offered much more: a morality fitted to meet the needs of the day, a recognition of the value of education and labor, and an insistence on what Christopher Hill has called "the spiritualization of the household." (See, below, the sermons of Richard Greenham and Thomas Gataker.) Thus the Puritanism of the first third of the century flourished in those areas where rapid transformations were taking place, in London and the market towns. The bourgeois virtues are the very virtues which Puritanism came more and more to encourage: hard work in one's calling, frugality, seriousness, and high moral standards. When the government's policies towards trade and colonization proved unsatisfactory to many of the newly rich, it was not unnatural for them to identify themselves further with the Puritans, who opposed another aspect of the government, its religious policy. Thus it became common in the 1620's and '30's to label as Puritans those opposed to the standing order in Church and State, hierarchy and court. This union of interests is nicely epitomized by John Preston, who was a leader of both groups of the opposition. (Preston is discussed below, pp. 236 ff.)

New support for Puritanism

During the period 1610-20 James had kept down opposition in the Commons by appointing those who sided against him to positions in the government or by seeing to it that they were defeated for election when next they stood. But by 1626 a genuine opposition party existed, united because its members had common views on questions of political power and constitutional rights, more than by opposition to the religious establishment. The development of this opposition party was doubtless a manifestation of the rise of the middle class, but the occasion for the crystallization of the opposition was the growing power of the arbitrary Buckingham and the new revolutionary Puritan leaders Pym and Sir John Eliot.

Meanwhile a fundamental change was taking place in the relationship of Church and State. In Elizabeth's reign considerable tension had existed between the two, for Church officials such as Parker considered the Queen to be unsympathetic to spiritual matters, while she found ecclesiastical officials unsympathetic to her need for Church lands with which to reward her faithful servants. Elizabeth had made problems for herself, for she chose good men for the episcopate. James, however, made preferment in the Church a matter of patronage operated by his favorites, notably Buckingham. Such a situation was very harmful to the Church, for those who now ruled the Church were men like George Abbot, successor to Bancroft in 1610 as Archbishop of Canterbury, and Bishop John Williams. As a modern scholar has said, almost all of James's bishops were "indifferent, negligent, secular." Only Bancroft's canons and officials who followed his policies after his death kept the Church from ruin during the eighteen years from 1610 until 1628, when William Laud became Bishop of London.

The history of Puritanism was profoundly affected by the six Archbishops of Canterbury who ruled the Church during the years 1559-1645. Parker (1559-75) had been moderate, if unsympathetic; Grindal (1575-83), suspended in his second year, was sympathetic to Puritanism but could do little to help it; Whitgift (1583-1604) and Bancroft (1604-10) were effective opponents of the Puritans. But Abbot (1611-33) was not interested in continuing their efforts; indeed, though he was not an active or effective administrator, he favored a mild kind of Puritanism. Abbot was suspended in 1627, and Laud (1633-45) was determined to crush the Puritans utterly.

Abbot's eighteen years in office were crucial for the Puritans. Had Bancroft lived longer or had James appointed as his successor an archbishop who followed his policies, it is doubtful that Puritanism could have flourished and triumphed as it was to do, though forces of real importance favorable to Puritanism were at work. One of these was the proposed marriage of Prince Charles and the Spanish Infanta, for any evidence of Roman Catholic sympathies at court created a backlash that helped Puritanism. Another factor the strength of which is difficult to determine, was a growing concern with the moral laxity that became more noticeable in the early seventeenth century. It seems likely that religious disagreements both in England and abroad contributed to a lowering of moral standards.

The Puritans were shocked when the King himself issued a proclamation that seemed to them to encourage dissipation. This was the so-called *Book of Sports*, which authorized Sunday games. (Charles reissued it in 1633.) Hard work for six days a week— including the hundred-odd holy days recognized by the Church, then a day for preaching and the Bible: this was the Puritan calendar. When they were not struggling against the bishops, the Puritans could devote themselves to this kind of morality and the accompanying bourgeois virtues.

The chief opponents of the Puritans in the 1620's and 1630's were the Laudians and the followers of Lancelot Andrewes, perhaps the first party except the Puritans, within the reformed Church of England, to develop a churchmanship which did not lean heavily on the State. The Puritans had been accused of seeking innovations. But the school of Andrewes, and later of Laud, clearly advocated changes; thus Puritans could now think of themselves as conservatives. Three aspects of the party's teachings were especially resented by the Puritans: its emphasis on ceremonial, its patience in dealing with sin, and its opposition to predestinarianism.

Puritanism, Crown, and Court

In Elizabeth's day both Puritans and episcopalians were Calvinists, as the Lambeth Articles suggest. In 1597, soon after the dispute over Barrett, the Puritan Samuel Ward observed ominously that "Lutheranism begins to be established," and by the early seventeenth century, Lancelot Andrewes's influence was felt. Yet as late as 1608 Calvin's *Institutes* were recommended at Oxford as containing the best system of divinity. In the early years of the century a reaction to Calvinism took place in England just as it did on the Continent, but James's fame as a Calvinist probably prevented it from spreading very fast, as did his moderate support of the strict Calvinists at Dort in 1619 and his attack on the liberal theologian Vorstius in 1611.

But in 1622 an Oxford clergyman preached that subjects may take up arms against their sovereign in defense of their religion. The sermon soon came to the King's attention. Upon investigation, James learned that the preacher had used as his authority Pareus's commentary on Romans. Since Pareus was a leading Continental Reformed theologian, James felt that the theology of the modern Calvinist divines was a threat to his position. Therefore he sent injunctions to Oxford and instructions to his Archbishop that students should no longer study the writings of the Reformers but only those of the Scriptures, the Councils, the Fathers, and the medieval schoolmen.

Soon it was clear that the way for a preacher to receive recognition was to preach the King's prerogative and to avoid the subject of predestination. The party most opposed to Puritanism identified itself with the King and his court and before long the King went so far as to instruct his Archbishop that the good example of the court clergy was to be followed: no one except the bishops was to preach on predestination, the efficacy of grace, or similar subjects. The court party could now be clearly distinguished from the Puritans, one focusing on the royal prerogative and the duties of a subject, the other still treating, not always discreetly, the prohibited subject of predestination. A theological split now existed in the Church. The debate continued, centering on the interpretations of the Thirty-nine Articles. The court party took the position that if a liberal interpretation was not to be given the Articles, at least the Calvinist interpretation was not to be given either. King Charles, who succeeded his father in 1625, accentuated the division by his support of the court party. In 1628 Charles published a declaration that the Articles were not to be disputed but accepted "in the true, usual, literal meaning of the said articles." The following year the House of Commons passed a resolution that the Articles were to be understood in the light of the Lambeth Articles.

To a certain extent it is strange that the episcopal party remained identified with Calvinism as long as it did, for the party did not follow Calvin or the Continental Reformed churches on such important matters as the retention of traditions and church polity. On these matters the Puritans were much closer to the Continental practice and therefore found it easier to remain attached to the predestinarian theology.

After the death of Calvin, theologians of the Reformed tradition systematized and dogmatized his teachings; the result is known as Protestant Scholasticism or High Calvinism. This theology is elaborately set forth in William Perkins's *A Golden Chain*, subtitled *The Description of Theology* (1590) and in *The Marrow of Sacred Divinity* (1623) of William Ames. Especially in this English form, High Calvinism emphasized double predestination or God's decrees of predestination and reprobation. (Perkins devotes six chapters to reprobation.) Just as the development of voluntarism or Arminianism on the Continent resulted in a stronger emphasis on the doctrine of the irresistibleness of God's saving grace, so in England every attempt by the court party to deny or ignore predestination led the Puritans to insist more on the centrality of the doctrine. This process culminated after the Puritan triumph in the official Calvinism of the Westminster Confession (1645–1647).

The struggle between King and Commons on the question of predestination, although perhaps of less importance than economic disagreements between the two parties, should not be considered minor. It was emotionally important to the increasingly influential Puritan members of Parliament, for they saw several changes, as threats to Protestantism: Arminianism, the increasing pomp and dignity of the bishops, and the related divine right theory of episcopacy (now a matter of vigorous contention between Puritans and episcopalians). (The term "Arminianism" came to denote in the 1620's and '30's not merely a theology but all that Puritans objected to in the Church.) Similarly threatening were the government's new friendliness to Catholic Spain and the concessions, small though they were, made to English Catholics. Francis Rouse's speech delivered in Parliament in January 1629 vividly stated the issues as he saw them:

. . . mark it well, you shall see an Arminian reaching out his hand to a Papist, a Papist to a Jesuit, a Jesuit gives one hand to the Pope and the other to the King of Spain; and these men having kindled a fire in our neighbor's country, now they have brought over some of it hither, to set on flame this kingdom also. Yea, let us farther search and consider whether these be not the men that break in upon the goods and liberties of the Commonwealth, for by this means they make way for the taking away of religion. It was an old trick of the devil: when he meant to take away Job's religion, he began at his goods, saying to God, "Lay thy hand on that he hath, and he will curse thee to thy face." Either they think thereby to set a distaste between prince and people, or to find some other way of supply to avoid or break Parliaments, that so they may break in upon our religion, and bring in their own errors. But let us do as Job did: he held fast his religion, and then his goods were restored to him with advantage; and if we hold fast God and His religion, these things shall be added unto us.

For Rouse, the basis for all of the disputes between the court and the bishops on the one hand and Parliament on the other was religion.

Although Elizabeth had known what it was to have her wishes opposed in Parliament, only in James's reign did the House of Commons establish itself as a separate power in English politics. The Stuarts had to deal with the Commons because of the court's financial needs. With the rise of political factions in the State, the government turned to the Church to strengthen its position, for although the Church was no longer by any stretch of the imagination a threat to the State (Elizabeth had supposed that it potentially was), the Church had powers which the Crown could use. And when the House of Commons attacked corruptions in the Church at the same time it defied James's demands, the bond between the bishops and the court, established by James's policy of patronage, grew stronger. The division of power in England which is suggested by Rouse's speech, a division with the House of Commons and Puritans on one side, court and episcopal power on the other, was the result.

The union of the court and the bishops was extended by William Laud. First as Bishop of London (1628), then as Archbishop of Canterbury (1633), Laud wielded immense power, for in addition to holding ecclesiastical offices he served as a privy councillor from 1626 and as chancellor of Oxford from 1633. He came to be virtually Charles's first minister. With Charles he pursued absolutist policies which were in every way anathema to Puritans. (C. V. Wedgwood has said that Charles's actions "might well be interpreted as those of a King who sought to strengthen the authority of the Crown by extending the authority of the Church.") Laud sought to eliminate presbyterianism in Scotland, forbade Englishmen abroad to attend Calvinistic services, and distressed Puritan lawyers by extending the role of the ecclesiastical courts. Most offensive of all was his policy which historians call "thorough." Because of lax administration during Archbishop Abbot's years, many Puritan practices had come to be accepted in parishes throughout England. Now Laud was determined to eradicate every manifestation of Puritanism. Puritans would have been thoroughly offended had Laud stopped here. But in addition he so emphasized and amplified the Church's ceremonies that he appeared to many to be leading England back to Rome, and he opposed Calvinism.

Laud helped to unite the leaders of the Church with the King's interests and with opposition to the House of Commons, which was inclined to Puritanism. Laud's distrust of Commons naturally affected his attitude towards political matters as well. If the House of Commons judged unfairly High Churchmen (those who stress the Church's authority), Laud seems to have reasoned, the House of Commons was also unfair to the King's political views. Laud continued the policy of rewarding those who emphasized the royal prerogative at the expense of Parliament. A notable example is the rise of Roger Manwaring, who in a sermon spoke of parliaments as of no importance and preached in the royal presence that not to obey the King is to incur damnation. The House of Commons impeached him and fined him a thousand pounds. Charles pardoned him, gave him a choice living, and soon made him a bishop. And no parliaments were called from 1629 to 1640.

Another indication of the sense of separation felt by both episcopalians and Puritans in the 1620's is the organization which Puritans established to make certain an increase in the number of Puritan clergymen. It is perhaps significant that the Puritan effort began in 1625, the year of King James's death, for soon after Charles became King, Laud prepared a patronage list for him, with each eminent divine labeled "O" or "P", Orthodox or Puritan. If they were to be considered heretics, the Puritans' establishment of an unincorporated, self-perpetuating trust to buy ecclesiastical livings was indeed a cautious protective reaction. The Puritan plan involved a strenuous training program for the ministers who were to receive the livings which the trustees held. Saint Antholin's Church, London, was used as trial ground; there at six o'clock in the morning, as often as six days a week, Puritan preachers held forth. After six years of trial, the trainee was ready for placement. The men in charge of the arrangements, the Society of the Feofees of Impropriations, including Richard Stock (John Milton's childhood rector, discussed below, 187 ff.), Richard Sibbes (the most noted Puritan preacher of his day), and later Nicholas Rainton (Lord Mayor of London), concentrated their attention on the placing of preachers in towns represented in the House of Commons, a process which occasionally involved getting rid of incumbents considered to be unsatisfactory. The Puritan program came to the attention of Laud, then Bishop of London, in 1632. He saw to it that the Court of Exchequer ordered the trustees to stop purchasing impropriations and to appoint to the benefices at their disposal men nominated by the Crown. Laud called the Puritan plan the "main instrument for the Puritan faction to undo the Church."

Although Laud stopped this Puritan project, he could not stop the influence of the projectors. This group, the Society of the Feofees, was an effective instrument for spreading what have been called parliamentary Puritan ideas in London; they were vigorous supporters of the parliamentary opposition to the Crown. This fusion of those opposed to the government of the Church and those opposed to the government of the State was a vital force in the creation of the Puritan Revolution.

Puritanism and the events of the 1630's

At this time a new course of action became open to the Puritans, for at the same time that Charles decided to rule without a Parliament, he granted a charter to the Massachusetts Bay Company, seven of whose members were also members of the Society of

Feofees. The timing was exceedingly fortuitous. About a thousand Puritans left England for Massachusetts in 1630, and by 1640 some twenty thousand had crossed the sea. Among them was Thomas Hooker, silenced in 1629, whereupon he fled first to Holland and then in 1633 to Massachusetts, in the same ship with John Cotton, rector of St. Botolf's, Boston (Lincolnshire), perhaps the most magnificent parish church in England. (Hooker is discussed below, pp. 219 ff.) Puritan New England provided for these men the long-awaited opportunity to establish a government and churches according to their understanding of God's Word. For those who remained behind, the New World was now available should the Old World meet disaster. Although much has been made of the fact that the men who led the New England Puritans were prominent men of the Church and State, it is surprising that more Puritan notables did not flee, for the England of the 1630's was not a happy place for Puritans. So few went that the Puritan movement felt no real loss of strength.

In spite of all that has been said about the silencings and persecution of Puritans in the reigns of Elizabeth and James, in some areas Puritanism flourished essentially unhampered until the days of Charles and Laud. Thus in the diocese of York Puritanism gradually spread during Elizabeth's reign with the encouragement of the successive Archbishops of York, who saw Puritanism as an effective instrument against the strong Roman Catholicism of the area. Leading Puritans were even members of the High Commission there. A typical Puritan lay leader, Sir Thomas Posthumus Hoby, was a member of both the Council of the North and the High Commission. After considering the various efforts to eliminate Puritanism in the sixteenth century, one reads with some shock an entry in the diary of Hoby's wife for April 14, 1605, "This day was the first day that the Common Prayer Book was read in our church."

Even the efforts of James came to little in York, however, and by the late 1620's nearly all the towns of the county were controlled or nearly controlled by Puritans. These included Leeds, Sheffield, Hull, Whitby, and York. It was not until 1632 and the election of Richard Neile as Archbishop of York that Puritans in the diocese began to feel threatened. Neile, chosen archbishop to bring the North to order, was faced with the task of undoing what his predecessors had encouraged. Despite vigorous efforts, Neile could do little more than create conflict. He did not, however, make clear his failure in his reports to Charles: even in 1639 he reports that all is well. As Ronald Marchant has put it, "The picture of universal calm officially recorded in 1639, however comforting it may have been to the government in London, must have been known by Neile and his subordinates to be completely false if conditions below the surface were examined." Quite naturally those who had flourished with official approval felt that men like Charles, Laud, and Neile were committing violence on the Church and sought to stop it.

By the middle of the 1630's it appeared that Laud and Charles had defeated the Puritans except in York. But ironically, the vehemence of Laud's efforts was leading to his downfall. Beginning in 1629, William Prynne, a lawyer of Lincoln's Inn, became one of the most outspoken and effective critics of Laud's policies, as well as of hair styles, Arminianism, and the theater. Prynne considered Laud an innovator who departed from the values of his predecessor, Archbishop Abbot, and of Elizabethan Anglicanism: Calvinism, austerity in worship services, and loyalty to the Crown. He managed to get several of his attacks published, and because of his learning and zeal, Prynne won many to his position. On the occasion of the publication of *Histrio-mastix*, an attack on stage plays, Laud saw to it that he was condemned for libel. (King Charles and the Queen were both patrons of the theater.) In 1634 Prynne was condemned for libel: he was pilloried and imprisoned for a life sentence, and his ears were partially cropped. Still not to be silenced, Prynne continued his writings in prison. He attacked the bishops as suppressors of the truth. When he and two other authors, John Bastwick and Henry Burton, were pilloried and lost their ears for their anti-episcopal writings, the London crowd that witnessed their disgrace treated them as heroes. (For an account of Bastwick, see below, pp. 251 ff.)

The transfer of altars to the east end of churches, one of the efforts at what Laud called "decency," made even loyal episcopalians resentful. The Puritans could thank the Scots for the events which turned the tide. When Archbishop Laud tried to carry his policy of "thorough" to Scotland, the united Scots revolted, and in the Scottish National Covenant declared their hatred for all non-Biblical religious practices and specifically rejected the episcopal government which had been established in Scotland in James's reign. These steps had profound consequences. First, the two "Bishops' Wars" of 1639–40 which Charles undertook to force the Scots to acquiesce were not only defeats for the King but so bankrupted the royal treasury that he was obliged at last to call a parliament. With the Long Parliament (1640) public opinion was unleashed and the Puritans found a vehicle for opposition to the policies of Laud and Charles. Second, the Scots were determined to destroy English episcopacy, which they regarded as a threat to their state. The Scots' assistance thus prepared the way for the victory of Puritanism.

The relationship between Puritanism and what used to be called the Puritan Revolution today seems less intimate than formerly. The modern emphasis on the economic and social forces operative in history has led some historians to call the Civil War a bourgeois revolution. Regardless of underlying factors, however, it must be said that the Parliamentary forces fought in the name of religion and liberty. Puritanism at the very least provided a rationale for many who otherwise could not have been stirred to take arms against their sovereign. To fight men needed words like these which Milton wrote in 1642 in *The Reason of Church Government*:

Though God for less than ten just persons would not spare Sodom, yet if you can find, after due search, but only one good thing in prelaty, either to religion or civil government, to king or parliament, to prince or people, to law, liberty, wealth, or learning, spare her, let her live, let her spread among ye, till with her shadow all your dignities and honors and all the glory of the land be darkened and obscured. But on the contrary, if she be found to be malignant, hostile, destructive to all these, as nothing can be surer, then let your severe and impartial doom imitate the divine vengance; rain down your punishing force upon this godless and oppressing government, and bring such a dead sea of subversion upon her that she may never in this land rise more to afflict the holy reformed church and the elect people of God.

The victory of the Puritans so transformed the victors that it makes the date of the beginning of their triumph, 1641, a desirable *terminus ad quem* for the materials which follow, and Milton's first pamphlet, *Of Reformation*, a fitting climax. Without the established religion which it had sought to purify, Puritanism disintegrated as a movement and as an ideal.

Puritan characteristics

Many Puritans of the 1630's and '40's looked back to the past with a sense of tradition. In recent books John F. H. New and Michael Walzer have tried to demonstrate that Elizabethan, Jacobean, and Caroline Puritanism had a set of distinctive characteristics, but Charles and Katharine George and Lawrence Sasek have argued that Puritanism had no such consistency. Indeed, one who seeks to characterize the Puritanism of the ninety years after 1550 finds it difficult to isolate specific characteristics which differentiate the nonconformist from his conformist brethren. The Puritan tradition was Calvinist; it was identified with strict moral standards and hard work, especially in the seventeenth century; and it stressed the importance of grace and the process of salvation. But it is difficult to be more specific. Consider, for example, the related matters of the Puritan sermon and the Puritan or plain style. The so-called Puritan sermon form with its doctrines, reasons, and uses is probably best understood as a form used by preachers of all tendencies except when the audience consisted largely of the learned. Millar Maclure, who has studied the sermons preached at Paul's Cross in the period 1534–1642, notes that most are "Puritan" in form, though the care taken in choosing preachers for this important pulpit would seem to indicate that Puritans were not often chosen. Such a notable episcopalian as the liberal Chillingworth used the standard "Puritan" form in his sermons.

One can say fairly that Puritans did differ from the conformists in their attitude towards the importance of the sermon. The difference is suggested by the dispute between Thomas Cartwright and Archbishop Whitgift in the 1570's. Whitgift was obliged to defend the status quo as established by Elizabeth: preachers were few and preaching was not considered a necessary part of proper pastoral care. Reading the service was enough. To Cartwright the sermon was very important. He taught that "as when the fire is stirred up and discovered it giveth more heat than when it is not, so the Word of God by preaching and interpreting (as it were stirred up and blown) maketh a greater flame in the hearts of the hearers than when it is read."

The Puritan emphasis on preaching resulted in excellence in Puritan preaching, but excellence of a particular kind. Puritan sermons, though they may be witty (as are Henry Smith's), learned (as are Thomas Gataker's), or emotional and personal (as are Thomas Hooker's), are unvaryingly clear. (Samples of all three follow.) Doubtless the sermons of Bishop Lancelot Andrewes and Dean John Donne are from the literary point of view superior, but no Puritan would consider beauty to be an essential quality of a good sermon. A good sermon is a means of grace: as Thomas Hooker put it, "the work of the spirit doth always go with and is communicated by the Word." John Preston defines preaching as "a public interpretation or dividing the Word, performed by an ambassador or minister who speaks to the people instead of God, in the name of Christ." Preston's phrase "dividing the Word," from St. Paul's second epistle to Timothy, serves as a justification for the Puritan ideal of clarity, for methodical division of a sermon led to clarity and also permitted the audience to remember the main points of the sermon. William Ames condemns those who depart from the established form, for their hearers "cannot commit the chief heads of a sermon to memory, that they may afterwards repeat it privately in their families, without which exercise the greatest part of that fruit doth perish which would by sermons redound unto the Church of God." Method was a help to the preacher as well as to his audience. It was the influential John Dod who set the example for young preachers: he took with him into the pulpit a paper containing only an analysis of the text, and a list of doctrines, reasons, and uses. (The practice of dividing, providing subheads, and numbering the parts of a sermon carried over into other Puritan writings, especially devotional literature, as is evidenced by the popular anthology *A Garden of Spiritual Flowers*, by Richard Rogers, Richard Greenham, William Perkins, and others.)

Nearly all Puritans insisted that "human authorities" have no place in sermons. Laurence Chaderton scorned "stories collected out of the writings of profane men," and saw true preaching as that which has the "least flavor of carnal wisdom." The very in-fluential William Perkins, while recommending the reading of the Fathers and the reformers in preparing sermons, warned of the need to conceal this reading. The Puritans' emphasis is nearly al-ways on the Bible, which they saw in sharp contrast to tradition and to *merely* human ideas and usages.

It is probably a mistake to try to say much about Puritan style. A careful student of the Elizabethan sermon, J. W. Blench, finds many preachers who could not be called Puritans (including Arch-bishop Whitgift) using the "Puritan" plain style. The English Puritan did not live in a closed society as did the American Puritan. Nor was Puritanism in England a static thing. Only in the 1620's and 1630's does one note the beginnings of a common style in such popular preachers as Richard Sibbes, John Cotton, and John Pres-ton, all of whom seem to have felt the influence of Laurence Chaderton, of Emmanuel College, Cambridge, and of William Perkins, whose influence through his writings continued long after his death in 1602. It is perhaps best to consider the style of a given Puritan writer as that of an individual and avoid generalizations about *the* Puritan style.

Likewise it is questionable whether one can make sound gener-alizations about Puritan economic attitudes or Puritan social theory though Perkins and seventeenth-century Puritans frequently express bourgeois values. Puritans had one thing in common, that which gives them their name—their desire to complete the purification of the Church of England begun in Elizabeth's day. And since they disagreed about what that state of purity should be, how could they agree on the ramifications of their position? In the pages that follow are to be found some of the varieties of Puritan style, thought, and attitudes.

John Hooper (*ca.* 1495–1555)

John Hooper, the martyred Puritan bishop, was a native of Somerset, where his family was a prosperous one. Although the facts about his early life are not certain, he seems to have commenced A.B. at Merton College, Oxford, in 1519. He then probably became a Cistercian monk and entered Cleeve Abbey in Somerset. There he remained until the dissolution of the monasteries in 1536. He returned to Oxford, where his study of the Scriptures caused the authorities to look on him with disfavor. In London as steward to Thomas Arundel, Hooper read in the writings of the Continental reformers Zwingli and Bullinger. Arundel sent him to Bishop Gardiner to be cured of his disaffection with the established religion, but the conference did not cause Hooper to change his mind. A Protestant by the early 1540's, he had to flee to Paris to escape the penalties of the Statute of Six Articles.

By January 1546 Hooper had arrived in Strasbourg, where he met and planned to marry a Flemish Protestant. They were to live on the Continent. First, however, he returned to his home to obtain part of his inheritance, though his father opposed him because of his religion. The journey took a full year and was highly dangerous. Twice Hooper found himself in prison. On his return he married and in March 1547 settled in Zurich. He lived here for a time with Bullinger, who gave him theological instruction, and here he wrote his first works, *A Declaration of Christ and His Office* (1547), dedicated to Somerset, the Protector now that Edward was King; *An Answer Unto My Lord of Winchester's Book* (1547), in which he argued against Bishop Gardiner's Catholic views on the Eucharist; and *A Declaration of the Ten Commandments* (1549), in which he teaches that each man's eternal fate is determined by himself, grace being available "to every and singular of Adam's posterity."

When he left Zurich is not certain, but it was after the birth of his child. According to Foxe the martyrologist, he parted from Bullinger with these prophetic words:

". . . you shall be sure from time to time to hear from me, and I will write unto you how it goeth with me. But the last news of all, I shall not be able to write: for there," said he (taking Master Bullinger by the hand), "where I shall take most pains, there you shall hear of me to be burned to ashes."

On his return to England, where he could now safely be a Protestant, Hooper was made chaplain to the Protector Somerset and preached usually twice a day, often to crowded churches. His pulpit manner was notably severe and remote, and he engaged in a number of doctrinal disputes which did not endear him to Cranmer. Nevertheless he was ordered to preach before the King during Lent of 1550. His choice of Jonah as text for the seven sermons was made, he wrote Bullinger, in order to "freely touch the duties of individuals." The sixth sermon, a portion of which is reprinted here, begins with a continuation of Hooper's argument against tran-substantiation, occasioned, if that is the word, by the text, "And the people of Ninevah believed God, and proclaimed fasting, and arrayed themselves in sack cloth, as well the great as the small of them." Hooper seems to have had no sense of sermon form. At the end of the time allotted for one sermon he stopped and the next time picked up where he had left off. But his outspoken attack on kneeling at Communion and what he regarded as Romish ritualistic practice makes the sermon a lively one, and the addresses to the King add to the interest of the work.

On April 7, 1550, Hooper was offered the bishopric of Gloucester by the King's Council, despite the opposition of many bishops, but he refused because of the "Aaronic habits" and the "impious" form of oath required. Like other, later Puritans opposed to vestments, Hooper preferred the Swiss custom of wearing the full black gown used by the academic and professional classes, an indication of the priesthood of all believers. Bishop Ridley of London and Arch-bishop Cranmer were unwilling for Hooper's desires to prevail, though the Council was sympathetic to him. Ridley, charging in-subordination, wrote to Hooper:

These things which you scruple, these ceremonies and vestments, are things indifferent: you call them sinful. Now I attach no more value to them in themselves than you do, but they are ordered, and you are wrong to oppose them.

Hooper's refusal provoked considerable argument. John à Lasco, head of the foreign Protestants' church in London, took Hooper's side; the great theologian Martin Bucer (then in England) opposed him though he maintained that the vestments ought to be abolished. Peter Martyr, another great theologian then in England, held with Bucer that the garments were indifferent. Hooper continued to preach his cause, now with such violence that the Council suspended him. Though he could not preach, he could write, and soon had published *The Confession of John Hooper's Faith*. Hooper's lack of civility offended many, but because the letters patent making him a bishop had already been prepared, it was necessary to try to make him a bishop whether he liked it or not. The result was a case of nonconformity. Other men, such as Robert Ferrar, Bishop of St. David's, were consecrated without the usual ceremonies, but Ridley refused to consecrate Hooper because of his public attacks on order. The Council now placed Hooper in Cranmer's hands, and Cranmer soon committed him to prison. At last Hooper gave way and accepted the vestments as indifferent. In March 1551 he was consecrated with all the required ceremonial.

Hooper's conduct of his diocese was as vigorous as might be expected. A thorough visitation of the diocese in 1551 revealed shocking ignorance among the clergy. Ten were found who could not repeat the Lord's Prayer and twenty-seven who could not name its author. Hooper's visitation articles anticipate some later Puritan views (the Church is defined as "the congregation of the faithful") and the accompanying injunctions have been called the most advanced pronouncement which had yet been made by any authority in the Church of England. They provided for quarterly meetings of clergy with the bishop to discuss problems. Perhaps these diocesan assemblies provided a model for the Puritan meetings of Elizabeth's reign (the "prophesyings"), for Parkhurst, a leader in the Elizabethan Puritan movement, was in Hooper's diocese at this time. Hooper appointed superintendents rather than archdeacons and rural deans; in this he followed the Swiss practice.

Hooper suppressed heresies, stirred the consistory court to action, and successfully arbitrated cases brought to the episcopal court. He was everywhere and into everything. We find him, for example,

writing to Cecil, the Secretary of State, in April 1551, requesting
help in dealing with the problem of high prices.

In early 1552 Hooper assumed episcopal duties in Worcester in
addition to his charge of Gloucester. His regular functions were
burdened by the extent of his rule as well as his resistance to the
spoilage of the Church in his diocese. Despite his complex responsi-
bilities, however, he found time to be hospitable. Foxe tells of seeing
in his house at Worcester "a table spread with good store of meat
and beset full of beggars and poor folk." Inquiring, Foxe learned
that Hooper made it a regular practice to feed the poor.

Two months after the death of King Edward, in September
1553, Hooper wrote to his old friend Bullinger that he had just been
committed to prison and feared that "all godly preachers are in the
greatest danger." In March of the following year he was deprived
because he would not practice celibacy and separate from his wife
(for which Bishop Tonstal called him "beast") and because he
denied the corporeal presence of Christ in the Sacrament. He remained in prison until January 1555, when he was examined several
times by Queen Mary's ecclesiastical commissioners. After one
examination Hooper had an opportunity to talk with John Rogers,
soon to be the first martyr under Mary. "Come, brother Rogers,"
Foxe reports Hooper to have said, "must we two take this matter
first in hand and begin to fry these faggots?" Rogers replied, "Yea,
sir, by God's grace," to which Hooper added, "Doubt not but God
will give strength."

In February Hooper was officially degraded and a few days
later was sent to Gloucester, where seven thousand watched as he
was horribly tortured. The green faggots which were to destroy
him failed to burn properly. After suffering for three-quarters of
an hour, Hooper finally died when the third fire built around him
burned. In April 1555 Anne, Hooper's widow, wrote to Bullinger
that her husband was "with all the holy martyrs and with Christ
the head of the martyrs." Hooper well deserves a place in any
collection of Puritan writings. His idealistic disdain of reason of
State, his strict moral sense, and his brave death caused later Puritans
to look upon him as a spiritual godfather.

How to celebrate the Lord's Supper

[This is] the form how to celebrate the Lord's Supper. Here must be marked two persons: the minister and he that communicateth with the minister. These must come and assemble as St. Paul saith (I Corinthians xi). The duty and office of the minister [is this]. He doeth best his office and is best instructed to minister the Sacrament if he in the ministration thereof go as near as is possible to the first institution of Christ and the apostles. For Christ was and is the Wisdom of the Father, and the apostles had received the Holy Ghost that brought them into all truth. Therefore it must needs follow, their doings and ministration to be most perfect, holy, and religious.

The minister should prepare himself inwardly and outwardly. The inward preparation is if his mind and soul be instructed and furnished with godly doctrine and a fervent spirit and zeal to teach his audience, to stablish them in the truth, and to exhort them to perpend and mark well the merits and deservings of Christ. The outward preparation, the more simple it is, the better it is, and the nearer unto the institution of Christ and His apostles. If he have bread, wine, a table, and a fair tablecloth, let him not be solicitous nor careful for the rest, seeing they be no things brought in by Christ, but by popes, unto whom, if the King's Majesty and his honorable Council have good conscience, they must be restored again; and great shame it is for a noble king, emperor, or magistrate, contrary unto God's Word to detain and keep from the devil or his minister any of their goods or treasure, as the candles, vestments, crosses, altars! For if they be kept in the Church as things indifferent, at length they will be maintained as things necessary.

When the minister is thus well prepared with sound and godly doctrine, let him prepare himself to the distribution of the bread and wine, and as he giveth the bread, let him break it, after the

[*An Oversight, and Deliberation upon the holy Prophete Jonas: made, and uttered before the kynges maiestie, and his most honorable councell* (1550), fols. 142^recto^-148^recto^.]

example of Christ. He should give the bread and not thrust it into the receiver's mouth, for the breaking of the bread hath a great mystery in it of the passion of Christ, in the which His body was broken for us, and that is signified in the breaking of the bread, which in no case should be omitted. Therefore let the minister break the round bread, for broken it serveth as a sacrament and not whole. Christ did break it (Matthew xxvi; Mark xiv; Luke xxii). And St. Paul saith, "The bread that we break, is it not the communion of Christ's body?" (I Corinthians x) Thus should the perfection of Christ's institution be had in honor, and the memory of the dead left out, and nothing done in the Sacrament that had not God's Word to bear it. But, alas! God is accounted a fool, for men can use the Sacrament more religiously, devoutly, godly, and Christianly than Christ, God's Son, as it appeareth! For His form and manner is put out, and man's device and wisdom is accepted for it.

The duty of the receiver resteth in three parts, to say: what he should do before the receiving of the Sacrament; what he should do in the receiving of it; and what after the receiving of it. Before the receiving, he should prepare and make ready his mind, as the commandment of St. Paul is (I Corinthians xi): "Let the man prove and search himself," and so forth. And this may be done two manner of ways: first, towards God; then, towards man. Towards God he should, from the bottom of his heart, confess his faults and sins, and acknowledge his just condemnation. Then should he persuade himself by true and lively faith that God would be merciful unto him for the death of His dear beloved Son Jesus Christ, done in His body torn and in His blood shed. He should prepare himself towards his neighbor also. First, in case he hath hurt his neighbor in fame or goods, he should reconcile himself again with restitution of them both again. He that thus prepareth himself doth eat worthily the body of Christ; and he that doth not thus prepare himself, eateth nothing but the Sacrament to his everlasting damnation.

I make no mention here of auricular confession, as though that were a thing necessary to be done before or after the receiving of the Sacrament. For this confession is not of God, as their law doth record (the gloss upon the decree of penance, *Distinct.* v, "In Pœnitentia").

In the receiving of this sacrament, there be things required both in the inward man and also in the outward man. The inward preparation is when, the man receiving the bread and wine (being subjects and matters under the judgment and censure of the senses), the mind is elevated and lifted up into heaven, persuading himself by faith that as truly appertaineth unto him the promises and grace of God through the merits and death of Christ as he sensibly and outwardly receiveth the Sacrament and witness of God's promises, and doubts no more of an inward friendship, familiarity, concord, peace, love, atonement, and fatherly pity and compassion through Christ, by the means of faith, than he doubted that his mouth outwardly doth receive the signs and sacraments of God's mercy. To excitate in us this faith and belief in the merits of Christ, the bread is called the body and the wine His blood, after the manner and phrase of the Scripture.

The outward behavior and gesture of the receiver should want all kind of suspicion, show, or inclination of idolatry. Wherefore, seeing kneeling is a show and external sign of honoring and worshipping and heretofore hath grievous and damnable idolatry been committed by the honoring of the Sacrament, I would wish it were commanded by the magistrates that the communicators and receivers should do it standing or sitting. But sitting, in mine opinion, were best for many considerations. The paschal lamb was eaten standing, which signified Christ yet not to be come, that should give rest, peace, and quietness. Christ with His apostles used this sacrament, at the first, sitting; declaring that He was come that should quiet and put at rest both body and soul, and that the figure of the Passover from thenceforth should be no more necessary; nor that men should travel no more to Jerusalem once in the year to seek and use a sacrament of the Lamb to come, that should take away the sins of the world.

After the receiving of it, there should be thanksgiving of all the church for the benefits of Christ's death. There should be prayer made unto God that they might persevere and continue in the grace of God received. They should help the poor with their alms. This form, methinketh, is most like unto the form of Christ and the apostles. How far the Mass differeth from this, all men know. I pray God the best may be taken and the worst left, throughout all the world. And all such as be yet infirm, by reason of long custom and lack of knowledge, let them pray God and search the Scriptures without affectation. Such as be perverse and obstinate and will admit no reason, for them the ire and displeasure of God is ready and prest to punish them when He seeth time, as it is to be seen by the Corinthians (I Corinthians xi), that for the abuse of the Supper many of them fell sick and into diseases. So will He do with us if we neglect His most perfect and godly institution.

Edward Dering (*ca.* 1540–1576)

Edward Dering, a leader in the first generation of Elizabethan Puritans while still a young man, was born of an old Kentish family about 1540. He was a student of Christ's College, Cambridge, commencing B.A. in 1560. He maintained a connection with the University for some years, receiving an M.A. in 1563 and later serving as University proctor and University preacher. In 1564 while the Queen was visiting Cambridge, Dering delivered an oration. Something of the Puritanism developing then at Cambridge is indicated by the fact that Thomas Cartwright and Walter Travers also took part in the University activities during the royal visit. In 1568 Dering received the benefice of the rectorship of his home parish, Pluckley. During this same year Dering's first work was published, a polemic directed against the Jesuit Harding. Dering's hatred of all things "papistical" is quite possibly the basis of his Puritanism.

Dering at one time served as chaplain to the Duke of Norfolk, for whose children he composed prayers, perhaps those contained in his published works. (Norfolk was the eldest son of Henry Howard, Earl of Surrey.) Dering also served as chaplain in the Tower of London and was probably a prebend in Salisbury Cathedral, but more important was his position as preacher in St. Paul's Cathedral, London.

Among Dering's most interesting extant writings are his letters to Sir William Cecil. In November 1570 Dering wrote to Cecil in the latter's capacity as Chancellor of Cambridge University. Cecil was officially responsible for new University statutes which had been drawn up to help limit the growing power of Thomas Cartwright, who had been preaching presbyterianism at Cambridge. While professing not to be a nonconformist, Dering makes it clear in this letter that he sympathizes with Cartwright; he finds the anti-Cartwright statutes "unrighteous" and Cartwright's opponents insufficiently anti-papist. Dering attacked John Whitgift, later Archbishop of Canterbury, simply because he failed to accept Cartwright's views. "So forward a mind against Mr. Cartwright, and other such, betrayeth a conscience that is full of sickness." The heads of the colleges "keep benefices, and be nonresidents. While they are clothed in scarlet, their flocks perish for cold, and while they fare deliciously, the people are faint with a most miserable hunger." The letter plainly labels Dering a Puritan. Fifteen months later, Dering wrote again to Cecil about Cartwright, then in Geneva. He sought Cecil's aid in encouraging Cartwright's return. In the letter he also attacked Cecil, rather gratuitously, for his lack of true religion.

More interesting still is Dering's sermon preached before the Queen in February 1570. In this altogether forthright sermon Dering instructed Queen Elizabeth on her duties as a ruler. She should, he directed, punish lying and swearing and permit more preaching, take power from the bishops and eliminate pluralities and nonresidence. If he could show her majesty the many abuses that exist, he

would first lead you to your benefices, and behold some are defiled with impropriations, some with sequestrations, some loaden with pensions, some robbed of their commodities. And yet behold more abominations than these. Look after this upon your patrons, and lo, some are selling their benefices, some farming them; some keep them for their children; some give them to boys, some to serving men; a very few seek after learned pastors. And yet you shall see more abominations than these. Look upon your ministry, and there are some of one occupation, some of another; some shake bucklers, some ruffians, some hawkers and hunters, some dicers and carders, some blind guides, and cannot see, some dumb dogs and will not bark. And yet a thousand more iniquities have now covered the priesthood. And yet you in the meanwhile that all these whoredoms are committed, you at whose hands God will require it, you sit still and are careless, let men do as they list. It toucheth not belike your commonwealth, and therefore you are so well contented to let all alone. The Lord increase the gifts of His Holy Spirit in you, that from faith to faith you may grow continually, till that you be zealous . . . to work His will.

For this performance Dering was silenced, though his sermon was very soon printed and had eight editions or issues within the decade. In dedicating the printed sermon to Elizabeth, Dering complains that the Queen had "misliked" him for a great many years and now had silenced him for a "long time." When he was restored is not known.

Dering's reputation in both London and Cambridge increased greatly during the next few years. In 1572 he was often with Edwin Sandys, the Bishop of London, as well as intimate with Cartwright, for whom he tried to win the favor of Lord Burghley. At Cambridge he was a leading preacher and had many followers, and Archbishop Parker, though he did not feel that Dering measured up to his reputation, admitted that he was thought by some "the greatest learned man . . . in England."

A series of twenty-seven sermons on the Epistle to the Hebrews, apparently preached towards the end of 1572, and a catechism published during that year reveal something of Dering's theological position as well as attesting to his popularity. There are no peculiarly Calvinistic articles in the catechism; indeed, less is made of the doctrine of predestination in it than in the catechism of Alexander Nowell, Dean of St. Paul's, which had appeared two years earlier. Dering's catechism treats of the commandments, the creed, the sacraments, and the Lord's Prayer. The sermons on the Epistle to the Hebrews make no more than a casual mention of election but are rigorously moral and vehement in their attacks on "papistry." For Dering the Bible is the touchstone to try the virtue of all things religious. "God spake it; therefore we must do it. God speak it not; therefore we have nothing to do with it." "Where said He, 'Keep unto me Lent or Advent, Ember weeks, or saints' eves'?"

These same qualities appear in the sermon reproduced here. When Dering speaks of crucifying the affections, that is, the passions, we recognize a Puritan in the modern sense of the word. When we see the Pope described as "a sick head of an ill-disposed synagogue," we are likely to think that things Roman Catholic are not greatly to the author's taste. Dering's unwillingness to rely on any authority but the Bible goes hand in hand with his abhorrence of "carnal reason," though he was not an anti-intellectual. In his sermons he does not parade authorities, yet one finds references to Eusebius, Aristotle, Augustine, and Plutarch, among others; and in *A Sparing Restraint*, references to Orosius, Tertullian, Suetonius, and Aegesippus. But, like Calvin, Dering had no respect for the ability of man's unaided reason to reach religious truth.

Dering's 1567 Tower of London sermon is interesting in part because of its dramatic context. The sermon was presumably preached in the Chapel of St. Peter ad Vincula, the place of worship for prisoners within the fortress. The audience probably included the Duke of Norfolk, who was imprisoned in the Tower at that time for his part in the Northern (Roman Catholic) Uprising. Norfolk, who had had John Foxe the martyrologist as his tutor, was no Catholic; one of his chaplains had been, as we have noted, Dering himself. Dering reminded Norfolk in a letter apparently written after Norfolk's condemnation that he had tried to persuade him "from your wicked servants, from your Popish friends, and from your adulterous women." Perhaps some of those imprisoned were among these friends: one of the prisoners was John Leslie, bishop designate of Ross in Scotland and an ardent supporter of Queen Mary.

Though Dering's sermon was addressed to Roman Catholics, it is critical not of their questionable loyalty to the Queen, but of their religious principles and practices. Had the sermon been preached a little later, one imagines that Dering would have discussed patriotism, for less than six months later the excommunication of Elizabeth was found nailed to the door of the Bishop of London's palace.

In form, Dering's sermon below is quite different from the carefully organized sermons of most later Puritans, with their many divisions and subdivisions. Dering takes up the first sentence of his text, the petitions of the Jews, explains it, compares the religious outlook of the Jews with other religious attitudes of Jesus's time, and then compares the needs of the Jews with the needs of his hearers. He then explains the significance of Jesus's reply, relates it to the teaching of Roman Catholicism, denounces the doctrine of transubstantiation, and preaches the doctrine of salvation by faith and the rewards of faith.

Dering's style is an excellent specimen of the plain style, but his plainness is prevented from being dull by his passion and by his mastery of the telling phrase. In one of his sermons on the Epistle to the Hebrews Dering denounces preachers who babble of "philosophy and vain things," "unknown tales and sweet words," "idle sounds, strong to tickle our ears with fond delight, strong to puff us up with pride of our wits, but more weak than water to teach us true repentance." No one, he argues, has ever been "converted by hearing stories or fables of poets." But his sermons do not lack rhetorical devices, such as repetition. Ten times, almost consecutively, he begins sentences in the sermon that follows with "There was never. . . ." Five consecutive sentences begin "He never tasted of Christ, that. . . ."

The year 1573 was a difficult one for Dering. He was silenced on two occasions for his teachings. Although many charges were alleged against him, it seems likely that it was his views on the episcopacy that led to his suspension. When questioned, he professed agreement with the sacraments of the Church and with the articles of faith, except for the article on the consecration of bishops and archbishops. He maintained that there should be no superiority among ministers, who should be chosen by the people. He spoke out against the use of vestments and musical instruments in worship and argued that the State should observe the judicial laws of Moses. His presbyterian views were much the same as Thomas Cartwright's.

After one suspension Dering was restored through the efforts of Sandys, who perhaps admired him though they disagreed. Sandys wrote to Burghley:

These be dangerous days, full of itching ears mislying their minds, and ready to forget all obedience and duty. . . . a soft plaster is better than a sharp corrosive to apply to this sore. . . . If Mr. Dering be somewhat spared, yet well scolded, the others, being manifest offenders, may be dealt with according to their deserts.

Dering was preaching again in 1574, although the Queen still "misliked" his sermons. In 1575 he was in ill health, and wrote in one of his *Godly Letters* (published in 1597) of coughing, spitting blood, and having difficulty in breathing. On June 26, 1576, while still in his thirties, he died. Among his last words were these words of wisdom addressed to preachers: "Dally not with the word of God; make not light of it. Blessed are they that use their tongue well when they have it."

Corrupt religion and true

John vi. 34. "Then they said unto Him, 'Lord, give us evermore of this bread.' And Jesus saith unto them, 'I am the bread of life; he that cometh unto me shall not hunger, and he that believeth in me shall never thirst.' "

We have, dearly beloved in our Lord and Savior Christ, we have in this portion of Scripture to consider, first, this petition or request which the Jews make unto Christ in these words, "Lord, give us evermore of this bread"; then, the answer that our Savior Christ maketh again, "I am the bread of life," etc. Their request riseth of certain words spoken immediately before, where Christ saith, "My Father giveth unto you from heaven the true bread. For the bread of God is He that cometh down from heaven and giveth life unto the world," through which words they brake out straight into this prayer, "O Lord, give us always this bread." These words they do not utter with any good affection or longing desires to be partakers of the mercies which are offered unto all in Christ Jesus, but rather of a distempered mind drawn into contrary desires, seeking by all means to fill themselves with happiness, and yet to jest and scoff at the doctrine of Christ. The thoughts of their minds are made manifest both by these words of Christ, "Ye seek me because you ate of the loaves and were filled," and also by their own words to the same effect, where they say, "Our fathers did eat manna in the wilderness," likewise requiring that Christ would so feed them full by miracle, and then they would follow Him.

And afterward also, when Christ had further taught them that He would in no such sort feed them daintily on earth but, if they would eat of the bread that He would give they must renounce such fleshly concupiscence, crucify themselves unto the world, and be with a lively faith incorporate into His body, then they should eat of living bread—as soon as they heard this, they murmured at Him, showing that He was not the bread that they did seek for,

[*A Sermon Preached at the Tower of London* (London, 1597), sigs. C^{recto}-C3^{verso}.]

and then declared what was their scoffing spirit, and said openly, "Is not this Jesus the son of Joseph, whose father and mother we know? How came he down from heaven?" Thus, dearly beloved, we learn what minds these men had that would so fain have been fed with the bread of life. They would live forever, but they would live as they list. They would follow Christ, but they would neither hunger nor thirst. They would do the will of God, but they would not crucify their affections. They would come unto heaven, but they would not be led by Jesus, the poor carpenter's son. Their carnal fancies beguiled them. Their scoffing at Jesus Christ made their hearts so blind; and their desire of happiness was nothing but the show of their own folly.

Now let us beware by other men's harms. Let us not fall after the same example of disobedience. If we bring our carnal fancies to the Word of God we shall never understand it. The natural man perceiveth not the things that are of God. Such gross imaginations deceived Nicodemus that he knew not what it was to be born anew. Such fancies made blind the woman of Samaria that she knew not how to ask for the water of life. Such carnal imaginations made the children of Zebedee to ask of our Savior Christ, they knew not what. Yea, all the disciples of our Savior Christ by such fleshly desires oftentimes understood Him not. And how much more ought we to take heed, that have so barren hearts, not watered so plentifully with God's Spirit? Whither shall we be led, if we bring unto God's Word our sensual appetites? Sure even thither whither these Jews are gone before us, to murmur against Christ and despise His cross. Let us then take heed while it is yet time, and in obedience of God's Word banish far from us our own understanding. And if we will be taught of the Lord God, let us lead into captivity all our own cogitations and seek no better estate for the Gospel of God than He Himself hath appointed by His holy wisdom. Otherwise it will surely come upon us that came so long ago upon these carnal Jews, and we shall have so good liking of our own delight that we shall contemn the poor Galilean, and with a proud countenance we shall think much scorn that the carpenter's son should be our master. This is the fruit that groweth out of man's wisdom. Here it is plainly testified in this Sixth of John. It is testified in the scribes and Pharisees that so often scoffed at our Savior Christ, in the soldiers that upon the cross had Him in such derision, in the whole multitude of the Jews that struck Him and spit on Him and bid Him aread who had hurt Him. Thus after that by carnal reason they would needs judge of Christ, they grew more and more in hardness of heart, till they thought it good wisdom to speak so great blasphemy.

Such gospelers there were many in the primitive Church, that thought themselves wise in making a jest of Christ. So Julianus the Apostate, when the Christians asked help against all their injuries, with mocks and scoffs he would ask why they did complain when the Galilean their master bade them do good for evil; if any would take away their coat, that then they should give him also their cloak. So many wicked magistrates spoiled the Christians of their money, and would taunt them merely with the saying of their God: "Quod Cæsaris scis, Cæsari da"—give that unto Caesar that thou knowest is Caesar's. Such gospelers at this day we have a great many in England, that laugh smoothly in their sleeves at their madness, as they think, that follow so earnestly the Gospel. So St. Peter hath borne witness generally of the wicked of all ages, that they shall think it much madness that other will not run to like effusion of riot. But let them alone that seek willingly to go so far astray. This is the time of their rejoicing; the days of repentance are not yet come. When they have done with their mocking, themselves shall be then mocked at, and for all their pleasant sporting they shall be called to judgment.

Another thing I noted unto you in the petition of these Jews, and that was a desire of happiness which they wished to come unto, and in the midst of their malice, yet an inward sighing of spirit that they might once eat of the bread of life. They pleased themselves exceedingly in fighting against Christ, and yet again in remorse of conscience they wished to be partakers of eternal life. And this is that sparkling of the grace of God which is kindled in the hearts of all men, of which St. John saith that "Christ lighteneth all men that come into this world." Cain had this light when the burden of his sin seemed so heavy unto him that it could not be pardoned. Esau had this light when for loss of his father's blessing he lifted up his voice and wept. Pharaoh had this light when in remembrance of all his plagues he cried at the last, "The Lord is righteous, but I and my people are wicked." The sorcerers of Egypt had this light when God confounded their wisdom in a most vile creature, and they confessed before Pharaoh, "This is the finger of God." Pilate had this light when he washed his hands and cried before all the Jews that he was innocent from the blood of Christ. Simon Magus had this light when he wondered at the signs and miracles that were wrought by the apostles and would have given money for the Holy Ghost. The Gentiles themselves, they had all this light; Antiochus, when he wept for all the evil that he had done at Jerusalem; Julianus, when he cried, "Vicisti Galilæe"—O man of Galilee, thou hast gotten the victory; Adrian at his death, when he spake unto himself, "Animula vagula, blandula, hospes comesque corporis, quae nunc abibis in loca, nec ut soles dabis locos, palidula, rigida, nudula?"; Brutus had this light when, the night before he was slain, he thought he saw a spirit that cried thus unto him, "Ego sum tuus malus genius, Brute; hodie me in Phillippis videbis."

But what need I, dearly beloved, to make this long by examples? You yourselves, I am sure, can witness with this truth. There is none of you so far given over to uncleanness but I am sure sometime you say with these unclean Jews, "O Lord, give us one day the bread of life." This is the triumph that virtue hath over vice, that wheresoever she is most hated, there she is often wished for. And this is the great punishment that God bringeth upon the wicked, even as the poet [Persius] said, "Virtute ut videant, intabes canta relicta" [Satire III]—that though they love not virtue, nor cannot like to follow her, yet they should pine away with a longing desire after her. And this I am sure, it striketh deep and woundeth the conscience of the wicked. Though they have set their heart as an adamant stone, and made their face like flint, yet grace pierceth throughout their concupiscence and they say sometime, "The way of virtue is better." There was never so impure and dissolute an adulterer but he hath said sometime, "The chaste body is best." There was never so blasphemous nor vile a swearer but sometime he hath trembled at God's majesty. There was never man so proud and ambitious but sometime he remembereth he is but earth and ashes. There was never such a usurer nor covetous wretch but sometime he thinketh his gold and silver shall canker and the rust of it shall be a witness against him. There was never so riotous a person, sumptuous and prodigal, but sometime he condemneth his own doing, and saith with the prophet, "The unrighteous man borroweth, and payeth not again." And what should I say more? There was never so high-minded nor vainglorious a king but he hath sometime thought his crown would fall from his head, and the crown of righteousness was better, which was in the kingdom of heaven.

And this, dearly beloved, as it is in a wicked life, so likewise it is in corrupt religion. Truth, that is strongest and overcometh all, in religion forceth the enemy oftentimes to confess her. There was never papist that so magnified merits and talked of his works of supererogation but oftentimes in his conscience he would surely confess that when he had done all, yet he was unprofitable. There was never any so great an enemy to faith but when his conscience was touched with the grief of sin he would cry aloud, "Faith alone doth justify." There was never, I am sure, papist yet so drunken, that made so much of all his fleshly worshippings, of organs and singing, of altars and altar cloths, of frankincense and sweet-smelling savors, of banners and streamers, of goodly tunes and melody, of silver crosses and chalices, but he hath said sometime, "Who required these things at our hands? The true worshippers do worship in spirit and verity." There was never papist in so deep a sleep of pardons and purgatory but he hath surely said that such weak engines can break down but paper walls, and such cold water can quench but painted fires. There was never pope nor general council so desperately bent to set up worshipping of images but their own hearts have often cried within them, "They have mouths and speak not, they have eyes and see not, they have ears and hear not, they have noses and smell not, they have hands and touch not, they have feet and walk not; thou shalt not bow down to them nor worship them." There was never papist so blinded with the great absurdity of transubstantiation but sometime, seeing the wine in the chalice, he hath been afraid to say, "By this and by nothing else let my sins be washed," and, seeing the cake in the priest's hands, "Thou alone hast redeemed me, and alone by thee I look to be saved."

This, doubt ye not, dearly beloved, is the working of the Lord in the hearts of all His enemies. Refuse Him how ye will in life or in religion, you shall carry day and night a witness in your breast against yourselves, and your hearts will condemn you, that cry evermore against you. The way unto true happiness is neither by sin nor superstition, neither by open rebellion nor yet by accursed idolatry.

And thus far out of this petition of the froward Jews I have noted unto you what I have thought best for our common instruction. The Lord grant us that we make the like request, but with a better spirit, and pray evermore unto Him, "O Lord, give us always the bread of life."

Thomas Cartwright (1535–1603)

He whom Thomas Fuller called the head of Elizabethan presbyterianism, Thomas Cartwright, fits the modern popular image of the Puritan rather too well. A strong advocate of discipline in the modern sense of the word, Cartwright would have made the Church much more of an instrument of oppression than it was under his opponent, Archbishop Whitgift. Though he has great historical importance, and may have been—as Theodore Beza maintained—as learned a man as was to be found, he left no great monument, for his career as a writer was devoted to controversy on a very confined issue.

Thomas Cartwright was born in 1535 at Royston, Hertford, not far from Cambridge, of a very respectable yeoman family. He matriculated at Clare Hall, Cambridge, while he was still very young, in 1547, and in 1550 he became a scholar at St. John's, where Thomas Lever, an extreme Protestant, soon became master. He commenced B.A. in 1554, along with John Whitgift. After serving briefly as a fellow, he left in 1556, probably because of the reestablishment of Roman Catholicism, and studied law. In 1560 he returned again, took up a fellowship, and commenced M.A. Two years later he was honored by being asked to participate in a public disputation held for the visiting Queen Elizabeth. Although the proceedings were thoroughly academic, it probably did Cartwright little good that the Queen should hear him on this occasion vigorously oppose the institution of monarchy.

The controversy over vestments had its academic headquarters at Oxford, but at Cambridge, St. John's, Cartwright's college, also actively opposed the wearing of the "popish rags." The leader of the opposition was William Fulke, a fellow. During the greater part of the controversy, however, Cartwright was not in England, for in 1565 he became domestic chaplain to Adam Loftus, Archbishop of Armagh, and in Ireland Puritans were not troubled for their nonconformity. These circumstances—the acquaintance with Lever and Fulke, and two years' service in Ireland—must have had a great influence on Cartwright, especially the latter, for it was common for those exposed to the superstitions of Roman Catholicism in Ireland to want a thorough housecleaning of the "remnants of Romanism" in the Church of England.

Shortly after his return to Cambridge in 1567, when he was awarded the B.D. degree, Loftus recommended Cartwright as his successor in Ireland, but the appointment went elsewhere. At this time Cartwright made a considerable impression on the Cambridge community in his capacity as preacher to the University, a result being his appointment as Lady Margaret Professor of Divinity in 1569. The consequences of this appointment were of great moment; they are discussed in the general introduction.

By June, 1571, Cartwright was in Geneva, where he lectured twice a week at the Genevan Academy. This institution for theological students was now headed by Theodore Beza, who became Cartwright's admirer. While in Geneva, Cartwright attended meetings of the local consistory in order to learn of the workings of this great Reformed church.

In Geneva for somewhat less than a year, Cartwright returned to England by way of Rouen, with Edward Dering, the London Puritan, preparing his way by obtaining Lord Burghley's approval of his return. But back at Cambridge Whitgift, now vice-chancellor, deprived Cartwright of his fellowship because he had not fulfilled the requirement of his fellowship oath to take priest's orders within a stated time. As a result, Cartwright was for a time without a regular occupation; he lived in various places and acted from time to time as a tutor.

In late 1572 Whitgift published an *Answer* to the Puritans' *Admonition to Parliament*, which had appeared earlier in the year. Cartwright busied himself to reply, and by April *A Reply to an Answer Made of Master Doctor Whitgift* was in circulation. By June a second edition appeared, despite a royal proclamation against the book. In an effort to restrain its circulation, the authorities called in all copies, but few were received. There was occasion for concern, for the book had great influence: many who had been loyal to the Establishment were now convinced presbyterians, and some of these preached Cartwright's doctrines from Paul's Cross, the outdoor pulpit of St. Paul's Cathedral.

The efforts to stay Cartwright culminated in the issuance by the Ecclesiastical Commissioners of a warrant for his arrest in December 1573. Cartwright therefore fled to Germany, where he enrolled as a student at Heidelberg. Here he wrote a preface to Travers's *Ecclesiasticae Disciplinae . . . Explicatio*, probably saw the work through the press, and translated it into English.

Meanwhile Whitgift issued a *Defence of the Answer* in February, 1574, and in 1575 and 1577 Cartwright issued his *Second Reply*, the end of the controversy. Opposition among some Puritans to his position that a minister should not abandon his charge because of the vestment requirement did not prevent his being recognized by all the hard-core Puritans, such as John Field and Thomas Willcocks, as the authority on further reformation in the Church.

The differences between Whitgift's and Cartwright's views on the Church are manifold. Since, however, their debate is central in Elizabethan Puritanism, their fundamental attitudes must be characterized. Whitgift held that in the Church of England "the Gospel is sincerely preached and the sacraments rightly ministered." Since the Church teaches all things necessary for salvation and since its worship is regulated by the Book of Common Prayer, "a godly book, without any error in substance of doctrine," it is wrong to break the peace of the Church. The Church's teaching is "agreeable to order" and "keepeth every man in his degree and calling." England is a Christian commonwealth, where there can be no clear separation of Church and State. In the Church nothing "against the Word of God" "in ceremonies, order, discipline or government" "is to be suffered" but "no one certain and perfect kind of government . . . is prescribed in the Scriptures."

For Cartwright, on the other hand, proper discipline (that is, the organization of the Church and the correction of its members) is necessary for salvation, and "the Word of God containeth the directions of all things pertaining to the Church, yea, of whatsoever things can fall into a man's life." Cartwright's basic position is well described in the epistle to the Church of England prefixed to his *Reply to . . . Whitgift*; this epistle is reprinted here.

D. J. McGinn, who studied the controversy carefully, argues that Cartwright lacked real skill in dialectics and was more eager to win converts than to find the truth. McGinn asserts that Cartwright so emphasized the way of life of the Old Testament that he lost sight of the virtue of Christian charity. This is a sweeping indictment, but few modern readers who carefully consider the controversy are likely to disagree with McGinn.

Whitgift's defense of the Establishment against Cartwright's attack is intelligent and able, but scarcely a defense within a clearly established philosophic framework. Such a defense Richard Hooker was to offer, and the Puritans had no spokesmen who could reply with a work of the breadth and depth of Hooker's *Laws*.

Returning to Cartwright's career, we find him at Basel for a year or two after leaving Heidelberg. Then he turns up at Middelburgh, in Holland, where he served as factor, or supervisor of sales, for the English Merchant Adventurers, who were strong supporters of further purification of the Church. Cartwright remained in Holland for eight years. While there he married the sister of John Stubbe, the strenuous Puritan who achieved fame by his opposition to Elizabeth's proposed marriage to the Catholic Duke of Anjou. It was impossible, one supposes, for Cartwright to have known that his great work was now behind him. His pastoral activities in Holland, beginning in 1580 as replacement for Walter Travers, were in a sense only something to be doing until the time should come for his return to England and action. There were some small satisfactions, for his church was presbyterian in character, and too he had the honor of being called to professorships at Leyden and St. Andrews, calls which he did not accept.

A more meaningful honor, seemingly, came to him when Sir Francis Walsingham, of the Queen's Council, asked him to serve Her Majesty's government by preparing a confutation of the Rhemish translation of the New Testament, which later became part of the Douai Bible. (This translation had anti-Protestant annotations.) For £100 a year, he was to answer this and other Jesuit books. Cartwright took up this task, eager to satisfy his Puritan supporters and hopeful that he might find his way back into the Queen's good graces.

Four years later, in 1586, the work nearly complete, Cartwright was forbidden by Whitgift to continue, for the latter, now Archbishop of Canterbury, thought quite rightly that the book would hurt rather than help the Establishment because of its author's presbyterianism. It was 1602 before even part of the book found its way into print through the work of Robert Waldegrave, the Puritan printer, then working in Scotland, and it was 1618 before the bulk of the work, which had suffered the ravages of time, was printed, through the work of the "Pilgrim Fathers" at Leyden.

During his stay in Holland, Cartwright had occasion to dispute in writing with Robert Harrison and Robert Browne, the separatists. Against them Cartwright defended the Church of England as a true church. This defense caused him to identify himself with the "impure" Church, and Cartwright became more moderate in his attitude towards episcopacy.

Since his health was bad, Cartwright listened receptively to the pleas of his supporters that he return to England. But soon after his homecoming, in 1585, Bishop Aylmer issued a warrant for his arrest. Cartwright, imprisoned, was visited by crowds who welcomed him. Hopeful that he might be less trouble if treated well, Elizabeth got him released, and even Whitgift treated him kindly.

In 1586 the Earl of Leicester made Cartwright Master of Leicester Hospital, an institution which he had established to relieve the poor in Warwick. Cartwright's stipend was £100 per annum. For the first time in England Cartwright preached regularly, in the nearby parish church. He also took an active part, though not it appears as leader, in the classical movement which established within the body of clergymen of the Church a kind of presbyterian organization. In 1588 he subscribed to the Book of Discipline and in the following year took part in such presbyterian meetings as the general conference held at St. John's College, Cambridge. As the authority on the presbyterian system, he was asked every imaginable kind of question, one being whether it was proper for women to set their hair out on wires.

When the movement was broken up by the authorities in 1590, Cartwright along with other leading presbyterians was called before the High Commission to answer charges made against them. He was said to have renounced his episcopal ordination and taken another in Holland (a false charge), to have established a presbyterian church there (half-true), to have preached in Warwick without a license and criticized the Church and the Prayer Book, to have had knowledge of Martin Marprelate's and John Udall's publications (little truth here, though Job Throckmorton, who was involved, was his neighbor), and to have taken part in the classical movement. Cartwright refused to take the *ex officio* oath and at length was imprisoned. Finally he was tried in the Star Chamber in 1591, but he refused to answer most of the questions put to him. He admitted having signed the Book of Discipline but said that the Book was never put into practice.

Though never found guilty, Cartwright continued to languish in prison. Even the support of James VI had no effect. Only Cartwright's signature to a declaration endorsing episcopacy and repudiating presbyterianism would, he was told, win him his release. At last, in 1592, in bad health, Cartwright and the other Puritans were set free.

Cartwright presumably returned to Warwick. Three years later he was appointed chaplain at Castle Cornet, at Guernsey in the Channel Isles, where his pastoral charge was the governor, his family, and the soldiers of the garrison. Here real disciplinary presbyterianism existed, and Cartwright was in his element at last. He sought successfully to end discord, and he reformed the system in operation. This post he held till 1601.

In 1596 Cartwright published *A Brief Apology* against the charges of Matthew Sutcliffe, who had attacked him in print. This work is of considerable biographical interest. We learn, for example, that "in the space of five years I preached at Antwerp and Middelburgh, I did every Sunday read the prayer out of the Book." Cartwright's attitude towards the Church in these last years is decidedly moderate: concerning his "judgment in sundry matters of the discipline," though differing from sundry learned men in our Church, I have the consent of many worthy Churches and godly learned both of this and other ages."

Cartwright lived out his life at Warwick something of an invalid. He was nevertheless selected to speak at the Hampton Court Conference, but his death in December, 1603, prevented his serving. His funeral sermon was preached by John Dod.

Although two works by Cartwright appeared after his death, in addition to the *Confutation*, it was through his debate with Whitgift, his lectures at Cambridge in 1569, and direct personal contacts that Cartwright had great influence. A strict believer in

Old Testament legalistic justice, Cartwright is scarcely appealing as a man of humanity. Although one has occasion to sympathize with the Elizabethan Puritans, especially under Whitgift, the ideals of Thomas Cartwright were surely an unattractive alternative.

Puritanism is renovation, not innovation

As our men do more willingly go to warfare and fight with greater courage against strangers than against their countrymen, so it is with me in this spiritual warfare. For I would have wished that this controversy had been with the papists or with other (if any can be) more petulant and professed enemies of the Church, for that should have been less grief to write and more convenient to persuade that which I desire. For as the very name of an enemy doth kindle the desire of fighting and stirreth up the care of preparing the furniture for the war, so I cannot tell how it cometh to pass that the name of a brother slaketh that courage and abateth that carefulness which should be bestowed in defense of the truth. But seeing the truth ought not to be forsaken for any man's cause, I enforced myself, considering that if the Lord might lay it to my charge that I was not for certain considerations so ready as I ought to have been to publish the truth, He might more justly condemn me if, being oppugned and slandered by others, I should not according to that measure which He hath dealt unto me and for my small ability defend it and deliver it from the evil report that some endeavor to bring upon it.

And as unto other parts of the Gospel, so soon as the Lord openeth a door for them to enter in there is for the most part great resistance, so in this part concerning the government and discipline of the Church, which is the order which God hath left, as well to make the doctrine most effectual and to give as it were a sharper edge unto the preaching of the Word, as also to be a wall to keep it

[*A Reply to an answer made of Master Doctor Whitgift agaynste the Admonition to the Parliament* ([1572]), sigs. B3^{verso}-B4^{verso}.]

and make it continue amongst us, I see there be sundry lets which do as it were with weapons stand up to stop the passage and to hinder, that it should not be settled amongst us. With the which albeit I wrestle hand-to-hand in this book, yet forasmuch as we have all drunk so deep of the cup of untruth that we do not only stumble at blocks which other men lay in our way, but oftentimes we gather lets unto ourselves in framing a prejudice against the truth, I thought good to note shortly what those stumbling blocks are, and although I cannot remove them, yet to give warning of them and to lend my hand to the weaker and simpler sort to help to overstride them.

The offenses which are taken herein be either in respect of the cause [i.e., presbyterian Puritanism] or in respect of those which seek to defend and promote the cause. The cause is charged first with newness and strangeness, then as author of confusion and of disorder, and last of all as enemy to princes, magistrates, and commonwealths. For the first, besides that it is no sufficient challenge to say it is new and strange, there is no cause why it should be counted new which is confessed of those which mislike it to have been for the most part used in the apostles' times, nor why it should be esteemed strange which is used now far and near, of this and that side the sea, and of no strangers but of those which are of the household of faith. And it shall more largely appear in this book that this is no innovation but a renovation, and the doctrine not new but renewed, no stranger but born in Sion, whereunto it, being before unjustly banished, ought now of right to be restored.

And of confusion and disorder it is yet more untruly accused. For justice may be as well accused for doing wrong as this doctrine for bringing in disorder, whose whole work is to provide that nothing be done out of place, out of time, or otherwise than the condition of every man's calling will bear; which putteth the people in subjection under their governors, the governors in degree and order one under another, as the elder underneath the pastor and the deacon underneath the elder; which teacheth that a particular church shall give place unto a provincial synod where many

churches are, and the provincial to a national, and likewise that unto
the general, if any be, and all unto Christ and His Word. When, on
the contrary part, those which stand against this doctrine are
thereby compelled to bring into the Church great confusion and
marvelous disorder, whilst the pastor's office is confounded with
the deacon's, whilst women do minister the sacraments, which is
lawful only for men, whilst private men do that which belongeth
unto public persons, whilst public actions are done in private places,
whilst the Church is shuffled with the commonwealth, whilst civil
matters are handled by ecclesiastical persons, and ecclesiastical by
those which be civil, and, to be short, whilst no officer of the
Church keepeth his standing and one member doth take upon it the
office of another. Which things as they hazard the army and destroy
the body, so they do presently hinder and will shortly, if remedy be
not provided, utterly overthrow the Church. And therefore, unless
good order be in that which was brought into the Church by
popery, and confusion in that which was left unto the Church by
the Apostles, and that it be order that public actions should be
done in private places by private persons and by women that is
appointed to be done by men, and confusion when the contrary is
observed, and finally, unless order have another definition or nature
than hitherto hath been read or heard of, there is no cause why this
doctrine which containeth the discipline and government of the
Church should be thus shamefully slandered with confusion and
disorder.

For the third point, which is that it is an enemy to magistrates
and the commonwealth: if it be enough to accuse without proof,
to say and show no reason, innocency itself shall not be guiltless.
This doctrine was in times past, even by their confession which
write against it, a friend unto princes and magistrates when princes
and magistrates were enemies unto it. And can it now be an enemy
unto princes and magistrates which are friends unto it? It helped
and upheld the commonwealths which were governed by tyrants;
and can it hinder those which are governed by godly princes? And
in what is it an enemy to princes and magistrates? Note the

variance; set down the enmity. If the question be whether princes and magistrates be necessary in the Church, it holdeth that the use of them is more than of the sun, without the which the world cannot stand. If it be of their honor, it holdeth that with humble submission of mind, the outward also of the body, yea, the body itself and all that it hath, if need so require, are to be yielded for the defense of the prince and for that service for the which the prince will use them unto, for the glory of God and maintenance of the commonwealth. If it be asked of the obedience due unto the prince and unto the magistrate, it answereth that all obedience in the Lord is to be rendered. And if it come to pass that any other be asked, it so refuseth that it disobeyeth not in preferring obedience to the great God before that which is to be given to mortal man. It so refuseth that it submitteth the body and goods of those that profess it, to abide that which God will have them suffer in that case. And if it be showed that this is necessary for the Church, it cannot be but profitable for the commonwealth. Nay, the profit of it may easily appear for that by the censures and discipline of the Church as they are in this book described, men are kept back from committing of great disorders of stealing, adultery, murder, etc., whilst the smaller faults of lying and uncomely jesting, of hard and choleric speeches, which the magistrate doth not commonly punish, be corrected. And undoubtedly, seeing that the Church and commonwealth do embrace and kiss one another, and seeing they be like unto Hippocrates's twins which were sick together and well together, laughed together and wept together and always like affected, it cannot be but that the breaches of the commonwealth have proceeded from the hurts of the Church, and the wants of the one from the lacks of the other. Neither is it to be hoped for that the commonwealth shall flourish until the Church be reformed. And it is also certain that, as the Church shall every day more and more decay until it be made even with the ground, unless the walls be builded and the ruins repaired, so the weight of it, if it fall, will either quite pull down the commonwealth or leave it such as none which fear God will take any pleasure in it.

For seeing Solomon saith that by wisdom, which is the word of God, kings do govern and princes do bear rule, it cannot be but as that wisdom is either contemned or neglected or otherwise abridged of her free and full course, so princes and magistrates and consequently their commonwealths either go to wrack or decay, or at the least want so much of their flourishing estate as there wanteth of that word of God which He hath appointed to be their stay.

And howsoever, before the coming of our Savior Christ amongst the Athenians, Lacedemonians, and Romans, and since His coming in divers places where this wisdom hath not been heard of, there may seem to have been some shows of either flourishing or tolerable commonwealths, yet neither have those endured, but, according to the prophecy of Daniel, have been broken all to pieces, so that there is not so much of them left as a shard to fetch fire in, neither yet can those kingdoms which have the knowledge of the Gospel revealed unto them look for that long-suffering and patience of God towards them wherewith these ignorant kingdoms have been borne with. For as the benefit is greater towards these than towards the other, so is the judgment swifter against them than against the other if that grace which was not offered unto them, being offered unto these, be refused and made light of. And in these especially is and shall be fulfilled that which the prophet Isaiah saith, that it shall be in the later days that every nation and kingdom which shall not serve the Church shall be destroyed, as of the other side the full and whole placing of our Savior Christ in His throne is the perpetual stay and staid perpetuity of all princes in their seats.

And therefore, if this book shall come into the hands of any that have access unto Her Majesty, the head of this commonwealth, or unto her most honorable Council, the shoulders thereof, my humble suit and hearty request in the presence of God is that, according as their callings will suffer them, they will put them in remembrance of these things which otherwise they know better than I, and that they would set before them the example of Moses, who was not contented to have brought the people out of Egypt, but would very fain also have conducted them into the land of Canaan: that is, would gladly have been the instrument of the full and whole deliverance of the people. And seeing that the Lord doth offer unto them this honor, which He denied unto His servant Moses, that they would not make themselves guilty of so great unthankfulness as will follow of the forsaking of so incomparable a benefit; that Her Majesty especially, and her most honorable Council would set before them the example of David, who although he made a great reformation of those things which were defaced by Saul, yet he was not content that the ark of the Lord should dwell under a tabernacle, and therefore desired marvelously that he might build the Temple unto the Lord; and seeing that the Lord hath granted that unto them which He denied unto His servant, that they would not be narrow and strait in themselves; seeing the Lord openeth the treasures of His goodness so largely unto them; that they would set before them the zeal of Zerubbabel, who, although he had, after the return out of captivity, abolished idolatry, laid the foundations of the Temple and set up an altar unto God, whereupon the morning and evening sacrifice was daily made: yet, being admonished by the prophet Haggai that God would not be pleased unless the Temple also were fully builded, did (all fear of the nations round about and other business laid aside) cause it forthwith and with all possible speed to be made an end of; finally, that it would please them to consider the examples of Josiah, Hezekiah, and Jehoshaphat, who are therefore to their everlasting commendation praised of the Holy Ghost for that they made whole and thorough reformations, whereas the honor of other some, albeit they were otherwise good, is stained and carrieth the mark of their imperfection by this and like exception, that although they did such good things and such, yet they left also such and such undone.

Which I do not speak as though we had not already by Her Majesty especially, and afterward by their honors' hands, received a singular benefit, but that we, having the whole, might have our hearts and mouths filled with the praise of God and continue the possession of that which we have, which otherwise for our unthankful refusal shall be taken away. Wherein as we have especial regard that the name of God should be magnified not by us alone but by our posterity to the world's end, so is it not the smallest part of our care that Her Majesty and your honors, to whom we are so deeply bound, and of whom we have received so singular benefits of peace and preaching of the Gospel, might with your successions continue and flourish amongst us forever. But the desire of reformation and fear of God's heavy wrath to come upon us hath carried me further herein than I purposed. I will therefore make an end of these points, considering that the untruth of these accusations of newness and strangeness, of disorder and confusion, of being enemy to princes and commonwealths shall better appear in the discourse of this book.

Walter Travers (*ca.* 1548–1635)

If Thomas Cartwright was the "head" of Elizabethan Puritanism, Walter Travers was the "neck," as some contemporaries would have it. Born about 1548, Travers was a native of Nottingham, where his father, a decided Protestant, was a goldsmith. In 1560 he went up to Cambridge, where he studied at Trinity College. Two years later, Cartwright was made a fellow of the college and their association began. Because of his abilities Travers was selected to deliver an oration before the Queen during her visit to Cambridge in August 1564, when he was about sixteen. In 1566 he was graduated B.A.; the following year he was elected junior fellow with the approval of the new master of the college, John Whitgift. In 1569 he commenced M.A. and was made a senior fellow. Shortly afterwards, however, he left England to study at Geneva, where he became an intimate friend of Theodore Beza.

It was in Geneva that Travers wrote *Ecclesiasticae Disciplinae et Anglicanae Ecclesiae ab illa Aberrationus Plena et Verbo Dei & Dilucida Explicatio*, published in 1574. This work, which was translated shortly afterwards by Cartwright as *A Full and Plain Declaration of Ecclesiastical Discipline*, was considered the authoritative statement of presbyterian principles by English Puritans. (A portion is reprinted here.) Mullinger, the historian of Cambridge University, went so far as to say that this work "in the latter part of the sixteenth and earlier half of the seventeenth century exercised an influence on religious thought in England unsurpassed by that of any other work." Perhaps this is an overstatement, but the influence of this work of Travers, along with that of the "Book of Discipline," which he edited later, was surely very great.

After his years in Geneva and thorough exposure to Continental Reformed thought, Travers returned to England and was made M.A. at Oxford in 1576. Because of his unwillingness to subscribe to the Church's articles of conformity, he could not obtain a position in the Church. Besides, he had not yet been ordained. Therefore he left England again, this time for Holland, after the English

ambassador had arranged for him to serve a congregation of English merchants at Antwerp. There Travers was ordained in May
1578, not by a bishop but by the local Protestant clergy. After
this service he was chosen, in presbyterian fashion, as minister by
the merchants' congregation. Under Travers' leadership this congregation did not use the Book of Common Prayer, and for this reason
the governor of the merchants closed the place of worship. Sir
Francis Walsingham, Elizabeth's Secretary of State, perhaps as a
result of a plea from the English ambassador, intervened on Travers's behalf and rebuked the governor. A compromise was eventually reached: Travers made some slight use of the Prayer Book
and was left alone. Nevertheless, minor disputes made Travers's
position uncomfortable.

In July 1580 Travers returned to England for a long visit. During
the early part of his absence from Antwerp, Thomas Cartwright
took his place. Once again their close identification is suggested.
Within six months of the time he left, Travers decided not to
return, though the merchants were eager to have him; in December he resigned and recommended Cartwright as his successor.
In the same year Travers and Cartwright were both invited by the
famous Andrew Melville to serve as divinity professors at St.
Andrews University in Scotland, but neither accepted.

We have noticed Walsingham's relationship with Travers. On
his return to England Travers established a very important relationship with another member of the Queen's Council, the immensely influential Lord Burghley, in whose house he became
chaplain as well as tutor to Burghley's son Robert Cecil, later chief
minister in King James's reign. Perhaps through Burghley's efforts,
in 1581 Travers was made reader at the Temple. Actually his
position was that of acting master, or chaplain, since the master,
Richard Alvey, was ill. This position, which did not require subscription to the articles of conformity, was that of minister to the
lawyers of the Inns of Court. In the early 1580's Travers appears
to have won over many lawyers to the cause of Puritanism. The
continuing support of Puritanism by members of the bar was of
immense importance in the development of the cause up to the
Civil War of the 1640's.

During this time Travers's abilities were recognized, perhaps through Burghley's efforts, even by the Queen. It seems likely that it was she who encouraged him to write a reply to a Catholic plea addressed to the Lords of the Privy Council to restore Roman Catholicism to England. In 1583 was published Travers's *Answere to a Supplicatorie Epistle,* a learned refutation of the Catholic argument.

In August 1584 Alvey died. Since the late master had recommended Travers for his post and since Burghley, who also recommended him, referred to him as "well learned, very honest, and well allowed of the generality of that house," the Temple, Travers expected to be made Alvey's successor. But Archbishop Whitgift, who had followed Travers's career since their days together at Trinity College, charged that Travers was ineligible since he had not been ordained according to the form used in the Church of England. Travers justified himself by replying that national boundaries do not affect the validity of ordination, according to ancient and widely recognized precedents. After much controversy, Elizabeth decided that the post should not go to Travers or to Whitgift's nominee but to Richard Hooker, who had been recommended by Edwin Sandys, Archbishop of York. Travers remained as reader.

The events which followed are famous in the chronicles of the controversy between Puritanism and the Establishment. We have descriptions from the two men intimately involved, for both Travers and Hooker wanted their positions known when, less than a year after Hooker's appointment, Travers was silenced by Whitgift. Both descriptions were printed at Oxford in 1612. The first is entitled *A Supplication Made to the Privy Council by Mr. Walter Travers;* the second, addressed to Whitgift, *The Answer of Mr. Richard Hooker to a Supplication Preferred by Mr. Walter Travers to the H.H. Lords of the Privy Council.* The conflict seems to have originated when those members of the Temple most inclined to Puritanism, under the leadership of Travers, tried to persuade Hooker, when he appeared as the new master, to have his appointment approved by the congregation, according to Puritan principles. Hooker refused, and likewise he refused to permit other Puritan practices to be followed, such as sitting or standing to receive Holy Communion.

The dispute soon entered a new phase, one of great significance for an understanding of the split between Puritans and those satisfied with the Church as established: the debate marks the beginning of the identification of theological liberalism with the episcopal party and theological conservatism with Puritanism. Hitherto there had been no real theological division, and though it is easy to overstate the differences between the two groups, especially since many clergymen were at most only loosely identified with either position, the liberal and conservative tendencies did in time increase antagonisms.

The basis of this dispute was a series of points of doctrine which Hooker presented or implied in his sermons and which Travers labeled unorthodox. Of the fifteen, the most important were these:

1. The Church of Rome is a true church.

2. The Fathers, who lived and died in popish superstition, were saved because they sinned ignorantly.

3. Predestination is not the absolute will of God but is conditional.

4. The reprobates are rejected for the evil works which God foresaw they would commit.

5. The assurance of things which we believe by the Word is not so sure as of those things which we perceive by means of the senses.

Travers attacked these points in his sermons. It was these sermons of Hooker and Travers which Fuller, from his vantage point many years later, described: "The pulpit spake pure Canterbury in the morning, and Geneva in the afternoon."

Although posterity has given the palm to Hooker, it was Travers who won the hearts of his hearers. Whereas, according to Fuller, Hooker's "voice as low, stature little, gesture none at all," "Mr. Travers' utterance was graceful, gesture plausible, matter profitable, method plain, and his style carried in it *indolem pietatis*, a genius of grace flowing from his sanctified heart."

An important consequence of this dispute was that Hooker found occasion for the studies which resulted in the *Of the Laws of Ecclesiastical Polity*, or, as he put it, "in this examination, I have not only satisfied myself but have begun a treatise in which I intend a justification of the laws of our ecclesiastical polity." Travers, on the other hand, was silenced because he lacked episcopal ordination.

For a number of years after this time Travers appears to have been paid his salary by the Temple authorities. He resorted to private meetings with Puritans in London and soon found himself occupied with the classical or presbyterian movement. A Book of Discipline having been prepared by some now unknown presbyterians, Travers was called on to edit it late in 1584, when he was too busy with his problems at the Temple to give the task much attention. After encouragement by the always busy John Field, Travers finally prepared a revised version which was available by March 1587. Though not published at this time, it is extant in five manuscript copies, all somewhat different, and a version was finally gotten into print in 1644, when it was called *A Directory of Church Government*. Originally in Latin, it bore the title *Disciplina Ecclesiae Dei Verbo Descripta*, and was intended to be a guide for establishing presbyterianism. In some ways it is a digest of Travers's earlier *Explicatio*, though the author had now changed his mind on some details. Travers's recent biographer, S. J. Knox, calls the book "an outstanding contribution to the spread of the presbyterian cause throughout Elizabethan England" and "the most dangerous instrument that had ever come into the hands of the Genevan revolutionaries."

Meetings were held in many places throughout England for discussion and critical examination of the book, the London meetings being held in Travers's house. Foreshadowing the break-up of Puritanism in the 1640's, the Elizabethan presbyterian Puritans could not agree on details of the work. Besides the Puritan debates over presbyterianism Travers found the episcopal establishment eager to debate also, and when John Bridges, Dean of Sarum, attacked the Puritan plan of church government in his huge *Defense of the Government Established* (1587), Travers answered with his *Defense of the Ecclesiastical Discipline Ordained of God* (1588), and Dudley Fenner replied to Bridges with *A Defense of the Godly Ministers* (1587). The first two of the Martin Marprelate tracts were also defenses of the Puritan position, though it is most unlikely that Travers and Fenner approved of Martin's manner.

The heat of the Marprelate controversy, the death of John Field, the lack of agreement among the presbyterians, and Bishop Bancroft's effective detective work soon brought on the collapse of the classical movement.

Although it is impossible to deal adequately in short space with Travers's voluminous writings on ecclesiastical discipline, some of his ideas are of fundamental importance for an understanding of presbyterian Puritanism. Travers's concept that God's Word provides a basis for discipline is of prime significance; it is set forth in the selection which follows. For Travers, "the church of Christ in all this matter of discipline hath received all her laws and decrees from the Jews," and therefore Old Testament precedents are as compelling as those of the New Testament. Hence princes have an obligation to maintain church discipline, just as did the leaders of the Jews.

Travers's attractive personality, much admired by his contemporaries, shines through his writings, but despite the favor with which men might consider him, Whitgift's attitude towards his nonepiscopal ordination barred him from any ecclesiastical living in England. His patron Lord Burghley eventually found a post for him: in 1594 he became head of Trinity College, Dublin. Adam Loftus, Archbishop of Dublin, called him as fit a man as lived for the position, "a wise and learned man." At Dublin one of Travers's students was James Ussher, later Primate of Ireland, though he was something of a Puritan. But Travers found that Ireland did not agree with his health, and within a few years he returned to England, now highly regarded for his work as educator and administrator.

There he lived obscurely, even for a time in poverty, a bachelor, preaching only rarely. As late as 1630, when he was in his eighties, he published *Vindiciae Ecclesiae Anglicanae: or A Justification of the Religion now Professed in England*. Despite the title, the book does not express satisfaction with the Church as it then existed. Rather Travers defends those doctrines held alike by Puritans and those identified with the Church as established. Addressed to Roman Catholics and those attracted to Rome, the work defends the use of the vulgar tongue, communion in both kinds, and the Word of God as the basis for faith. Its attacks on such Roman Catholic practices as the use of images are moderate and gentle.

At his death in 1635 he was sufficiently prosperous to leave one hundred pounds each to Emmanuel College, Cambridge, earlier noted for its Puritanism, and Trinity College, Dublin, both sums to assist candidates for the ministry. Travers's influence was felt in the decade after his death: his Book of Discipline was used in the preparation of the Westminster Assembly's *Form of Presbyteriall Church-Government* (1645). One leaves a consideration of the life of the gentle Walter Travers with the conviction that here was a great waste of talent.

Church discipline and the Gospel

The manner of government in all human societies is of greatest force and power either to the preservation or overthrow of the same, for there is no commonwealth, be it never so small, no, not a house, that can be preserved without some certain manner of government and discipline. And those kingdoms and commonweals have always most notably flourished and longest continued which first of all were set in good order of government, and afterwards kept the same without any alteration or change. As contrariwise the destruction of greatest commonweals and most flourishing states have followed where either the order of government was ill appointed in the beginning or else being well begun was afterwards altered and neglected. For policy, government, and good laws are in city or any commonwealth whatsoever as the helm is to the ship, the wrest to the instrument, order to an army, and as the soul is to the body.

Hereof it came that Athens, which was so famous a city, after it could no longer hold and steer this helm, was tossed with every wave and storm, and in the end perished and was overthrown. And hereby also that ancient city of Lacedaemon, changing the severe laws of Lycurgus, changed also her estate, even as a song is changed by altering the time and note in which it was first set. Hereby the

[*A Full and Plaine Declaration of Ecclesiasticall Discipline owt off the word of God, and off the declininge off the church off England from the same* (1574), pp. 1–10.]

Romans' commonwealth, or army rather, after that they left the severity of the law of arms and warlike discipline whereby they did always more prevail than by might and power, lost also their ancient glory and renown. And to conclude, hereof cometh that we see now everywhere so many towns fallen to ruin and lying like the dead carcasses of the cities which sometimes they have been, because that by changing their old government by little and little, at the last the whole state was lost and went away as the soul from the body.

And even as the monuments of the Greek and Latin writers do witness these things to have chanced to many commonweals and other societies and companies, even so we read in the holy histories that the Church (which is a certain society and company of such as profess the true service of God) with no less danger neglected the discipline and order which God, their most loving and wise lawgiver, had appointed them to be ruled by, yea, to their much greater loss and punishment, for that, besides those incommodities which are wont to chance unto others by changing good laws, they always found by experience that the Lord God, their lawgiver, was ready to punish and revenge the contempt of His discipline and order. For, to pass over the punishment of God upon the church of the Jews, whosoever doth diligently and attentively read the history of the Christian Church shall well understand that the calamity of the former times, in which the Church lay dead as it were by the space of many years, came of no other cause than of the contempt of the most wholesome and most holy ordinances whereupon it was grounded by our Lord and Savior Christ, that it might have endured forever. Therefore it is a wonder to see, whereas our merciful God of His unspeakable goodness and by a singular miracle even now of late within the memory of our fathers hath raised up the Church as it were out of the grave again by the voice of the Gospel, that so few are careful for the maintaining and preserving of this life, and that being content as it were to be in good health by preaching of the Gospel, they care not for discipline, whereby this health may be the better preserved, and also the strength and beauty which was lost by former sickness be recovered and gotten again.

And surely it is greatly to be feared lest that they, if they go thus on still and continue to condemn so necessary an aid, fall again into the calamities of the former times, and lest that these later times become worse and more miserable than the former. But I am most of all afraid for our Church of England, which, by the space of so many years as it hath already embraced the Gospel, not only thinketh not of instituting a lawful discipline therein, but in a manner useth only that which it hath received from the papists, nor will not be persuaded to receive and embrace that discipline which Christ and His apostles have left unto us; whose state hitherto hath been this until the time of King Henry the Eighth's reign. For a long space before it had lain dead and as it were without any life. Then at the length by the greater favor and grace of God towards us, divers notable men rose up who, as Elias and Elisha raised up the children which were dead, so they likewise by most earnest prayer and cherishing it by all means got at the last some life into it, so that at the length it began as it were to wax warm and neese [sneeze], and by certain articles of sound doctrine to show some tokens of a church reviving again.

And afterwards, in the time of Edward the Sixth, a prince of singular hope and towardness in all godliness and virtue, was fully revived and recovered not only her life but also her health again. But our Church, being thus recovered, was contented with physic only and good diet for her health, and used no exercise to get her color and strength again, for although many did exhort to abolish that popish tyranny which then was still remaining in the policy of the Church, and to place instead thereof a just and lawful manner of government according to the Word of God (which thing especially that famous man Martin Bucer, being then a stranger in England, did in that book which he wrote of the kingdom of Christ), yet could not England be brought to leave that form of governing the Church whereunto it had been accustomed under popery, but divided and separated as under the doctrine and discipline of the Gospel, two things which both by their own nature and also by the commandment of God are to be joined together. But forasmuch as health cannot long be kept and preserved without due and moderate exercise, not long after—namely, in those most cruel times of Queen Mary—it fell sick again, that it was not only in danger of death but in a manner past all hope to recover again. And surely even then our Church had out of doubt been utterly destroyed, as indeed it was brought all to ashes, unless that heavenly Son Jesus Christ had quickened it, being more than half dead, and raised it up like a phoenix out of the ashes again, and except our most noble Queen Elizabeth had risen up as a mother in Israel, to travail with and bring forth our Church again.

But this new birth hath not as yet been any more happy touching the restoring of discipline than were the former times. Therefore I thought it my duty even for the kind affection which I bear to that Church in which I have been both born and brought up and therefore love most dearly for good causes (even as the apostle saith to live and die together)—I thought it, I say, my duty to desire and beseech this Church earnestly and carefully to think of this so great a benefit, whereby it may be established forever, and most earnestly to exhort and admonish it to abolish that popish tyranny which yet remaineth in the government thereof, and to restore again the most holy policy of ruling the Church which our Savior Christ hath left unto us, and to fear lest that the Lord will punish us and will be revenged of us if we continue still to despise His discipline.

But forasmuch as there be many who, because they delight rather in a fair outward show than the true simplicity of the Gospel, strive and contend to retain still this popish hierarchy and counterfeit manner of governing the Church, blaming that order for many causes which we persuade unto, this whole controversy is fully and at large to be disputed of, that, when they understand the good cause that we have to reprive the one and require the other, they may join together with us in earnest prayers unto God and humble suit unto Her Majesty that, this popish tyranny being at the last utterly abolished and clean taken away, in place thereof a better and more holy government of the Church according to God's Word may be established.

Which cause I purpose so to handle that, first drawing out the right pattern and platform of the lawful policy and government of the Church as Christ and His apostles have left it unto us, together therewithal I will note our faults and errors in every point, that by this comparison the truth may more clearly shine and appear. First, therefore, seeing we have not to do with such as reject all discipline of the Church, that it may be better understood what it is whereof we dispute, I will declare what the lawful discipline of the Church is.

I call, therefore, ecclesiastical discipline the policy of the Church of Christ ordained and appointed of God for the good administration and government of the same. That I make here God the author of discipline, whereupon it followeth that we have to fetch the rules thereof from no other fountains but from the Holy Scriptures, had need be more fully proved, because it is denied by many who dare affirm that there is no precept given touching this matter, but contend that it is wholly left unto judgment of the magistrate and of the Church. First, then, let them tell us why they deny that God hath thus carefully provided for Christian churches, and why they affirm it to be left free for us to rule it as we list, seeing that in the old church of the Jews all things which pertained not only to the government of the civil state but also of the ecclesiastical (for although with them God was author of both, yet He would have them distinguished the one from the other) were so diligently and exactly distributed and both commanded by God and commended to writing by Moses, that it was expressly forbidden that nothing should be added unto it nor taken from it. For it appeareth manifestly that that exact pattern of discipline came not first from Moses but from God, by this, that Moses testifieth so often that the Lord had appointed the manner of creating and ordaining ecclesiastical officers and their power and authority, Who was always ready to punish the transgressors of His ordinances with most grievous plagues and punishments.

There is a notable history in the ninth of Numbers, of certain unclean persons who, thinking it no sufficient cause why they should not eat the Passover with the rest of Israel because they were polluted with touching of a dead body, which they must needs do, seeing there died daily some amongst them (as of necessity it cometh to pass in so great a multitude), went to Moses and Aaron desiring that they might not be secluded from that solemn communion of the church. But what doth Moses in this case? What taketh he upon him? Surely nothing at all, but referreth the cause wholly unto God, by Whose answer they were forbidden to eat the Passover with the rest of Israel and were put off unto the next month. Of which cause properly belonging to this discipline which we handle and referred to God, it may be clearly understood that Moses in all the government of the church did nothing by his private authority, but only delivered unto them that which the Lord had commanded; which thing also Moses himself doth plainly testify by his often repeating of these words, "As the Lord had commanded." And this is that faithfulness which the Apostle [in the epistle] to the Hebrews commendeth in him, that he ruled not the house of God by his own will, but by the authority of the Lord, the master of the household.

And how precisely is it commanded in the Tabernacle that all should be made after the fashion and pattern which had been showed by the Lord in the mountain. Neither so long as kings were in any tolerable state, any either kings or priests took upon them any such authority to appoint matters belonging to the church, but all things were ruled and governed according to the will and authority of God. For whereas in the fashion and building of the Temple and in the offices of the Levites and of the singers certain things were somewhat otherwise appointed by David and Solomon than they had been commanded by Moses, that change and alteration was not made by the authority of David and Solomon as kings, but by the will of God Himself, who appointed it so by His prophets, as appeareth in the Second Chronicles. Therefore also the fashion and pattern of the Temple after it was overthrown was so exactly drawn out by Ezekiel that the new Temple might be builded again according to the pattern of God showed by His prophet. Wherefore also Ezra and Nehemiah exacted all their reformation to the pattern of Moses, David, and Ezekiel.

Seeing then so stable and certain a rule of governing the Church continued unto Christ, the laws and ordinances were appointed by God Himself, and that it was accounted wicked and unlawful for any man boldly to have taken anything in hand in these matters, and that such as did so escaped not the grievous punishment and vengeance of God, why do they now at the last deliver God of this care, or rather spoil the Church of her patron and defender, by Whose government it might be preserved, and Who, sitting in the stern at the helm, it never feared any storms or tempests but was always safe in all danger? And how absurd and unreasonable a thing is it then especially to think the love and care of God to be diminished towards His Church when He hath testified it with a most certain and undoubted testimony, that is to say, by the sending of His only begotten Son to take away our sins and, as the prophet of God, to declare all the Lord's will and counsel towards us and to rule the Church by His own authority. For this is that Prophet like unto Moses Who should plainly and perfectly declare unto us of God all things which do belong unto our duty, Whom we ought to hear and to obey, as the Holy Ghost by the mouth of Peter hath expounded that promise, and by that heavenly voice which testified of Him from heaven that He was the dear and only begotten Son of God, in Whom the Father was well pleased and commanded us to hear Him. But how should we think Him to be like unto Moses if He either hath wholly omitted, or not so clearly and perfectly (as far as was needful for us) showed and declared this doctrine of the manner of governing the Church, being so necessary, and which Moses hath so diligently and faithfully declared?

Therefore we must conclude, if we acknowledge Christ to be that Prophet, that He hath fully and perfectly declared unto us whatsoever was needful for the government of the Church, except we will rob Him of some part of the prophetical office, or prefer a servant, be he never so faithful, before the only begotten Son, and as it were Eliezer before Isaac in his father's house, which surely they do who think the servant to have omitted nothing in this behalf, [and] that the heir hath omitted all, and that Moses left all things perfect but Christ either began them not or did not finish that which He began. Now whereas I affirm that Christ hath left us so perfect a rule and discipline, I understand it of that discipline which is common and general to all the Church and perpetual for all times, and so necessary that without it this whole society and company and Christian commonwealth cannot well be kept under their Prince and King, Jesus Christ. And surely we must needs either confess that Christ hath left us such an order to live by or else spoil Him of His kingly office. For what doth more belong unto the name, office, and duty of a king than to give laws unto his citizens and subjects and to make such decrees and ordinances whereby all the parts of his kingdom may be maintained? The papists indeed deny it, and dispute against us and contend that it is lawful for their high priest to rule and order the Church of God as he listeth; but we who do detest and abhor this blasphemous voice and according to God's Word acknowledge and confess Christ to be the only King of the Church—how can we say either that He neglected so great and so necessary a point of His kingly office, or that He hath left it us to order as we please?

Anthony Gilby (*ca.* 1510–1585)

The only Marian exile represented in this study is Anthony Gilby, one of the most prominent Puritans of the exiles, especially in the field of propaganda. Little is known of his early life. Born about 1510 in Lincolnshire, he commenced B.A. in 1532 and M.A. in 1535 at Christ's College, Cambridge. He appears to have been a minister in Leicestershire and soon became a follower of Calvin's theology.

Like Hooper and Cranmer, Gilby wrote a reply to Stephen Gardiner's *A Detection of the Devil's Sophistry, wherewith he Robbeth the Unlearned People of the True Belief in the Sacrament of the Altar* (1546). Gilby's work, published in 1547, is entitled *An Answer to the Devilish Detection of Stephen Gardiner*. This long, dull work attacks the concept of the sacrifice of the Mass and transubstantiation. A significant point is the sense of a Protestant tradition which Gilby demonstrates in the prefatory epistle through a reference to the burning of poor Bilney, dead sixteen years. In 1551 Gilby published a commentary on the prophet Micah, a thorough, competent, solid, but dull work which shows clearly the author's adherence to Calvinist theology, as does his treatise on election and reprobation, published later, in Elizabeth's reign.

On Mary's accession he fled to Frankfort, where he allied himself with the anti-Prayer Book group of radical English Protestants: Knox, Whittingham, Foxe, and others. These drew up the service order which later became known as the Order of Geneva. When a group of Prayer Book Anglicans under Richard Cox joined them, Gilby sought to win them over to his side for the sake of peace, but he failed and the Coxians triumphed. Soon Gilby found himself heading a group which appealed to the Frankfort magistrate to stop Cox, on the grounds that the Gilby-Whittingham-Knox group was much closer to the local religious practices than Cox was. The effort failed, and on August 27, 1555, we find Gilby and others of his group, including Christopher Goodman, writing to the English congregation at Frankfort to indicate their intention to leave. Shortly thereafter they did, some going to Basel with Foxe, some to Geneva. Among the latter were Gilby, his wife and son, and Whittingham, who described Geneva as the place where "God's word is truly preached, manners best reformed, and in earth the chiefest place of true comfort."

The Geneva group formed a congregation and elected Knox and Goodman pastors, but since Knox was in France, Gilby temporarily took his place. Gilby's chief activity at Geneva, however, was his work, with Whittingham, on a translation of the Bible. Their version, which came to be known as the Geneva Bible, was distinctly the most scholarly and accurate version to be published in English before the Authorized Version of 1611. Appearing first in 1560, it had ninety-six complete editions by 1640. This very popular translation was richly annotated with a Calvinist commentary: indeed, some of the notes were Calvin's. A Calvinist catechism was later added, though it was almost superfluous. To a substantial degree the Geneva Bible was responsible for the permeation of the Elizabethan Church by Calvinism.

On Mary's death the Genevan party had high hopes that their position would be adopted by the Church of England. For this end Gilby and seventeen other radical Protestants circulated a letter praying that all the exiles be reconciled to one another to form a united front to seek the establishment of Genevan practices. The Frankfort group showed a disinclination to adopt this position, and none of Gilby's group achieved much recognition when they returned to England.

Gilby fared better than most, for he found a position with Henry Hastings, Earl of Huntington and brother-in-law of Lord Leicester. At Ashby-de-la-Zouch, near Leicester, Gilby exercised his ministry till his death in 1585. Because of Hastings, Gilby was not harassed for his nonconformity, though there is clear evidence that he was a nonconformist. In 1571 Parker commanded the Archbishop of York, Grindal, to prosecute Gilby, but Grindal refused, saying that Ashby was not in his diocese.

In 1572 Gilby met with Willcocks, Sampson, Field, and Lever, and agreed that an admonition should be addressed to Parliament. Gilby did not take part in the composition of the work, which was assigned to Willcocks and Field, but he may have been responsible for the better *Second Admonition to the Parliament* (1572), which describes the presbyterian program that the Puritans would substitute for the corruptions pointed out in the first *Admonition*. Correspondence is extant between Gilby and Humphrey, Sampson, and Willcocks. The letters addressed to Gilby were written with great respect; he is addressed as "good Father Gilby."

Gilby very probably wrote *A Pleasant Dialogue Between a Soldier of Barwick and an English Chaplain,* composed about 1575. It was not published until 1581 because, according to a prefatory note, soon after it was written "there was hope of reformation." But now "no hope remaineth," and "the folly of the persecutors" of the Puritans should be made known. It is from this dialogue that the selection below was taken. The dialogue proper is preceded by an epistle to a number of leading Puritans: Coverdale, Turner, Whittingham, Sampson, Humphrey, Lever, and Crowley. Like everything else of Gilby's, the epistle is outspoken. To him the bishops are "our enemies and persecutors" who are "strangely bewitched," for they desire services "with crossing, with coping, with surplicing, with kneeling, with pretty wafer cakes, and other knacks of popery."

He maintains that "the cross and candlesticks upon the Queen's altar are superstitious, though they be kept there I wot not for what policy." For him, all those who follow the leadership of the conformist leaders are selfish knaves, unworthy of the ministry. But if only one "symbol of popery," the vestments, were done away with, numbers of really able men would take up the Christian ministry. Many other remnants of the superstition of the past remain, according to Gilby, who lists one hundred remaining points of popery. Among these are the title of archbishop, organs, deans, dispensations, pluralities, simony, and "lewd plays" on the Sabbath.

Although Gilby was a very learned man proficient in three languages, apparently it was his status as a former exile which brought him great prestige in the Puritan movement. Unlike Whittingham, who ultimately conformed, Gilby remained a strict Puritan until his death in 1585. Gilby is not an attractive figure. Stern, angry, stubborn, he seems to have been embittered by the lack of success of Puritan efforts. His *Pleasant Dialogue* is an interesting and influential work, though scarcely pleasant.

Of popish traditions in the English Church

The Speakers

MILES MONOPODIOS, *the soldier, lame of one foot.*
SIR BERNARD BLINKARD, *a formal priest and a lord's chaplain.*

MIL. What, Bernard, mine old companion? Well met. I scarce knew thee, thou art so disguised and changed. Thou didst jet up and down so solemnly in the church, and so like an old popish prelate, that a great while I doubted of thee. What, man, art thou so strange? Hast thou forgotten me? Thou hast a good mark whereby I must needs know thee, and if I had not been, thou shouldst have had none eye this day to see withal.

BERN. Yes, Miles, I knew thee, and remember that thou wast ever an honest fellow towards me, and thou savedst my life then, I confess.

MIL. But Bernard, I pray thee, tell me of thine honesty, what was the cause that thou hast been in so many changes of apparel this forenoon, now black, now white, now in silk and gold, and now at the length in this swooping black gown, and this sarcenet flaunting tippet, wearing more horns also upon thy head than ever did thy father, unless he were a man of the same order? I pray thee, of good fellowship tell me how thou art come to this change, since thou leftest our company. For surely I have gotten nothing by my long service but stripes and wounds, and now I must needs leave off this trade, because I want my legs, and ashamed I am to beg. I would therefore very fain enter into this thy glorious trade, wherein thou art so well trimmed and appareled, if I might do it safely. Belike thou wantest none other thing, for one quarter of thy gown would make me a coat, and a sleeve of thy surplice would make me a shirt. There must needs be plenty where there is

[*A Pleasaunt Dialogue, Between a Souldior of Barwicke, and an English Chaplaine. Wherein are largely handled & laide open, such reasons as are brought in for maintenaunce of popishe Traditions in our Eng. Church.* (1581), sigs. B2^{recto}-B7^{recto}.]

so great superfluity. And I that have lived in scarcity, in peril and labor all my life long, would now in my old age find some ease and safety. As for our learnings, they are both like, thou knowest, unless of late thou hast been at some university.

BERN. No, I have been at no university, but in my lord's house a year only, and I know that thou hast more learning than I. But I must admonish thee of two things, the one touching me, the other thee: in thy talk thou must use me more reverently, and tie a "Sir" by your girdle when you speak to me.

MIL. What in the vineyard, are you entered into the order of knighthood? You were of late in the order of the four and twenty, amongst the number of other good fellows.

BERN. You may not thus jest with me; I am within the holy orders of priesthood.

MIL. Is it even so, sir? Then will I pose you. Of what order, I pray you, of the order of Aaron, or of Melchizedek, or of the popish order? There was but one after the order of Melchizedek, and the other ceased at Christ's coming, so that it were a denial of Christ to renew that order. Therefore I suppose you are of the third, even of the popish order, and so methought by your attire.

BERN. Nay, I would thou knewest it, I defy the Pope, I am none of his order, I know not what he is: whether a man, a woman, or a beast. No, nor I care not, for I had none orders at his hand. Therefore I am no popish priest, if thou list to take it so.

MIL. Why, sir, where the devil then got you your orders, having so small learning?

BERN. Where? Of my metropolitan, my lord of Canterbury's good grace. God save his grace, for he helpeth many such as I am, forth of the briers, with his licenses and dispensations.

MIL. God send him better grace, and pardon him of his manifold sins, that promoteth you and such companions to this state.

BERN. Why man, thou knowest not what a state this is, for though he find us never so very dolts, yet can he and the other bishops by the laying on of their hands give us the Holy Ghost. For so said they to me and my fellows: "Hold, take the Holy

Ghost." So that I am no more of the lewd laity, but of the holy spirituality, and I have gotten a good benefice or twain, and am called "Master Parson," and may spend with the best man in our town, and do keep company with gentlemen of the country in hawking, hunting, dicing, carding, and take my pleasure all the day long; so that I do come to the church sometime in the morning and read a little whiles dinner be made ready.

MIL. This is an easy order that thou talkest on, if it be as good as it is easy; and I pray thee, how might I come into the same order and state with thee?

BERN. I will tell thee all for old fellowship's sake, and I will help thee to avow some for money; and that is the surest way. But if thou have no money, then must thou fawn upon some gentleman that either hath some impropriations or other benefices in his hand, or else by other means, to seek some little gain by it, or hath some in his gift. Get his letters to the bishop and thou needst not to doubt of orders.

MIL. Yes, peradventure the loss of my leg will be a hindrance; yet I think there be thousands in England on whom benefices are worse bestowed, for I will fight for the realm and the Holy Church, as lame as I am.

BERN. I tell thee, thy fighting will not serve thee so much as the want of the comely wearing of thy gown, thy cope, and thy surplice will hinder thee.

MIL. Why sayest thou so? Such swooping clothes will hide my stump foot.

BERN. Nay, I tell thee, my lords the bishops will have all things comely, and thou canst not go in [to] them but thou wilt swing them on the lame side evil favoredly.

MIL. Why fool, all the grace is in swinging, and swingeing of them, and I can do that decently. But I marvel how thou, wanting thy finger and one of thy eyes, wast admitted, for by the Pope's law thou shouldst not have been received.

BERN. Yes, by dispensation for money, and now is less danger, for there is no lifting, and therefore less money will serve.

MIL. But what is that, I pray thee, whereof thou saidst thou wouldst admonish me concerning myself? For I see that thou art come into a high estate above me and hast gotten some other spirit and therefore knowest much more now than when thou wast a poor soldier.

BERN. Thou dost use too much to scoff at our priestly apparel and our church gear. This must thou leave, or else canst thou neither have benefice thyself nor be welcome to any man of worship that taketh profit by benefices. No, thou canst come to no company to be quiet, for there are very few that can agree to the Genevans' fashion, to have nothing in the church but naked walls and a poor fellow in a bare gown telling a long tale and brawling and chiding with all his auditory. Nay, my lord, my master will none of that. As for my lord, I heard him say that he could never go to any of these Genevans' sermons, that he came quiet home, but that there was ever somewhat that pricked his conscience. He thought always that they made their whole sermon against him. But in the hearing of matins, evensong and pricksong at Paul's, or in my reading of my service in his chapel, he saith, he feeleth no such thing, for he is never touched, but goeth merrily to his dinner.

MIL. Thus said wicked Ahab, by the good prophet Micah. But as for me, I use to say nothing but that I have heard good preachers teach openly in the pulpit that all popish priests' apparel are superstitious; and such church ware as they did wear is infected with idolatry. Wherefore as the idols themselves were detestable, and the Pope to all Christian men and to all true English hearts execrable, so all the monuments of idolatry and all the usual liveries and garments of the idolatrous priests and Pope's chaplains ought to be rejected of the servants of Christ as abominable. And all that you say against the Genevans might be brought against Christ and His disciples in the same words and sentences.

BERN. I know that you have learned this lesson of the London ministers. But I have read a book of late, written by a proctor for our English priesthood, which calleth them stark fools and answereth them, I warrant you, in all points. I warrant you, Miles, he is a man of great authority that dare so boldly revile them and handle them like abjects, and my lords the bishops do take our parts against those busy fellows and keep some of them in prison and put others from their livings. And I may tell thee in secret, if we had not found such a master to maintain our ceremonies, and also unless the bishops had played the lords indeed, these prating preachers would have made some of us to have turned our tippets and for very shame to have forsaken our benefices. Yea, if they had had liberty but a little longer they would have disgraced my lord's grace, the Archbishop of Canterbury, and have made all England to believe that our gracious metropolitan (whose glorious grace, long might it last, for we poor ignorant priests shall never fail, unless he fall) had been but an idle shepherd, and an English Pope; and (which grieved the other bishops at the hearts) they began shrewdly to shake the lordly state of all the clergy. They would not have a bishop nor a minister known by his apparel, but by his preaching. A shameful heresy. They cry, "Pasce, pasce, pasce"; I cannot tell what they mean. They would have men such fools, to turn to that poor beggarly estate that was amongst the apostles, and always toil and travail with the people, and brawl and chide when anything is amiss. But I tell thee plain, they had then lost the greatest part of their number, a jolly sort of gentlemen swooping in their sarcenets, and many other good fellows too. Therefore I do account (with Master Examinator) all these poor beggarly London ministers stark dolts and thrice fools, for their preachings, their writings, and their beggarly living in their offices. I tell thee, my lords the bishops that were their fellows beyond the seas in Queen Mary's days are now ashamed of them, and care not for their companies, they are so beggarly, so busybodies, and will allow nothing but God's Word in the churches.

MIL. As for the bishops, they are not all so far gone, I trust in God. But I pray thee, Sir Bernard, in what part of his book doth your Master Examinator call them fools?

BERN. Marry, at the first word, and applieth Solomon very eloquently (as I heard Master Doctor say) to serve his purpose.

MIL. Is this Master Doctor's eloquence? He had need to have great corners in his cap to hide his ass's ears. Let him not begin his oration thus among soldiers. But what is the cause, I pray you, that you and your master of ceremonies dare so proudly (at the first chop) call God's ministers and faithful teachers of His holy Word in London, fools? Let me talk with you a little for old fellowship's sake. Is it because they have labored so faithfully to feed the flock of Christ (which you mock with "Pasce, pasce") that few can be named comparable to them in pains, in travails, in perils and diligence? Master Examinator, whosoever he was, should not thus against reason have railed on such, whom their very enemies the papists do reverence for their pains, their care and diligence. Ask at the churches of Antholine, Peter, Bartholomew, and at other churches also, what painful travails from time to time they have sustained, what perils in the plague they adventured. Have not the poor sick persons and prisoners by them been comforted and the people most diligently instructed? If this be true (as it is most true) for the reverence of Him, Whose servants they are, they should have been more gently handled and more brotherly answered, than thus to have been called fools, at the first word, though in some points they had failed as men and not satisfied the great wisdom of Master Examinator. Neither doth the rhetorical art of your master teach him thus rudely to begin, with them whom he should persuade. Neither Christian charity (if either of you were ever entered into that school) doth permit you to call your brother fool, as you may read in our Savior Christ's first sermon, Matthew v, which He beginneth with blessing and not with brawling.

Laurence Chaderton (*ca.* 1537–1640)

Laurence Chaderton, the Puritan Methuselah, was the son of Thomas Chaderton of Chaderton, Oldham, Lancashire, near Manchester. His father was a prosperous gentleman who intended to settle his lands in Manchester and Lichfield, with three to four hundred pounds a year, on Laurence, his third son, who was born sometime between 1536 and 1539. His entrance to a university was delayed, first by a lack of interest in learning, the result of bad teaching, and then perhaps by a stay at the Inns of Court. He entered Christ's College, Cambridge, apparently in 1565, and commenced bachelor in 1567, when he became a fellow. He was made deacon in 1568, M.A. in 1571, and B.D. in 1578. Although Christ's was not yet known as a Puritan college, one of the fellows in Chaderton's early years there was the young and brilliant Edward Dering.

Chaderton's stay at Christ's was marked by his rejection of the Catholicism of his father, who promptly all but disowned him. "Dear Laurence," he wrote, "If you will renounce a new sect which you have joined you may expect all the happiness which the care of an indulgent father can secure you; otherwise I enclose a shilling to buy a wallet with. Go and beg for your living. Farewell!"

Chaderton's connection with Christ's continued through 1577. During these years he established a great reputation as a scholar, especially in theology, classical and modern languages, and logic. He was the earliest expounder in England of Peter Ramus's art of logic, on which he lectured. He aroused great interest in this non-Aristotelian method of arguing, which as a result later became popular among Puritans. He was responsible for William Perkins's interest in Ramus and is the direct philosophical ancestor of the logician William Ames and also of John Milton, another Ramist. Another aspect of Chaderton's career at Christ's is his tutelage of Arthur Dent, who later became his brother-in-law when the two married sisters.

Around 1570 Chaderton became lecturer at St. Clement's, Cambridge, a post he may have acquired because of the acclaim which met his preaching to the prisoners in Cambridge. A little over ten years later, Chaderton's pupil Perkins similarly was chosen lecturer of a Cambridge church after successful preaching before local prisoners. Chaderton's lectures on Cicero's *Topica* and *Pro Marcello* were likewise well received, but he could not be persuaded to publish them. His only printed works are two sermons, one preached at Paul's Cross in 1578, and the one of which part is reprinted here, and also a short treatise *De Justificatione Coram Deo et Fidei Perseverantii non Intercisa*, published along with the writings of some other men by the Jesuit Antonius Thysius. The sermon on Romans which appears here was published anonymously and went through four editions. It was referred to as an authoritative statement of Puritan principles, for example by Dudley Fenner (in *A Defence of the Godly Ministers*, 1587), by John Udall (in *The State of the Church*, 1588), and by the anonymous author of *An Humble Motion* (1590, perhaps by John Penry). None of these identifies the work as Chaderton's but merely as *A Sermon on the Twelfth of Romans*.

In 1581 Chaderton's reputation was such that he was offered the preachership of Lincoln's Inn, but he refused. Out of his fellowship because of his marriage, in 1584 he was made the first master of Emmanuel College, which Sir Walter Mildmay, favorer of the Puritans, founded in part because of his respect for Chaderton and in part to prepare learned ministers. Chaderton held this post for thirty-seven years, during which time the college became the seedbed of Puritanism.

Although Chaderton's Puritanism was famous, he was protected from persecution by the fact that Bancroft, Whitgift's chief ferreter-out of Puritans, had been his dear friend since undergraduate days when Chaderton had rescued him in a town-gown fight. Chaderton was an active presbyterian and worked with Cartwright in the organization of the discipline in the 1580's. In the Emmanuel chapel a non-Prayer Book service was used and the surplice was omitted. Holy Communion was celebrated with the receivers sitting around a table. It is hardly surprising that Emmanuel produced some of the stricter Puritans of the time. Among them were the New Englanders Thomas Hooker, John Cotton, Thomas Shepard, and John Harvard. During the Commonwealth, Emmanuel supplied the masters of eleven other houses at Cambridge.

Chaderton's influence on the development of the Puritan sermon is hard to measure but may well have been crucial. His interest in Ramistic logic, which made much of methodicalness and orderliness, is reflected in the sermon given here as well as in his Paul's Cross Sermon. (Gabriel Harvey, Spenser's friend, characterized him as "methodicum.") As a result, his sermons are very different from most sixteenth-century Puritan sermons but resemble strikingly those of the famous Puritan preachers of the seventeenth century, many of whom were Emmanuel men. The lengthy analysis of the religious hypocrite's seven marks in the Paul's Cross sermon is precisely the kind of matter that we find in Thomas Hooker's sermons.

Chaderton's biographer, William Dillingham, had many personal memories of the master of Emmanuel; he speaks of his "astonishing influence in the pulpit." "Having once preached for two hours," Dillingham reports,

he said that he had tired his hearers' patience and would leave off; upon which the whole congregation cried out: "For God's sake, sir, go on, we beg you, go on!" He accordingly continued the thread of his discourse for another hour, to the great pleasure and delight of his hearers.

Because of his widespread influence among Puritans and the respect in which he was held, Chaderton was one of the four Puritan representatives at the Hampton Court Conference of 1604. However, he had very little to say, requesting only that some ministers might be permitted to omit the wearing of the surplice and the use of the cross in baptism. One of the few Puritan requests granted at the Conference resulted in the King James Version of the Bible. Chaderton was one of the eight men who translated the books of the Old Testament from I Chronicles to Ecclesiastes. Another honor which came to him was the degree of Doctor of Divinity, conferred on him in 1613 at the behest of the Count Palatine.

In 1622, at the age of about eighty-five, he resigned his mastership, but only after he was sure that an able man would succeed him; John Preston was selected. But despite Chaderton's advanced age he retained his faculties. He is reported to have read a Greek Testament in very small print without glasses during his retirement. Besides continuing his studies he found time for his hobby, grafting and planting trees. The following lines on Chaderton, of unknown authorship, reveal the contemporary attitude towards him:

> We are young, alas, and know thee not;
> Send up old Abram and grave Lot,
> Let them write thy epitaph and tell
> The world thy worth; they kenned thee well.
> When they were boys, they heard thee preach,
> And thought an angel did them teach.
> Awake them then and let them come,
> And score thy virtues on thy tomb;
> That we at those may wonder more
> Than at thy many years before.

The government of the Church

. . . for from these two pestilent fountains, self-love and ambition, flow envying of the good, bitter contention and striving with the equal, disdain and contempt of the inferiors. Hence it is that the governors of the Church think too well of themselves, not humbly begging the direction of God's Spirit, but expound the Word according to their own fancies; that they desire to rule as they list, devise new offices, confound those which the Lord hath wisely distinguished, challenge unto themselves new titles, new names, princely prerogatives, and unlawful jurisdiction over their brethren. All which vices, as they sprung up first in the Church of Rome (notwithstanding this admonition of Paul for the preventing of them), so having now deadly wounded the body and wholly de-

[*A Fruitfull Sermon, upon the 3.4.5.6.7. and 8. verses, of the 12. Chapiter of the Epistle of S. Paul to the Romanes, very necessary for these times to be read of all men, for their further instruction and edification in things concerning their faith and obedience to salvation* (London, 1584), pp. 20–27.]

stroyed and defaced that Church, they have spread their boughs and branches into many places of the Lord's vineyard, wherein they have taken such deep root that it is to be feared that as they now do overshadow the tender plants of the orchard of God, so they will in time consume and destroy the whole growth with the poison of their corruption, except they be plucked up by the roots. For my part, examining the matter with an indifferent mind, I can see no other root whence these rotten and unnatural boughs should spring, than from this high and lofty mind whereby men do presume to think of themselves and of the treasure of grace which they have, more than they ought to do. Why would not Diotrephes receive John and the other faithful ministers of the Word? Wherefore did he prattle with malicious words against them? Why would he neither himself receive, nor suffer others to entertain the brethren? Was not this the only cause, because he loved to have the preëm-inence in the Church? Read the third epistle of John. What caused the scribes and Pharisees to condemn and disdain the base estate and low degree of Christ and His poor disciples? They loved the chief places at feasts and desired the chief seat in the assemblies and greeting in the markets, and to be called of men "Rabbi, Rabbi"; was not this because they were high-minded? Why did James and John, and their mother, moved by them, desire to be chiefest in the kingdom of Christ? Or why did the other disciples disdain at this request? Was it not only because their hearts were puffed up with pride, vainglory, and ambition? Why did some preach to add affliction unto Paul's bonds? Was it not because they thought better of themselves and their gifts than of him and his gifts, and by envying him troubled the Church?

Oh, therefore, how necessary is it for us that be of the Church to beat down this brazen wall of pride, presumption, and ambition which cause all these disorders among us, that God may rear up in our hearts the new fortress of a sound, discreet, humble, and sober mind, and so make us sincere observers of this general law. All these things I have spoken do sufficiently teach how some churches have been and are at this day sore wounded, others destroyed by these two horrible monsters of pride and ambition which will not be subject to any, nay, which will, if they be suffered, lift up their heads into the throne of the Lord.

Now to the commonwealth, wherein if we shall ask the wisest men of all ages that be past, either religious or profane, they will tell you that which by long and certain experience they have learned: namely, that this proud and ambitious surprising of gifts, disliking of men's proper dealings, have been the disturbers, I might say the destroyers, of families, tribes, towns, cities, kingdoms, and empires. So Moses, Joshua, David, and the prophets have left in their writings this to be learned of such as will read them. The profane writers, both Grecians and Romans, which have registered the diversities, changes, overthrows, and ruins of commonwealths, do teach the same better than the time will suffer me particularly to rehearse. But to omit the ancient monuments and histories of the old time, and to come to our own country: did ever any man harden his heart here in England against lawful regiment, which hath not been full of pride and ambition? Can the sober-minded man, resting and taking his felicity in his base and low calling, lift up his hand to pluck the regal crown from the head of the lawful governor? No, no, dearly beloved, no more than a heavy stone can ascend into the highest region of the firmament. It is the light head and the aspiring mind which through pride and ambition flieth into the prince's palace.

Seeing, then, that these two vices of pride and ambition do not only eternally condemn such as are infected with them, which is most fearful, but also wound and destroy the society of the saints and the policy of kingdoms; seeing that the Lord by His apostle here doth so straitly forbid them as the most dangerous enemies unto this general law, I am to charge you in the name of Christ, from the highest to the lowest, to throw down yourselves before the majesty of God, craving earnestly the grace of His Spirit to mortify these evil affections, so that they may have in them neither poison to kill the soul nor power to hurt the Church or commonwealth. And for you that are the ministers of God, and our governors, if you will learn how to establish this general law and to remedy all the abuses thereof, behold: this must be your wisdom.

First pluck up by the roots, through the ministry of the Word and the authority of the sword, all proud and high looks, arrogant and ambitious persons; set before your eyes the godly zeal of David. "Him," saith David, "that hath a proud look and high heart, I cannot suffer." Again, "Betimes will I destroy all the wicked in the land, that I may cut off all the workers of iniquity from the city of the Lord." Oh, that all Her Majesty's Council and all other magistrates in this land had kindled in their breasts such a zeal of God's glory, such a hatred of all sin, namely of pride and ambition, and such a love of His sober and sound judgment, which breedeth humbleness of heart and a mind fully contented with any estate whereunto the Lord calleth us. Secondarily, above all things, it behooveth you that be the Lord's servants in magistracy to establish, everyone within his charge and jurisdiction, this general law, providing that every man have wherein to occupy himself and his gifts, according to the tenor of this law, in his own standing place and vocation, and that he do discharge it according to the measure and proportion of his gifts which he hath received for that purpose. For none in the Church and house of God must want his office; none must walk inordinately; none must be idle in his calling, or unprofitable. As, therefore, you know your enemies and how to vanquish them, and also the law of the Lord, how to establish it, take heed unto yourselves and dally not in the Lord's matters. For if you shall not betimes by the sword of justice cut off all that deserve death by the law, not suffering your eye to take pity upon any, and also correct other malefactors according to their desert without partiality, know for certainty that the just God will require their blood at your hands. Again, if you shall prefer your own policies and devices before the establishing of this general law of God, assure yourselves that your Lord and Master, Whose person you sustain, will never suffer such contempt of Him unpunished. Therefore as you hate these vices and all other sins, as you love this undefiled law of the Lord, let your hatred be showed in abolishing the one, and your love declared in establishing the other.

John Udall (*ca.* 1560–1592)

John Udall lived a short yet very eventful life. His fate as a martyr and his connection with the Marprelate controversy make his career one of considerable importance to the history of Puritanism in England. Nothing definite is known about Udall's early life. He matriculated as a sizar at Christ's College, Cambridge, and commenced B.A. at Trinity in 1581 and M.A. in 1584. While at Cambridge he became a close friend of John Penry, who was executed the year following Udall's death. Also during these years he became a Hebrew scholar good enough to translate and later enlarge Peter Martinus's *Key to the Holy Tongue.*

Sometime before 1584 Udall became lecturer or curate-in-charge of Kingston-upon-Thames, Surrey, where he soon established a considerable reputation as a preacher. During 1584 three volumes of his sermons were published. But his outspoken ways equally soon alienated some members of his church. A letter of reprimand was consequently sent to Udall and the members of his church by an official of the Archdeacon of Surrey, Cottington. In part it reads as follows:

Many and sundry complaints have been made unto me . . . of the contemptuous disorders and church matters of certain newfangled people of this town and parish. . . . I am credibly informed that . . . the form of common prayer set forth by act of Parliament is had in contempt, the laudable ceremonies of the Church obstinately broken and violated, the authority of my Lord's grace of Canterbury and other . . . bishops . . . and their proceedings authorized by her majesty openly resisted and spoken against, new ceremonies, new form of prayer, new feasts and fasting days, private meetings, singing of psalms, and lectures or readings and interpretings [?] of Scripture in private houses, contrary to the laws and customs of the Church of England, invented. . . .

Udall's efforts to establish the presbyterian discipline resulted in his being silenced. Later he was thoroughly examined by the Bishop of Winchester and others, and also by Archbishop Whitgift and the High Commission. At the latter hearing Udall complained about the discipline of the Church and the presentment of benefices; he also declared that ministers should be called by Scriptural names only, to which remark Whitgift retorted, "There will be an Archbishop when you shall not be preacher of Kingston." Aid came from the Countess of Warwick and Sir Drue Drury, both of whom were sympathetic to Puritanism. When the chief witnesses against Udall died before they could present their charges, Udall was released on his promise not to speak against his opponents.

Another clash with the authorities, one which led to the end of his career at Kingston, occurred sometime before 1588. Udall himself describes the incident in a somewhat fictionalized version in the entertaining though bitter dialogue entitled *The State of the Church of England Laid Open in a Conference Between Diotrephes a Bishop, Tertullus a Papist, Demetrius a Usurer, Pandochus an Innkeeper, and Paul a Preacher of the Word of God*. It is reprinted here in part. Notes on his silencing which Udall had shown to John Field and other Puritans, and the story of it, found their way into the first of the Marprelate tracts, the first part of *Oh Read Over Dr. John Bridges*. Both works were published in 1588. Here is Martin's version.

. . . Doctor Cottington, Archdeacon of Surrey, being belike bankrupt in his own country, cometh to Kingston-upon-Thames of mere good will that he beareth to the town (I should say to usurer Harvey's good cheer and money bags), being out at the heels with all other usurers and knowing him to be a professed adversary to Mr. Udall (a notable preacher of the Gospel and vehement reprover of sin) taketh the advantage of their controversy and, hoping to borrow some of the usurer's money, setteth himself most vehemently against Mr. Udall, to do whatsoever Harvey the usurer will have him, and taketh the help of his journeyman Doctor Hone, the veriest coxcomb that ever wore velvet cap and an ancient foe to Mr. Udall because (indeed) he is [a] popish dolt, and (to make up a mess) Stephen Chatfield, the vicar of Kingston, as very a bankrupt and dunce as Doctor Cottington . . . must come and be resident there that Mr. Udall may have his mouth stopped. And why? Forsooth because your friend Mr. Harvey would have it so, for, saith Harvey, he raileth in his sermons. Is that true? Doth he rail when he reproveth thee (and such notorious varlets as thou art) for thy usury, for thy oppressing of the poor, for buying the houses over their heads that love the Gospel and the Lord's faithful minister (Mr. Udall)? . . .

Hone, the bawdy doctor, chargeth him to be a sectary, a schismatic, yea, he affirmeth plainly that the Gospel out of his mouth was blasphemy.

Udall's identification with this story of the abuse of prelatical power presumably did him no good when later he was tried for sedition.

In *The State of the Church*, Udall has his spokesman identify himself in an interesting way with the nonconformist tradition. For a better understanding of the form which church government should take, he recommends to the bishop Walter Travers's *Ecclesiastical Discipline* (1574); William Fulke's *A Brief and Plain Declaration Concerning . . . Discipline and Reformation* (1584, running title: *A Learned Discourse of Ecclesiastical Government*); Dudley Fenner's *A Counterpoison* (*ca.* 1584); Laurence Chaderton's *A Fruitful Sermon* (1584), and Thomas Cartwright's *Second Reply*. (Portions of the first and fourth of these key Puritan treatises are reprinted here.)

In addition to his dialogue *The State of the Church of England*, Udall wrote another important work at this time, *A Demonstration of the Truth of that Discipline which Christ Hath Prescribed in His Word, for the Government of His Church*. An attempt to prove the validity of the presbyterian arrangement logically from Scripture, this work of course belongs in the Cartwrightian tradition. It is prefaced by a rather violent letter to the archbishops and bishops; probably it was this piece that caused Udall's later difficulties and led to his death. The work was reprinted twice later: in 1593 in *A Part of a Register* and in 1642 as *The True Form of Church Government*.

The work was printed by Robert Waldegrave, a Puritan printer whose press had been confiscated as a result of his printing of Udall's dialogue. Waldegrave had left London carrying with him a box of type. He printed Udall's *Demonstration* at East Molesey, very near Kingston, shortly after Udall was finally silenced there. Within three months Waldegrave began issuing the Marprelate papers, the first of which was printed at East Molesey.

Udall now felt that his career as a preacher was over, and for six months he prepared for a return to private life. But a pleasant surprise interrupted his plans: he was called to preach at Newcastle-upon-Tyne. At the time Newcastle was suffering greatly from the plague; in 1588–89 1,727 people died there. One of Udall's sermons occasioned by the plague appears in a volume of sermons printed in 1596. In it Udall warns that the plague is only the beginning of God's punishments, which will not cease until the poor are required to attend religious services, where they may be taught to amend. Udall apparently considered himself to be a plague-stopping preacher.

This sermon, as well as Udall's other extant sermons (six volumes in all were published), represent an intermediate step between the loosely organized sermons of Dering and Gifford and the elaborately methodical sermons of many seventeenth-century Puritans. Thomas Fuller credited Udall with adding an important new element to the sermon, proofs of doctrine. Udall's frequently printed *Commentary upon the Lamentations of Jeremy* provides in its introductory pages an important discussion of this contribution to the sermon. Part of it makes clear a common view of Puritans towards the sermon:

. . . the end wherefore Christ Jesus when he ascended into heaven . . . gave gifts unto man, was for the edification of the body of Christ, Ephesians iv.12; that is to build up God's people in the true knowledge of the holy Word, and so to confirm them in the faith, and reform them in their lives. Now to the end that this may be done . . . the workman whom God hath fitted to this great work must be . . . taught unto the kingdom of heaven . . . furnished with all kinds of knowledge meet to express God's will to His people in most effectual manner. . . . [T]he first thing that is to be done in the right teaching of the same to God's people, must needs be the clear and evident deliverance of the sense of the text in hand; that out of the same, as from a fountain that runneth clearly, all that He is further may be seen to be derived. Secondly, seeing whatsoever was written aforetime was written for our learning, Romans xv.4, it must needs be that every sentence of the Holy Scripture containeth in it at least one general doctrine; and therefore the sense being once understood, the next thing that is to be understood is the collecting of the same out of the text, in such plain and manifest manner, as must needs be acknowledged in the conscience of the hearer to be so; which being enlarged by the examples and testimonies of Scripture, and manifested by the force of reason grounded upon the same, must needs take such root in the conscience of the hearers, as they shall either be thoroughly persuaded of the truth of it (if it be rightly and effectually handled), or leave such a part therein as shall convince the same. Thirdly . . .

the right use [is] to be propounded unto them on the same doctrine . . . [for] the apostle . . . saith that the whole Scripture is
profitable to teach (that is, to learn doctrine out of it) . . . to improve (that is, to confute all errors contrary to wholesome doctrine),
to correct (that is, to reprove the misbehaviors of them that walk
disorderedly), to instruct in righteousness (that is, to direct God's
people in all the ways of godliness), II Timothy iii.16, yea, and to
arm us with patience and comfort in all kinds of trouble, Romans xv.4.

During the period of his connection with Newcastle, in 1589
Udall visited Edinburgh, where he preached before King James on
June 17. Perhaps because of this sermon, James later came to Udall's
aid while he was imprisoned. In 1603, when James came to England, he is reported to have been disappointed to learn of Udall's
death, exclaiming, "By my sal then the greatest scholar in Europe's
dead."

Udall's last years were filled with unhappiness. In December
1589 he was fetched to London in the midst of extremely cold
weather to be examined by the Privy Council. He was later tried
under statute 23 Elizabeth.c.2 for being the author of the anti-
episcopal books *A Demonstration* and *The State of the Church of
England*. The peculiar reasoning behind his trial and eventual condemnation is as follows. The law condemned any person who in-
tentionally wrote any "false, seditious, and slanderous matter to
the defamation" of Queen Elizabeth or stirred up insurrection or
rebellion, the punishment to be death. The Queen had established
episcopal government in the Church. Therefore to strive against
the bishops was to strive against the Queen's person. (Udall answered that if the bishops had informed the Queen of the state of
the Church, she would have redressed the ills and he would never
have had to complain.) This unjust trial appears to have resulted
from Udall's close connection with Waldegrave, Penry, and the
Marprelate tracts, which had much offended officials of both
Church and State.

After his friends had made many efforts to have him released,
(one of which involved his being offered a chaplaincy abroad,
working for the "Turkey merchants"), Udall was finally pardoned, but too late. He fell ill and died in June 1592. His brilliant
defense during his trial and the courage with which he stood by

his convictions helped to increase his reputation, and his death was regarded as a martyr's. He was remembered by Robert Harris as late as 1652 as one of England's four greatest preachers.

The state of the Church of England

DIOT[REPHES]. Mine host, I pray you stay with me and my friend Mr. Tertullus, and tell us some news, for we are lately come out of Scotland and would hear, before we come near London, in what state things do stand, lest we, coming on a sudden, speed as ill as we did at Edinburgh and St. Andrews.

PAND[OCHUS]. Good my lord, I can tell you no great news, for I go not so far as to church once in a month, but if I do happen to go, one of my servants doth come for me in all haste, to make merry with one guest or other; but there be two in this house that came from London, if it please your lordship. I will entreat one of them to come unto you; it may be he can tell you something.

DIOT. I pray thee do so. You are welcome, my friend. I understand that you came from London; I pray you tell me some news, for I, having been in Scotland some space, have not heard much of the state of England.

DEM[ETRIUS]. My lord, I hear no news, but that our bishops (God's blessing have their hearts for it) say pretty well, by one and by one, to these precise and hot preachers, for some of them are put to silence, some of them close prisoners in the Gatehouse, some well loaded with irons in the White Lion, and some in the Clink. I hope to see them one day all put down, for they trouble the whole land and are neither contented to obey the authority of these holy fathers, neither yet will suffer us to live as our forefathers have

[*The State of the Church of England, Laid Open in a Conference Between Diotrephes a Bishop, Tertullus a Papist, Demetrius a Usurer, Pandochus an Inn Keeper, and Paul a Preacher of the Word of God* ([1588]), sigs. A3^{recto}-C2^{recto}.]

done before us. And here is a good fellow which I met yesterday upon the way, who is just of their opinion.

PAND. I know not what religion he of whom you speak is of, but I am sure that he hath many of our preacher's qualities, for which I like him the worse, for since our preacher came I have not gained half so much as heretofore I did, but if I had but every night such a guest, within one month all men would refrain from coming to mine house, and so I might beg.

DIOT. Why, mine host, what are his qualities that you dislike so much?

PAND. What? I will tell you. As soon as ever he lighted, my man that took his horse chanced but to swear by God, and he was reproving of him by and by; and a gentleman cannot come all this evening, in any place where he is, but he is finding fault with him for one thing or another. And when he should go to supper with other gentlemen, sitting at the lower end of the table, he would needs say grace, forsooth, before and after supper, and so stay them that were hungry from their meat the longer, and from their sleep afterward. But one wiser than the rest served him in his kind, for he started up, saying, 'My father had no grace before me; neither will I have any.'

DIOT. I perceive he is one of these peevish Puritans that troubled the Church when my friend and I went into Scotland. Have not the bishops yet suppressed them, neither by countenance nor by authority?

TERT[ULLUS]. Suppressed? No, my lord, a friend of mine wrote unto me that one of their preachers said in a pulpit, he was persuaded that there were ten thousand of them in England, and that the number of them increased daily in every place of all estates and degrees.

DIOT. I am sorry for that; I marvel that you never told me of it.

TERT. I did of purpose conceal it, lest, together with your ill success that you, and so consequently I, had in Scotland, your grief should have been aggravated, for I know how that the growing of them doth grieve you.

DIOT. You may be sure that it would have grieved me; if you had told me that when you told me of the increasing of your friends the papists, I think I should have died for sorrow.

TERT. I know that; therefore did I keep it close. But if news had come in like manner of the growing of the Catholic religion unto your man, that Puritan knave, he would have told it you at the first and so have molested you the more.

DIOT. You say well, and I perceive it is better to have a papist than a Puritan in a house, and more charity to do for them.

PAND. Your lordship asked me for some news, but your speech of your being and ill success that you had in Scotland giveth me occasion to inquire of you, if I may be so bold, some Scottish news.

DIOT. Ah, my host, though it grieve me to think upon it, yet it easeth my stomach to tell it out. The Puritans in Scotland had got up their discipline and utterly overthrown all the sovereignty of bishops, by which they prevailed so mightily that we feared our fall in England shortly to ensue. Whereupon I was sent, together with this my friend, who came out of France into England, to go and seek the subversion of their great assemblies and the rest of their jurisdiction, wherein I prevailed a while, but now it is worse than ever it was.

PAND. How came it to pass that when you had gotten some ground you held it not?

DIOT. Because the whole land cried out for discipline again, and the noblemen so stiffly did stand to it; and lastly, the ministers that came home from England dealt so boldly with the King that I was utterly cast out without all hope ever to do any good there again, and now I make homeward in haste lest I lose all there also. But I pray you help me to speak with that Puritan; I shall learn more by him because he is better acquainted with the cause than either of you.

DEM. He may soon know more in that case than I, for I promise you, mine only study is in my counting house, to see my money, and when each parcel is due unto me.

PAND. And I meddle with nothing but my innkeeping; as for

these controversies and this Scripturing, I never trouble myself with it, but I will go to him to see whether I can get him to come to your lordship. But before I go, I must beseech you to say nothing to him as from me, for you know I must be friendly to all, lest I lose my custom and drive away some of my guests.

DIOT. Great reason, for every man must live of his trade. Neither must you tell him what I am.

PAND. Sir, here be certain gentlemen in another chamber that, hearing of your coming from London, would gladly speak with you.

PAUL. Whence are they, can you tell?

PAND. They are Englishmen, but they are new come out of Scotland.

PAUL. I am willing to go to them, though it be late, and so much the rather, because I long to hear some good news from thence.

PAND. Here is the gentleman that you desired to speak withal.

DIOT. You are welcome, my friend. I was desirous to speak with you for that I perceive you came from London; I pray you, can you tell us any good news?

PAUL. No, surely, for I am a very ill observer of such things.

DIOT. You seem to be a minister; can you tell me what good success my lords the bishops have in their proceedings?

PAUL. They have too good success: they wax worse and worse; they grow even to the height of their iniquity, so that I hope their kingdom will not stand long.

DIOT. Why, sir, what do they, that they offend you so grievously?

PAUL. They stop the mouth of the shepherds and set at liberty the ravening wolves, and turn the foxes among the lambs.

DIOT. I must desire you to express your mind more plainly, for you seem to be so possessed with discontentment that it maketh you to speak, as it were, snatchingly.

PAUL. I confess myself discontented and greatly grieved, but yet not so much as to make me less able to express my mind.

DIOT. I pray you, therefore, lay open your former speeches that I may understand your meaning.

PAUL. My meaning is this: that there are three abominations committed by them. The first is that they do bear such an enmity against the kingdom of Jesus Christ that they put to silence one after another and will never cease, if God bridle them not, until they have rooted out of the Church all the learned, godly, and painful teachers. The second is that they enlarge the liberty of the common enemies the papists. The last is that they commit the feeding of the flocks of Christ unto those that prey upon them and either cannot or will not labor to reclaim the wandering sheep. So that the conclusion that may be gathered upon their actions must needs be the eversion and overthrow of the Gospel, and so consequently the bringing in of popery and atheism.

DIOT. They put none to silence but the Puritans, who do indeed more hurt than good.

PAUL. I know no Puritans. If there be any, it is meet that they be put to silence. But Satan taught the papists so to name the ministers of the Gospel, and you are his instrument in continuing the same term.

DIOT. I mean them that are not contented with the state but mislike the government of the Church and would have a new form of government which would mar all.

PAUL. Would you have them contented with antichristian prelates to be rulers of the spouse of Christ, whereas the Word of God hath prescribed expressly another form direct contrary to that?

DIOT. I am a doctor of divinity at the least, and yet could I never read anything in the Word of God contrary to this government, neither yet to speak of any other, but that the ordering of the Church is left to the discretion of the wise and learned.

PAUL. Yes, you have read it, if God had given you eyes to see it. But if your study had been principally to advance God's glory and benefit His Church (which you never aimed at, but rather preferred vainglory and gain), you should easily have found it. I pray you, therefore, when you come to London, see if you can get these books: the *Ecclesiastical Discipline*; *A Learned Discourse of Ecclesiastical Government*; *The Counterpoison*; *A Sermon upon the Twelfth to the Romans*; and Mr. Cartwright's last reply, some of which books have been extant this dozen years, and yet are none of them answered; and you shall find it otherwise.

DIOT. If their lordships were taken away, the credit of the Gospel would fall to the ground and men would not regard it.

PAUL. Nay, their jurisdiction maketh it not to be regarded, for the simplicity of the Gospel cannot match with such outward pomp. It was of more credit before their calling was hatched than ever it was since.

DIOT. I hope never to see them overthrown, and I think they will never give over their bishoprics.

PAUL. I am of your mind, that they will never give them over, they have such experience of the gain of them. The use of the bag prevailed so much with one of the apostles that rather than he would lack money he would sell Jesus Christ Himself.

DIOT. You speak too unreverently and uncharitably of these holy fathers.

PAUL. Surely I have so much experience of their impious dealing that I can no better esteem of them in respect of their places than of the enemies of God, but as they be men, I will not cease to pray for them, that God would open their eyes, that they may see their sins and repent, which is the best way to deal charitably with them.

DIOT. I pray you tell me why these men be put to silence. I am sure it is for their notorious misdemeanor.

PAUL. I will tell you wherefore some of them were put to silence: one had conference with a bishop about subscription, and he was restrained for that he gave his friend a copy of his conference, another because he taught that the church of Antichrist was no part of the Church of God, another because his prayers before and after sermons were too long, and such like.

DIOT. Away! It is rather for not observing the Book of Common Prayer than for any such thing as you speak of.

PAUL. Indeed, many are suppressed therefore, but if any man

will give them their titles and authority they will give him leave to use his discretion with the Book, as we see by experience, for they use the Book and ceremonies as bridles to curb them that kick at their lordliness, which is the only thing that they mind.

DIOT. Well, I love not to hear these reverend fathers so abused, and therefore I pray you talk no more of it, but if it please you, you may depart.

PAUL. I am contented; only let me request you this one thing, that for so much as God hath given you learning you would pray unto God to guide you with His grace, that you abuse it not to your own destruction but employ it to His glory and the good of His Church.

DIOT. I thank you for your good counsel, and so fare you well; we will talk more in the morning.

PAUL. With a good will; I pray God our talk may tend to a good end.

Henry Smith (*ca.* 1557–1591)

Henry Smith, "Silver-Tongued Smith" as he was commonly called, was doubtless the most popular preacher of the Elizabethan period. Among his contemporaries who regarded him highly was Thomas Nashe, who said of him, "I never saw abundant reading better mixed with delight, or sentences which no man can challenge of profane affectation, sounding more melodious to the ear or piercing more deep to the heart."

Smith was born about 1557 in Withcote, Leicestershire, of gentle parents. He went up to Cambridge as a fellow-commoner at Queens' in 1573, but soon left to study with Richard Greenham at Dry Drayton, only five miles away. From 1576 to 1579 he was a member of Lincoln College, Oxford, seemingly a strange choice, as these were years when Lincoln was one of the least distinguished Oxford colleges. He appears to have commenced M.A. at St. John's, Oxford, in 1583.

He was probably connected with the church at Husbands Bosworth, Leicestershire, but sought no pastorate, for he did not wish to subscribe to the Thirty-nine Articles. The one permanent post he occupied was that of lecturer at St. Clement Danes, near Temple Bar, London. The system of lectureships developed largely as a result of the Puritan demand for sermons. As lecturer, Smith was paid through voluntary contributions from the parishioners. He soon became regarded, in Anthony à Wood's phrase, as "the prime preacher of the nation."

Smith's sermons are characterized by a lack of theological discussion but a multiplicity of Biblical quotations, a wide variety of subject matter, a pungent, epigrammatic style, and a pleasing informality. Thomas Fuller notes one other attribute, a rare one among Puritans: if Smith "chanced to fall on a sharp reproof, he wrapped it up in such pleasing expressions, that the persons concerned therein had their souls divided betwixt love and anger at the hearing thereof."

Smith differs from most Puritans in another important respect.

He was not primarily an expository preacher, seeming rather to choose a text that would fit the topic he had selected. As a result, he has whole sermons devoted to such topics as drunkenness, usury, marriage, baptism, the Lord's Supper, and giving alms to the poor. He was thus able to provide attractive titles for his sermons: "A Caveat for Christians," "The Ladder of Peace," "Food for Newborn Babes," "The Poor Man's Tears," and "The Benefit of Contentation" (that is, being content) are examples.

Smith's efforts to make his sermons appealing occasionally resulted in some tasteless displays of wit. Thus, commenting on Genesis ix.22 (Noah naked in his drunkenness), Smith says:

It is said that drunken porters keep open gates; so when Noah was drunken, he set all open. As wine went in, so wit went out; as wit went out, so his clothes went off. Thus Adam, which began the world at first, was made naked with sin (Genesis iii), and Noah, which began the world again, is made naked with sin, to show that sin is no shelter, but a stripper. This is one fruit of the vine more than Noah looked for.

The sermon which is presented here was not delivered at St. Clement Danes but at Paul's Cross, an open pulpit outside St. Paul's Cathedral. At Paul's Cross many famous sermons were preached, including Hugh Latimer's famous sermon on the ploughman.

Smith's very first sentence reveals that he was afraid his preaching might cause him difficulties with the authorities. He was in fact suspended briefly later, in 1588, because he was reported to have spoken against the Book of Common Prayer. He was, however, soon restored through the assistance of Lord Burghley. He was not made rector of St. Clement's when that position opened, apparently because of ill health.

Smith's attitude towards Puritanism is revealed in his very popular *God's Arrow Against Atheists*, of which not fewer than twenty-four editions had been printed by the year 1675. The last chapter of this defense of Protestantism in general and the Church of England in particular denounces roundly the separatists. Smith holds that ". . . a church may be, yea, a true church may be and is, though it have neither elders, nor deacons, nor discipline in it . . . for the desired discipline is not an essential part of the church." The errors of the Church of England are great, Smith ad-

mits, but since it includes preaching of the Word and proper administration of the sacraments it is a true church. Smith was thus a
conforming presbyterian Puritan.

Among Smith's works are two Latin poems, of about 850 lines
in all. But when he was forced to resign his lectureship in 1590
because of illness, Smith went to work preparing for the press his
greatest works, his sermons, fifty-five of which are extant. In the
middle of 1591 Smith died, still in his early thirties. His sermons
kept his fame alive for many years. By 1610 at least eighty-three
editions of his separate sermons and collections had been published.
As late as 1700 John Strype speaks of the sermons as "a common
family book even to this day."

The trumpet of the soul sounding to judgment

Ecclesiastes xi.9. "Rejoice, O young man, in thy youth; and let
thy heart be merry in thy young days; follow the ways of thine
own heart and the lusts of thine eyes. But remember, for all these
things thou must come to judgment."

When I should have preached under the Cross, I mused what
text to take in hand to please all and to keep myself out of danger;
and musing, I could not find any text in the Scripture that did not
reprove sin, unless it were in the Apocrypha, which is not of the
Scripture. This text bids them that be voluptuous, be voluptuous
still; let them that be vainglorious, be vainglorious still; let them
that be covetous, be covetous still; let them that be drunkards, be
drunkards still; let them that be swearers, be swearers still; let them
that be wantons, be wantons still; let them that be careless prelates,
be careless still; let them that be usurers, be usurers still. But saith
Solomon, "Remember thy end, that thou shalt be called to judgment at the last for all together." This is the counsel of Solomon,
the wisest then living. What a counsel is this for a wise man, such a
one as was Solomon?

[*Foure Sermons* (London, 1598), sigs. A2recto-B2verso.]

In the beginning of his book he saith, "All is vanity," and in the end he saith, "Fear God and keep His commandments." In the twelfth chapter he saith, "Remember thy maker in the days of thy youth." But here he saith, "Rejoice, O young man, in thy youth." Here he speaketh like an epicure, which saith, "Eat, drink, and be merry." Here he counsels and here he mocks, yet not after the manner of scorners, although they deserved it in showing their foolishness, as it is in the first of the Proverbs, "He laughed at the wicked in derision." As in the second Psalm, God seeing us follow our own ways. For when He bids us pray, we play; and when He bids us run, we stand still; and when He bids us fast, we feast and send for vanities to make us sport. Then He laughs at our destruction. Therefore when Solomon giveth a sharp reproof and maketh you ashamed in a word, he scoffingly bids you do it again. Like a schoolmaster which beateth his scholar for playing the truant, he biddeth him play the truant again. Oh, this is the bitterest reproof of all.

But lest any libertine should misconstrue Solomon and say that he bids us be merry and make much of ourselves, therefore he shutteth it up with a watchword and setteth a bridle before his lips and reproveth it as he speaketh it before he goeth any further, and saith, "But remember that for all these things thou must come to judgment." But if we will understand his meaning, he meaneth when he saith, "Rejoice, O young man": "Repent, O young man, in thy youth," and when he saith, "Let thy heart cheer thee": "Let thy sins grieve thee"; for he meaneth otherwise than he speaketh. He speaketh like Micaiah in the [first] book of Kings, [twenty] second chapter, "Go up and prosper," or like as Ezekiel, "Go up and serve other gods," or as St. John speaketh in the Revelation, "Let them that be wicked, be wicked still." But if there were no judgment day, that were a merry world. Therefore, saith Solomon, when thou art in thy pleasures flaunting in the fields and in thy brave ruffs and amongst thy lovers with thy smiling looks, thy wanton talk, and merry jest, with thy pleasant games and lofty looks: "Remember, for all these things thou shalt come to judgment."

Whilst the thief stealeth, the hemp groweth, and the hook is covered with the bait. We sit down to eat and rise up to play, and from play to sleep, and a hundred years is counted little enough to sin in, but how many sins thou hast set on the score, so many kinds of punishments shall be provided for thee. How many years of pleasure thou hast taken, so many years of pain. How many drams of delight, so many pounds of dolor. When iniquity hath played her part, vengeance leaps upon the stage. The comedy is short, but the tragedy is longer. The blackguard shall attend upon you; you shall eat at the table of sorrow, and the crown of death shall be upon your heads, many glistering faces looking on you. And this is the fear of sinners: when the devil hath enticed them to sin, he presumeth like the old prophet in the book of Kings, who when he had enticed the young prophet contrary to the commandment of God to turn home with him and to eat and drink, he cursed him for his labor because he disobeyed the commandment of the Lord, and so a lion devoured him by the way. The foolish virgins think that their oil will never be spent; so Dinah straggled abroad whilst she was deflowered. What a thing is this, to say rejoice and then repent? What a blank to say, take thy pleasure and then thou shalt come to judgment? It is as if he should say, steal and be hanged, steal and thou darest, strangle sin in thy cradle, for all the wisdom in the world will not help thee else. But thou shalt be in admiration like dreamers which dream strange things and know not how they come. He saith, "Remember judgment." If thou remember always, then thou shalt have little list to sin; if thou remember this, then thou shalt have little list to fall down to the devil though he would give thee all the world and the glory thereof.

Solomon saith [that] the weed groweth from a weed to a cockle, from a cockle to a bramble, from a bramble to a brier, from a brier to a thorn. Lying breeds perjury, perjury breeds haughtiness of heart, haughtiness of heart breeds contempt, contempt breeds obstinacy and brings forth much evil. And this is the whole progress of sin: he groweth from a liar to a thief, from a thief to a murderer, and never leaveth until he have searched all the rooms in hell, and yet he is never satisfied. The more he sinneth, the more he searcheth to sin; when he hath deceived, nay, he hath not deceived thee. As soon as he hath that he desireth, he hath not that he desireth. When he hath left fighting, he goeth to fighting again. Yet a little and a little more, and so we flit from one sin to another. While I preach, you hear iniquity engender within you, and [it] will break forth as soon as you are gone. So Christ wept; Jerusalem laughed; Adam brake one, and we brake ten, like children which laugh and cry, so as if we kept a shop of vices—now this sin and then that, from one sin to another. "O remember thy end," saith Solomon, "and that thou must come to judgment." What shall become of them that have tried them most? Be condemned most. "Rejoice, O young man, in thy youth."

But if thou mark Solomon, he harps upon one string; he doubles it again and again, to show us things of his own experience, because we are so forgetful thereof in ourselves, like the dreamer that forgetteth his dream, and the swearer his swearing. So we beg of every unclean spirit until we have bombasted ourselves up to the throat, filling every corner of our hearts with all uncleanness, and then we are like the dog that cometh out of the sink, and maketh everyone as foul as himself. Therefore saith Solomon, if anyone will learn the way to hell, let him take his pleasure. Methinks I see the dialogue between the flesh and the spirit. The worst speaketh first, and the flesh saith, "Soul, take thine ease, eat, drink, and go brave; lie soft. What else should you do but take your pleasure! Thou knowest what a pleasant fellow I have been unto thee. Thou knowest what delight thou hast had by my means."

But the soul cometh in, burdened with that which hath been spoken before, and saith, "I pray thee, remember judgment. Thou must give account for all these things, for unless you repent, you shall surely perish."

"No," saith the flesh, "talk not of such grave matters, but tell me of fine matters, of soft beds and pleasant things, and talk me of brave pastimes, apes, bears, and puppets, for I tell thee the forbidden fruit is sweetest of all fruits, for I do not like of your telling me of judgment."

But take thou thy jewels, thy instrument, and all the strings of vanity will strike at once, for the flesh loves to be brave and tread upon corks. It cannot tell of what fashion to be of and yet to be of the new fashion.

Rejoice, O young man, in thy youth.

Oh, this goes brave, for while wickedness hath cast his rubs, and vengeance casts his spurs and his foot, and thus she reels and now she tumbles and then she falls: therefore this progress is ended.

Pleasure is but a spur; riches but a thorn; glory but a blast; beauty but a flower; sin is but a hypocrite, honey in thy mouth, and poison in thy stomach. Therefore let us come again and ask of Solomon in good sooth whether he meaneth in good earnest when he spake these words. "Oh," saith Solomon, "it is the best life in the world to go brave, lie soft, and live merrily, if there were no judgment." But this judgment mars all. It is like a damp that puts out all the light, and like a box that marreth all the ointment, for if this be true, we have spun a fair thread that we must answer for all, that are not able to answer for one. Why, Solomon maketh us fools and giveth us gauds to play withal. What, then, shall we not rejoice at all? Yes, there is a godly mirth, and if we could hit on it, which is called, "Be merry and wise." Sarah laughed, and was reproved. Abraham laughed, and was not reproved. And thus much for the first part.

But remember that for all these things thou shalt come to judgment

This verse is as it were a dialogue betwixt the flesh and the spirit, as the two counsellors. The worst is first, and the flesh speaketh proudly, but the spirit comes in burdened with that which hath been spoken. The flesh goeth laughing and singing to hell, but the spirit casteth rubs in his way, and puts him in mind of judgment: that for all these things now ends "rejoice," and here comes in "but"; if this "but" were not, we might rejoice still. If young men must [be judged] for all the sports of youth, what then shall old men do, being as they are now? Surely if Solomon lived to see our old men live now, [he would say] as here he saith of young men, so high as sin rageth, yet vengeance sits above it, as high as high Babel. Methinks I see a sword hang in the air by a twine thread, and all the sons of men labor to burst it in sunder. There is a place in hell where the covetous judge sitteth, the greedy lawyer, the griping landlord, the careless bishops, the lusty youth, the wanton dames, the thief, the robbers of the commonwealth. They are punished in this life because they ever sin as long as they could, while mercy was offered unto them; therefore because they would not be washed, they shall be drowned.

Now put together "rejoice" and "remember": thou hast learned to be merry; now learn to be wise. Now therefore turn over a new leaf and take a new lesson; for now Solomon mocketh not as he did before. Therefore a check to thy ruffs, a check to thy cuffs, a check to thy robes, a check to thy gold, a check to your riches, a check to your beauty, a check to your musk, a check to your gloves [?]; woe from above, woe from below, woe to all the strings of vanity. Dost thou not now marvel that thou hadst not a feeling of sin? For now thou seeth Solomon saith true. Thine own heart can tell that it is wicked, but it cannot amend. Therefore it is high time to amend. As Nathan cometh to David after Beelzebub, so cometh accusing conscience after sin. Methinks that everyone should have a feeling of sin. Though this day be like yesterday and tomorrow like today, yet one day will come for all, and then woe, woe, woe, and nothing but darkness; and though God came not to Adam until the evening, yet He came. Although the fire came not upon Sodom until the evening, yet it came, and so comes the Judge although He be not yet come. Though He have leaden feet, He hath iron hands. The arrow stayeth and is not yet fallen; so is His wrath. The pit is digged, the fire kindled, and all things are made ready and prepared against that day. Only the small sentence is to come, which will not long tarry. You may not think to be like to the thief that stealeth and is not seen. Nothing can be hid from Him, and the Judge followeth thee at the heels, and therefore whatsoever thou art, look above thee and do nothing but that thou wouldst do openly, for all things are opened unto Him. Sarah may not think to laugh and not be seen, Gehazi may not think to lie and not be known: they that will not come to the banquet must stand at the door. What, do you think that God doth not remember our sins which we do not regard? For while we sin, the score runs on, and the Judge setteth down all in the table of remembrance, and His scroll reacheth up to heaven.

Item—for lending to usury. Item—for racking of rents. Item—for deceiving thy brethren. Item—for falsehood in wares. Item—for starching thy ruffs. Item—for curling thy hair. Item—for painting thy face. Item—for selling of benefices. Item—for starving of souls. Item—for playing at cards. Item—for sleeping in the church. Item—for profaning the Sabbath Day. With a number more hath God to call to account, for everyone must answer for himself: the fornicator for taking of filthy pleasure (O son, remember thou hast taken thy pleasure; take thy punishment); the careless prelate, for murdering so many thousand souls; the landlord, for getting money from his poor tenants by racking of his rents. See the rest; all they shall come like a very sheep, when the trumpet shall sound, and the heaven and earth shall come to judgment against them; when the heavens shall vanish like a scroll, and the earth shall consume like fire, and all the creatures standing against them. The rocks shall cleave asunder, and the mountains shake, and the foundation of the earth shall tremble, and they shall say to the mountains, cover us, fall upon us and hide us from the presence of His anger and wrath Whom we have not cared for to offend. But they shall not be covered and hid. But then they shall go the black way to the snakes and serpents, to be tormented of devils forever. Oh, pain unspeakable! And yet the more I express it, the more horrible it is, when you think of the torment passing all torments and yet a torment passing all that; yet this torment is greater than them and passing them all.

Imagine you see a sinner going to hell, and his summoner gape at him, his acquaintance look at him, the angels shout at him, and the saints laugh at him, and the devils rail at him, and many look him in the face; and they that said they would live and die with him forsake him and leave him to pay all the scores. Then Judas would restore his bribes. Esau would cast up his pottage. Achan would cast down his gold, and Gehazi would refuse his gifts. Nebuchadnezzar would be humbler. Balaam would be faithful, and the prodigal son would be tame. Methinks I see Achan running about. "Where shall I hide my gold that I have stolen, that it might not be seen nor stand to appear for a witness against me?" And Judas running to the high priest, saying, "Hold, take again your money; I will none of it. I have betrayed the innocent blood." And Esau crying for the blessing when it is too late, having sold his birthright for a mess of pottage.

Woe, woe, woe, that ever we were born. Oh, where is that Dives that would believe this before he felt the fire in hell, or that would believe the poorest Lazarus in the world to be better than himself, before that dreadful day come when they cannot help it, if they would never so fain, when repentance is too late? Herod shall then wish that he were John Baptist. Pharaoh would wish that he were Moses, and Saul would wish that he had been David; Nebuchadnezzar that he had been Daniel; Haman to have been Mordecai. Esau would wish to be Jacob, and Balaam would wish he might die the death of the righteous: then he will say, "I will give more than Hezekiah, cry more than Esau, fast more than Moses, pray more than Daniel, weep more than Mary Magdalen, suffer more stripes than Paul, abide more imprisonment than Micah, abide more cruelty than any mortal man would do, that it might be, "*Ite*, go ye cursed," might become "ye blessed." Yea, I would give all the goods in the world, that I might escape this dreadful day of wrath and judgment and that I might not stand amongst the go[n]e. Oh, that I might live a beggar all my life, and a leper. Oh, that I might endure all plagues and sores from the top of the head to the sole of the foot, sustain all sickness and grief, that I might escape this judgment.

The guilty conscience cannot abide this day. The silly sheep when she is taken will not bleat, but you may carry her and do what you will with her, and she will be subject. But the swine, if she be once taken, she will roar and cry and think she is never taken but to be slain. So of all things, the guilty conscience cannot abide to hear of this day, for they know that when they hear of it, they hear of their own condemnation. I think if there were a general collection made through the whole world that there might be no Judgment Day, then God would be so rich that all the world would go a-begging and be as a waste wilderness. Then the covetous judge would bring forth his bribes; then the crafty lawyer would fetch out his bags; the usurer would give his gain; and the idle servant would dig up his talent again and make a double thereof. But all the money in the world will not serve for one sin, but the judge must answer for his bribes, he that hath money must answer how he came by it, and just condemnation must come upon every soul of them. Then shall the sinner be ever dying and never dead, like the salamander that is ever in the fire and never consumed.

But if you come there, you may say as the Queen of Sheba said of King Solomon, "I believed the report that I heard of thee in mine own country, but the one half of thy wisdom was not told me." If you came there to see what is done, you may say, "Now I believe the report that was told me in mine own country concerning this place, but the one half as now I feel, I have not heard of." Now choose you whether you will "rejoice" or "remember"; whether you will stand amongst "you blessed" or amongst "you cursed"; whether you will enter while the gate is open or knock in vain when the gate is shut; whether you will seek the Lord whilst He may be found, or be found of Him when you would not be sought, being run into the bushes with Adam to hide yourselves; whether you will take your heaven now, here, or your hell then, there; or through tribulation to enter into the Kingdom of God, and thus to take your hell now, here, or your heaven then, there, in the life to come with the blessed saints and angels so that hereafter you may lead a new life, putting on Jesus Christ and His righteousness.

Job Throckmorton (1545–1600)

Was Martin Marprelate really Job Throckmorton? Perhaps we shall never be completely certain that he was, but evidence definitely points towards him. At any rate, Throckmorton's intimate connections with the publication of the Marprelate papers and with other Puritan activities make a consideration of his career helpful in understanding Elizabethan Puritanism.

Throckmorton was born in 1545, the son of Clement and Katherine Throckmorton and grandson of George Throckmorton. Job's father had been cupbearer to Queen Katherine Parr, to whom he was related. In 1556 Queen Mary granted Haseley Manor, a few miles northwest of Warwick, to Clement Throckmorton, though he was devoted to the Protestant cause. On the death of Clement in 1573, the property went to Job, the eldest son.

Job Throckmorton went up to Oxford, where he was educated at Queen's College; he commenced B.A. in 1566. Clement Throckmorton was four times member of Parliament for Warwick and Warwickshire, and so perhaps it was natural that Job sat in Parliament at the age of twenty-six.

Throckmorton's identification with Puritanism is suggested by the fact that Thomas Cartwright preached at Haseley in 1586, when it is reported of Cartwright that "more he said than ever he did in his life before," presumably on the subject of the defects existing in the Church. Perhaps as a result of this meeting, Throckmorton campaigned eagerly for election to Parliament, where it was hoped something could be done for the Puritan cause. Knowing of his interests, some of the magistrates of Warwick opposed his election, but Throckmorton won nevertheless.

In the Parliament of 1586–87 Throckmorton was prominent. Three speeches which he made are extant and have been excerpted at some length by Sir John Neale in his *Elizabeth I and Her Parliaments*. One argues for the execution of Mary Queen of Scots. Another supports eloquently and powerfully Anthony Cope's sweeping bill which would have authorized the use of a Genevan prayer book and done away with the whole existing ecclesiastical structure. (The Queen quickly put a stop to discussion of the matter.) A third speech of Throckmorton's deals with foreign affairs. In urging acceptance of the sovereignty of the Netherlands, Throckmorton was critical of James VI of Scotland. For this speech he was imprisoned briefly. The speeches of Throckmorton reveal an eloquent stylist and an outspoken Puritan. And with his sharp wit he does indeed, as Neale says, "display the qualities of the Marprelate tracts."

For the story of the tracts, which played an important part in Throckmorton's career, we must go back to 1584. In that year critics of the Establishment had published a book by William Fulke, earlier identified with their cause. Written eleven years earlier, *A Brief and Plain Declaration* (also known as *A Learned Discourse*) condemns the ignorance of the clergy and the form of the Church, and argues for the rights of the laity in ecclesiastical matters. Fulke's work was replied to in 1587 by John Bridges, in his 1400-page *Defence of the Government Established*. Dr. Bridges, Dean of Salisbury, addresses the Puritans as "our brethren" and treats them with gentleness and moderation.

Dudley Fenner, the forceful Puritan controversialist, replied with *A Defense of the Godly Ministers* (1588), in which he indicates that Bridges in his good-natured manner neglected to recognize the cruelty with which the episcopal authorities had treated the Puritans. In the same year Walter Travers too replied to Bridges. His work, *A Defense of the Ecclesiastical Discipline*, is a vindication of Travers's earlier work as well as an attack on Bridges.

The printer of Fulke's *Learned Discourse* was Robert Waldegrave, who sympathized with the Puritans and who had in the same year printed Chaderton's famous sermon on Romans and a Puritan prayer book. In London, during April 1588, Waldegrave published Udall's *State of the Church*, one effect of the publication being a raid on Waldegrave's house and the seizure of the press and copies of Udall's book. Waldegrave himself escaped with a box of type and after a delay of several months managed to set up his press again, this time in Surrey, where he printed Udall's *Demonstration of Discipline*, a presbyterian tract.

About the middle of October 1588 there issued from Waldegrave's press the first of the Marprelate papers, *Oh Read Over Dr. John Bridges, For It Is A Worthy Work, or An Epitomie of the First Book . . . by John Bridges*, actually only a prefatory epistle "To the right puissant and terrible priests, my clergy masters of the Confocation House." It was said to be written by "the reverend and worthy Martin Marprelate, gentlemen." Here as in the works that followed was a thoroughly readable mixture of vituperation, serious analysis of episcopacy, and humorous buffoonery. Here and in the other Marprelate pieces Martin establishes a theatrical frame of reference: acting as a comic monologist who occasionally becomes serious, Martin pretends to set his opponents on the stage before his audience that he may better ridicule them.

In the later *Hay Any Work for Cooper* Martin defends his satirical method:

There be many that greatly dislike my doings. I have my wants, I know, for I am a man. But my course I know to be ordinary and lawful. I saw the cause of Christ's government and of the bishops' antichristian dealing to be hidden. The most part of men could not be gotten to read anything written in the defense of the one and against the other. I bethought me, therefore, of a way whereby men might be drawn to do both, perceiving the humors of men in these times (especially of those that are of any place) to given to mirth. I took that course. I might lawfully do it. Aye, for jesting is lawful by circumstances, even in the greatest matters. The circumstances of time, place, and persons urged me on. I never profaned the Word in any jest. Other mirth I used as covert, wherein I would bring the truth into light.

But unfortunately, Puritan preachers such as Thomas Cartwright lacked a sense of humor or disagreed with Martin over what was decorous; they expressed their disapproval.

With John Penry, the Welsh Puritan, in charge, Waldegrave's press was secretly moved to Fawsley in Northamptonshire to the estate of Sir Richard Knightley, who had served in Parliament with Throckmorton in 1584. Here was printed the promised "Epitomie" of Bridges's book, a portion of which is reprinted here. By this time the Queen had been infuriated by Martin's libels, and the High Commission was in hot pursuit of the press.

In early January the press was moved from Fawsley and hidden at a farm at Norton-by-Daventry, where a third Marprelate tract was printed, a broadside, *Certain Mineral and Metaphysical School-points to be Defended by the Reverend Bishops*, and also a work by John Penry. In late March Job Throckmorton made an important appearance on the scene, though he may have been working backstage for some time. Penry, Waldegrave, and Throckmorton conferred at Haseley, Throckmorton's estate, just after the completion of a fourth Martin piece, *Hay Any Work for Cooper*, a reply to Bishop Thomas Cooper's *Admonition*, published two months earlier. This latter work is a defense of the bishops against Martin's attacks. (Martin's title is a play on the London street cry, "Ha' ye any work for a cooper?")

Because Waldegrave found that many Puritan preachers disliked Martin's approach and because he now believed he had a chance to print Cartwright's eagerly awaited *Confutation of the Rhemists' Translation*, he decided to print no more of Martin's writings. The meeting at Haseley was to decide how the next and most important work, *More Work for Cooper*, was to be printed. Throckmorton commissioned Humphrey Newman, who had been distributing Martin's writings, to find a new printer.

New printers, located in London, reported to Haseley and were told that they should go to Wolston Priory, where the press was now to be found, and where they would soon have a new manuscript to print. Before they had gone "about one bird-bow shot" from Throckmorton's house, they found a roll of paper, the text of the first part of *Theses Martinianae*. This they printed in July, along with a sixth work, *The Just Censure and Reproof of Martin Junior*. Both Throckmorton and Penry were at Wolston while the printing was being done. Here a revealing incident took place. Throckmorton asked one of the printers if he could make out the copy of *Theses* in a place where there were interlineations. Having no knowledge of the authorship of what he had been printing, the printer was surprised to find that Throckmorton read the obscure passage aloud "distinctly and readily."

In the house at Wolston where they worked the printers discovered part of the copy of *More Work for Cooper*. Before they could print it, it was time for the press to move on, for the authorities had keen detectives on the trail. The printers set up next just outside Manchester, the press having now covered about

250 miles in its journey since leaving Surrey. But an accident had befallen the traveling printers at Warrington, twenty miles from Manchester. Some of the type had been spilled on the ground from its box. An attempt to cover up had been made, but three days after printing had begun, officers of the law seized the press.

Word of the arrest came to Throckmorton at Haseley. Together with Penry, he appears to have put together another tract, containing a summary of the unpublished *More Work*. Somehow they managed to have it printed at Wolston as *The Protestation of Martin Marprelate*, in September 1589. Although there is a report of other pieces by Martin, *The Protestation* is the latest one extant.

The basis of the Marprelate papers seems to have been materials gathered by John Field, the organizer behind many Puritan activities, with an assist by John Udall. These were apparently put together by Throckmorton with Penry's aid. The project cannot be accounted a success. Neither Martin's jests nor the accounts of the bishops' oppressive measures really helped the Puritan cause, except insofar as they inflicted bruises on the bishops' dignity. Though Martin did not do what he intended, he did leave for posterity the chief satirical work of the Elizabethan age.

This account of the Marprelate affair leaves out many details, such as the story of the replies to Martin and the examination and tortures of the printers. Let us instead look at the further adventures of Job Throckmorton. When the printer Waldegrave left the printing of Martin's tracts he moved to La Rochelle, where he printed, among other works, a tract by Penry and another probably by Penry, *Master Some Laid Open in his Coulers*, a defense of Penry against the charges made by Robert Some in a book published in 1588. These books he turned over to Throckmorton at Haseley. Since little is known of this treatise, an excerpt is worth presenting to show how like Martin is the "Oxford man" to whom the printer ascribes *Master Some*.

The bishops, this controversialist declares, commend Bridges's book

unto us for the sufficiency, and we on the other side hold the flat contrary, that it was one of the reproaches of our land that ever it was suffered to pass the press. Now in this case who must be the judge? If I should name Oxford men unto you, it may be you would think me partial. Therefore, seeing Master Bridges himself is a Cambridge man, let him hardly be tried by his peers of the same university, and let the grandfathers (if they dare) put it to the censure of Dr. Fulke, Dr. Whitaker, Master Cartwright, and Master Chaderton [Puritans all], men I hope as well able to judge as all the lord bishops in Christendom. And if by the verdict of these it be not found as I have said, one of the poorest, grossest, and rawest pieces of work of that bigness that came out in English since Her Majesty's reign, let the conquest hardly be theirs, and let them possess their seats in peace, and the reproach light on the Puritans forever. If otherwise, then let them yield themselves guilty and resign. But I believe as well as they love Master Bridges, they had rather see him in Purgatory or fast bound in the House of Inquisition, than to hazard the least of their bishoprics upon any such trial.

With what reason can Master Some so distemper himself against Master Penry for one poor error, if it be an error, crying out loud and so often, "Blasphemy, blasphemy," and I know not what, and in the meantime suffer that clothead of Sarum to go away with a whole fardle of errors and absurdities, and not to say black was his eye.

Here the voice of Martin speaks, if not in his most eloquent accents.

For reasons not wholly known, Throckmorton escaped punishment for his part in the Marprelate affair, though he was convicted in the Warwickshire Assizes in the fall of 1590 for participation in the printing of the pieces. Nor was he severely troubled when Matthew Sutcliffe in 1595 published a damaging indictment, charging at length and seemingly with good reason that Throckmorton was Martin Marprelate. Sutcliffe had evidence in the form of letters which Throckmorton wrote to Penry, on the basis of which he charged that the "phrase and manner of writing" is the same in these as in the Marprelate pieces. Sutcliffe's case is very convincing, though Throckmorton in a published *Defence* (1594) had flatly denied that he was Martin. Another charge made against him, that he was involved in the plans of the madman Hacket, a self-proclaimed messiah, was dismissed as frivolous.

The last years of Throckmorton's life were uneventful. In 1595 he edited the *Apology* of Thomas Cartwright, who had preached at the baptism of his son in 1590. The gayest of the Puritans, Throckmorton is said to have worried for years about the eternal state of his soul. To achieve a sense of assurance, he spent the last days of his life with the famous preacher John Dod. He died in 1600. His last words were reported to be these: "Oh, Mr. Dod, I beseech you, stand by me. The joy and comfort of God's fate which I have labored for this thirty-four years is now come into my soul. I beseech you, give God the praise in prayer with me."

Throckmorton's intimate connection with the printing of the Marprelate pamphlets, his speeches in Parliament, the evidence cited by Sutcliffe, and the lack of a better candidate make it seem more than likely that Martin was Job Throckmorton, a most eminent Puritan layman and, strange as it may seem, a most eminent wit.

Bishops a brood of petty popes

Martin Marprelate, gentleman, primate, and metropolitan of all the Martins in England, to all the clergy masters wheresoever, saith as followeth:

Why, my clergy masters, is it even so with your terribleness? May not a poor gentleman signify his good will unto you by a letter, but presently you must put yourselves to the pains and charges of calling four bishops together, John Canterbury, John London, Thomas Winchester, William of Lincoln, and posting over city and country for poor Martin? Why, his meaning in writing unto you was not that you should take the pains to seek for him. Did you think that he did not know where he was himself? Or did you think him to have been clean lost, that you sought so diligently for him? I thank you, brethren, I can be well though you do not send to know how I do. My mind towards you, you shall from time to time understand by my pistles.

As now, where you must know that I think not well of your dealing with my worship and those that have had of my books in their custody. I'll make you rue that dealing of yours unless you leave it. I may do it, for you have broken the conditions of peace

[*Oh Read over Dr. John Bridges, for it is worthy worke, or An Epitome of the fyrste Book . . . by . . . John Bridges . . . wherein the arguments of the puritans are wisely prevented* . . . ([1588]), sigs. A2recto-B1recto.]

between us. I can do it, for you see how I am favored of all estates, the Puritan only excepted. I have been entertained at the Court; every man talks of my worship. Many would gladly receive my books if they could tell where to find them. I hope these courtiers will one day see the cause tried between me and you. I have many sons abroad that will solicit my suit. My desire is to have the matter tried, whether your places ought to be tolerated in any Christian commonwealth. I say they ought not. And I say John of Canterbury and all ought to be out of his place. Every archbishop is a petty pope; so is every lord bishop. You are, all the pack of you, either hirelings or wolves. If you dare answer my reasons, let me see it done. Otherwise I trow my friends and sons will see you one day deposed.

The Puritans are angry with me. I mean the Puritan preachers. And why? Because I am too open. Because I jest, I jested; because I deal against a worshipful jester, Dr. Bridges, whose writings and sermons tend to no other end than to make men laugh. I did think that Martin should not have been blamed of the Puritans for telling the truth openly. For may I not say that John of Canterbury is a petty pope, seeing he is so? You must then bear with my ingramness [ignorance]. I am plain; I must need call a spade a spade, a pope a pope. I speak not against him as he is a Councilor, but as he is an archbishop and so Pope of Lambeth. What, will the Puritans seek to keep out the Pope of Rome, and maintain the Pope at Lambeth?

Because you will do this I will tell the bishops how they shall deal with you. Let them say that the hottest of you hath made Martin, and that the rest of you were consenting thereunto, and so go to our magistrates and say lo, such and such of our Puritans have under the name of Martin written against your laws, and so call you in and put you to your oaths whether you made Martin or no. By this means Mr. Wiggington, or such as will refuse to take an oath against the law of the land, will presently be found to have made Martin by the bishops, because he cannot be gotten to swear that he made him not; and here is a device to find a hole in the coat of some of you Puritans. In like sort to find the printer, put every man to his oath and find means that Schilders of Middleborough shall be sworn to, so that if any refuse to swear, then he may be thought to be the printer. But bishops, let your fatherhood tell me one thing: may you put men to their oath against law? Is there any law to force men to accuse themselves? No. Therefore look what this dealing will procure at the length. Even a plain praemunire upon your backs for urging an oath contrary to statute, which is a piece of the foreign power banished by statute.

For the rest that will needs have my books and cannot keep them close, I care not how the bishops deal with such open fellows. And bishops, I would I could make this year 1588 to be the wonderful year by removing you all out of England. Martin hath told the truth—you cannot deny it—that some of you do injuriously detain true men's goods, as John of London; and some have accounted the preaching of the Word to be heresy, as John of Canterbury etc. All of you are in an unlawful calling and no better than a brood of petty popes. It will be but folly for you to persecute the courtier Martin until you have cleared yourselves (which you can never do) of the crimes he hath laid to your charge. Alas, poor bishops, you would fain be hidden in a net, I perceive. I will grow to a point with you. Have but a free disputation with the Puritans for the unlawfulness of your place, and if you be not overthrown, I will come in and do unto you what you think good, for then I will say that you are no popes. There was the *Demonstration of Discipline*, published together with mine Epistles, which is a book wherein you are challenged by the Puritans to adventure your bishoprics against their lives in disputation. You have gotten a good excuse to be deaf at that challenge, under color of seeking for Martin. Your dealing therein is but to hold my dish while I spill my pottage: you defend your legs against Martin's strokes while the Puritans by their *Demonstration* crush the very brain of your bishopdoms. Answer that book and give the Puritans the overthrow by disputation, or else I see that Martin hath undone you. Be packing, bishops, and keep in the pursuivants, or if you will needs send them abroad to molest good men, then pay them their wages and let them not pull it out of poor men's throats like greedy dogs as they do. You strive in vain; you are laid open already. Friars and monks were not so bad: they lived in the dark; you shut your eyes lest you should see the light. Archbishop Titus and Timothy will never maintain your popish calling. I have pulled off your vizard; look to yourselves, for my sons will not see their father thus persecuted at your hand. I will work your woe and overthrow, I hope. And you are already clean spoiled unless you will grant the Puritans a free disputation and leave your persecuting.

> Either from country or court
>   Mr. Martin Marprelate will do you hurt.
>   Rhyme doggerel
> Is good enough for bishops, I can tell,
>   And I do much marvel
> If I have not given them such a spell
>   As answer it how, they cannot tell.
> Doctor Bridges up and down
>   Writeth after this fashown.

The Epitome of the first book of this worthy volume written by my brother Sarum, Dean John, sic fœliciter incipit.

The whole volume of Mr. Dean's containeth in it sixteen books, besides a large preface and an Epistle to the Reader. The Epistle and the preface are not above eight sheets of paper and very little under seven. You may see, when men have a gift in writing, how easy it is for them to daub paper. The complete work (very briefly comprehended in a portable book, if your horse be not too weak, of an hundred threescore and twelve sheets of good demy paper) is a confutation of the *Learned Discourse of Ecclesiastical Government*. This learned discourse is a book allowed by all the Puritan preachers in the land, who would have all the remnants and relics of Antichrist banished out of the Church, and not so much as a lord bishop (no, not his grace himself), dumb minister (no, not dumb John of London himself), nonresident archdeacon, abbey lubber, or any such loiterer tolerated in our ministry. Insomuch as, if this stronghold of theirs be overthrown, ho, then all the fat is run to the fire with the Puritans. And therefore hath not the learned and prudent Mr. Dean dealt very valiantly (how wisely, let John Canterbury cast his cards and consider) in assaulting this sort of our precise brethren, which he hath so shaken with good vincible reasons very notably out of reason, that it hath not one stone in the foundation more than it had?

Richard Greenham (*ca.* 1535–1594)

About Richard Greenham's early life almost nothing is known. He seems to have been born about 1535, but the first definite fact we have about him is his admission to Pembroke College, Cambridge, as a sizar in 1559, presumably when he was in his middle twenties. He commenced bachelor in 1564 and M.A. in 1567, being elected fellow in 1566. Greenham may have served briefly as Edmund Spenser's tutor at Pembroke. The college had been decidedly Protestant since Edward's reign, when its most important member had been John Bradford, the Marian martyr. And two other martyrs, Nicholas Ridley and John Rogers, had also been Pembroke men. It is not surprising that in Greenham's day and after, Pembroke had a strongly Puritan flavor.

In 1570 Greenham moved to Dry Drayton, three miles from Cambridge, to serve as rector. During the twenty years that he held this post he was close enough to the center of Puritan activities to be of great importance in the movement. Robert Browne, the father of that kind of separatism known as Brownism, studied briefly with Greenham, but Greenham was too much devoted to the peace of the Church to please Browne. Henry Smith came to study with him later, and Greenham recommended him to Burghley for the post at St. Clement Danes. He was also the father-in-law of John Dod, who was called Greenham's Elisha. Another Puritan connection is the letter he wrote in 1570 to the Chancellor of Cambridge on behalf of Thomas Cartwright.

Greenham's identification with Puritanism is most clearly perceived in a letter written to the Bishop of Ely in 1573 at the Bishop's request. "I neither can nor will wear the apparel," wrote Greenham, "nor subscribe unto it or the communion book, no, not so far as I think it may be observed." Greenham humbly and modestly declines to defend his attitude, protesting that he cannot argue because his learning does not match that of the Bishop. He refers vaguely to the fact that he has not changed his mind; he feels exactly as he did three years ago. He would willingly "use some ceremonies and stay from speaking against some abuses so far forth as I might not hurt my conscience or give offense to others. But subscribe to anything but the Word of God I durst not."

Presumably his humility saved him, for he continued to serve at Dry Drayton. And his service was energetic. Although a little man of poor health, he rose regularly at four o'clock the year around. He preached twice on Sunday and once each on Monday, Tuesday, Wednesday, and Friday, and preached so hard that his shirt was drenched when he was through. On Thursday the service at Dry Drayton was catechetical. Besides conducting services, Greenham regularly visited his people in their shops and in the fields.

Although his pay was unusually high, a hundred pounds per annum, he frequently needed to borrow money to pay the harvest laborers, for the hundred pounds did not go far with the generous Greenham. But his reputation as a Puritan saint did go far. As a result, men of troubled spirits came from the surrounding area to get Greenham's advice. Frequently his visitors lived with him, gathering twice a day for devotions. Some idea of what went on at these gatherings has come down to us. After Bible reading, each one present might speak his thoughts. Among the group might be a neighboring minister such as John Dod. Many went away refreshed and unburdened. One visitor, after much conferring and praying, apologized for taking so much of his time. Greenham replied, "Oh my brother, not so; I never felt ill by well-doing, and if I may pleasure you, it is as joyful to me as any thing can be, for, for this cause I live." Some of Greenham's bits of advice have come down to us in his *Works*, where they are entitled "Grave Counsels and Godly Observations."

Despite his many efforts, Greenham was more appreciated by visitors than by his parishioners, and finally he left, announcing to his successor, "I perceive no good wrought by my ministry but one family." About 1589 he moved to London, where he preached in many churches, finally becoming preacher at Christ Church, Newgate, in 1591. But he kept in touch with his Puritan brethren, and is even reported to have been a member of presbyterian gatherings around 1590 with such other Puritan notables as Cartwright and Travers.

The reader of Greenham's sermons may well be confused at his connection with these men, who belong to a class entirely different from the Dod-Greenham-Henry Smith school. For the Cartwrightians were rigorously logical presbyterian Calvinists, whereas Greenham showed little interest in the intellectual side of religion and indeed was far from a clear or logical thinker. One suspects that when Greenham attended a presbyterian meeting he was more interested in discussing problems of "wounded consciences" than in organizing a classical movement.

When the hard core of Puritan agitators—the Cartwrights, Traverses, Willcockses—failed in their effort to refashion the Church of England according to the Genevan model, such men as Greenham provided an alternate outlet for Puritan energies: a reform of individuals was possible, if not a reform of churches.

The sermon reproduced here is a good example of Greenham's interests, ideas, and techniques. The subject is eminently practical: the education—in the Latin sense—and rearing of children. The sermon is almost planless. It is based on experience, not theory. One aspect only perhaps needs some explanation, Greenham's teaching on baptism. Greenham insisted that the parents of children about to be baptized have a solid Christian faith, "lest otherwise he [the minister] seal to a blank and so profane the sacrament, which appertaineth but to the faithful." The underlying idea here is that of the covenant, a concept which had been a part of much Puritan thinking since Edward's day. Infants have a right to be baptized, according to the theory, if they belong to the chosen people and are thus heirs of the divine promise. The sacrament is in this view not so much God's redemptive instrument as it is a "seal," an outward sign of what already exists. To baptize the child of a nonbeliever would be to provide an outward sign which corresponded to no inner reality.

Greenham's collected writings occupy a folio volume of nearly nine hundred pages and include seventeen sermons; seventy-five chapters of godly instructions on such topics as "Of Physic and Diet," "Of Fear," "Of Temptation," "Of Conscience," "Of Ceremonies, Things Indifferent, and of Turning Christian Liberty into Unchristian Licentiousness"; various meditations; and essays on religious subjects, nearly all very practical.

The prefatory matter to the collected edition of Greenham's works suggests that many of the manuscripts used to prepare the edition were in bad order, one being described as "most distracted and corrupt." Perhaps we have here an explanation of the unevenness of style which one notes as he turns the pages of the volume. Occasionally one finds a passage, such as this one, wherein Greenham shows real feeling for prose rhythm and a sense of imagery:

If Satan can make our youth an unprofitable age, in all the ages following, little good is to be looked for. For if ye once nip the blossom, where is the hope of the autumn? Where may we look for fruit? Well, if we needs use our pleasures, then must we set down some measure. The devil's rules never have exceptions, but God's saints must learn restraint; we must never make our hearts the stewards of our affections, that our thoughts wander not in them, and lest in desiring things too much, we exceed when we have them. There must be the least lusting of these outward things, because there is least use of them. If a man cannot want them, he will abuse them when he hath them. It is true that Jerome saith, "The beginning is honest, but the greatness is deformed." And that also sin is very reasonable in the beginning and very shamefaced.

In 1592 appeared Greenham's *Treatise of the Sabbath,* of which Thomas Fuller said, "No book is that aye made greater impression on people's practice." The work is one of the most important contributions to the strict Puritan theory of the Sabbath. It is interesting to note that the standard Puritan treatise on the Sabbath was written in 1595, the year after Greenham's death, by his son-in-law, Nicholas Bownd.

A hundred years after Greenham began his career, Richard Baxter recommended the reading of his works because of their emotional appeal. Greenham was probably remembered longest for his part in the exceedingly popular devotional collection *A Garden of Spiritual Flowers,* in which William Perkins also had a part. The book went through eleven printings from 1607 to 1638. In this volume and elsewhere in Greenham's writings much is made of a concept which later was used as the subject of sermons by many prominent Puritans. If a man believes he is saved, are there means by which he can tell quite certainly? Yes, teaches Greenham, and he provides at length the signs by which one can tell: the forgiving of our enemies, a delight in God's saints, the regular use of the means of grace (praying, receiving the Sacrament, hearing sermons), and the like. To detect within oneself all these signs of election is indeed to recognize oneself as a saint, Greenham taught.

Despite Greenham's emphasis on devotional reading, praying, and advising with one's minister, his great concern is of course the sermon. A final eloquent quotation puts the matter well:

It is good still [always] to attend upon hearing the Word, although we feel not that inward joy and working of God's Spirit, which either we have felt, or desire to feel. The preaching of the Word is God's ordinance: if it hath not wrought heretofore, though it work not presently, it may work hereafter. And because we know not who is the man, what is the time, where is the place, which is the sermon that God hath appointed to work on us, let us in all obedience attend on the ministry of every man, watch at all times, be diligent in every place, and run to every sermon which we can conveniently, because though the Lord touch us not by this man, in this place, at this time, through such a sermon, yet He may touch us by another.

Of the good education of children

Proverbs xvii.21. "He that begetteth a fool getteth himself sorrow, and the father of a fool can have no joy."

The Holy Ghost, speaking in the Scripture of foolish sons (as that he that begetteth such a one getteth himself sorrow, and that the father of a fool hath no joy), meaneth it not so much of natural idiots and such as are destitute of common reason (although it is true that this is a lamentable judgment of God and a heaviness to the parents of such a child) as of wicked children, such as are either ignorant in the Word, not knowing how to order one right step to the kingdom of God, or else, having some knowledge of God, ungodlily abuse it to maintain their carnal lust and appetite. For this cause, as it would grieve parents to have natural fools to their children, or such as either through some imperfection of nature are

[*The Workes . . . Revised, Corrected, and Published, for the further building of all such as love the truth, and desire to know the power of godlinesse* (London, 1612), pp. 276–279.]

dismembered or deformed and misfigured in the parts of the body, so much more should it grieve them to have such children as either for want of knowledge and heavenly wisdom cannot walk in the fear of God, or, abusing the knowledge given them, prostitute themselves to all sin and wickedness.

It is marvelous to see how greatly parents can bewail the want of one natural gift proceeding of some imperfection and how easily they can pass over without any grief the want of all spiritual graces, springing from corrupt education. In like manner it is strange that men can take the matter so heavily when their children break into such offenses as either have open shame or civil punishment following them, and yet can make no bones but boast over such sins as are against the majesty of God, accompanied with everlasting confusion and unspeakable torments, wherein what do most part of men bewray but their great hypocrisy, in that neither their joy nor their grief is sound to their children and that they love themselves more in their children than either their salvation or the glory of God? The tender love and care whereof no doubt did increase the sorrow of David for the death of his son Absalom, who was not so much grieved for the loss of a son as for that untimely end of his son.

Let us learn therefore to correct our affections to our children and be grieved for our ignorance, impiety, and sins; whereof either our carnal compassion, the not lamenting of our own natural corruption, the want of prayer for a holy seed, or profane education armed with the wrath of God may be a most just occasion. Can a man hope for a holy posterity? Or do we marvel if the Lord cross us in the children of our bodies when we make as bold and brutish an entrance into that holy ordinance of the Lord as in the meeting of the neighing horse with his mate, when, being joined in that honorable estate of matrimony, either as mere natural men without all knowledge of God we beget our children, or as too carnal men without the fear and reverence of the Lord, neither bewailing our corruption which we received of our forefathers, nor praying against our infirmities which may descend to our posterity, we abuse the marriage bed? Lastly, when, having received the fruit of the womb, we have no care by virtuous education to offer it to the Lord, that our child by carnal generation may be the child of God by spiritual generation? Surely no. And yet men without all looking up to God's providence and secret counsel, without all bethinking themselves of their corrupt nature from which their children are descended, without all looking back into their wicked and godless bringing them up, will fret against their sins and fume against their children. Yea, often they will correct them, and that to serve their own corruptions, not so much grieved for that they have sinned against God as that they have offended them. Christians therefore must know that when men and women raging with boiling lusts meet together as brute beasts, having none other respects than to satisfy their carnal concupiscence and to strengthen themselves in worldly desires, when they make no conscience to sanctify the marriage bed with prayer, when they have no care to increase the Church of Christ and the number of the elect, it is the just judgment of God to send them monsters, untimely births, or disfigured children, or natural fools, or else such as, having good gifts of the mind and well-proportioned bodies, are most wicked, graceless, and profane persons.

Again on the contrary side we shall find in the Word of God noble and notable men commended unto us for rare examples of virtue and godliness, who were children asked and obtained of God by prayer. Our first parents, Adam and Eve, being humbled after the birth of their wicked son Cain, obtained a righteous Abel, of whom, when by his bloody brother they were bereft, they received that holy man Seth. Abraham, begetting a child in the flesh, had a cursed Ishmael, but waiting by faith for the accomplishment of God's covenant, he obtained a blessed Isaac. Jacob, not content with one wife according to the ordinance of God, was punished in his children; yet after being humbled, he received a faithful Joseph. Elkanah and Anna, praying and being cast down, had a prophet that did minister before the Lord. David and Bathsheba, lamenting their sins, obtained Solomon, a man of excellent wisdom. Zacharias and Elizabeth, fearing the Lord, received John the Baptist and fore-runner of Christ. Look what sins we have naturally; without God's great blessing, without prayer and humbling of ourselves, we shall convey them to posterity. And although the Lord do grant some-times natural gifts unto the children of carnal and natural men, yet for the most part they receive their natural sins withal. But if the children of God by regeneration do see into themselves and lament their sins of generation, praying that their natural corruptions may be prevented in their posterities, they shall see the great mercy of God in some measure freeing their posterity from their sins.

Now when thou shalt see such sins to be in thy children, enter into thine own heart; examine thyself, whether they are not come from thee. Consider how justly the hand of God may be upon thee, and when thou wouldst be angry with thy child have a holy anger with thyself, and use this or suchlike meditation with thine own soul: "Lord, shall I thus punish mine own sin, and that in my child? Shall I thus prosecute the corruptions of my ancestors? Nay, I see, O Lord, and prove that thou art displeased with me for the too carnal desire of posterity. I lay then in some sin; I asked not this child of Thee by prayer. Be merciful unto me, O God, and in Thy good time show some pity upon my child." Thus thinking when thou goest about to correct the corruption of nature in thy child, which he could not help, arming thyself with prayer, repenting with Jacob, thou shalt be so affected that as thou art desirous to draw thy child out of sin, so yet to do it with the mildest means and with least rigor.

And one thing is most wonderful—that some will teach their children to speak corruptly and do wickedly whilst they are young, and yet beat them for it when they are come to riper age. Again, some will embolden their children to practice iniquity towards others which, when by the just judgment of God they afterwards practice against their parents themselves, they are corrected for it. And yet deal with these and such like men for the evil education of their children, and they will answer, "Do not we as much as is of us required? We send our children to the church to be instructed of the pastor and to the school to be taught of the master. If they learn, it will be the better for them. If not, they have the more to answer for another day. What can we do more?" But remember, O man, consider, O woman, whosoever thus speakest, that for thy sins' sake and thy want of prayer there may be a plague upon the pastor's pains and a curse upon the teacher's travail. If parents would have their children blessed at church and at school, let them beware they give their children no corrupt examples at home by any carelessness, profaneness, or ungodliness. Otherwise, parents will do them more harm at home than both pastors and schoolmasters can do them good abroad. For the corrupt example of the one fighteth with the good instruction of the other, which is so much the more dangerous because that corrupt walking is armed with nature, and therefore more forcibly inclineth the affections of children to that side. And further, experience teacheth us that children like or mislike more by countenance, gesture, and behavior than by any rule, doctrine, precept, or instruction whatsoever. Some there be also that will not have their children taught until they be ten or twelve years old, because (as they say) before that age, they have but an apish imitation. To whom I answer that, although indeed they cannot then deeply discern nor profoundly conceive things, yet how many things before those years both will they receive and remember? And I demand, if children be apish in imitating evil whilst they be young, which they will have the habit of when they be old, why may they not much more better do apishly good when they are young, which they may do carefully when they are old? Besides, let them so go untaught and they will grow so headstrong that they will sooner be broken than bended. And sure it is that one stripe or two words will do more good to a child in the beginning than a hundred stripes afterward. And here let parents be admonished of their indiscreet correction, who do their children more harm in showing a merry countenance after their discipline used than they do good by their chastising, although in their anger they be corrected. Neither do I purpose to take away natural affections and a Christian kind of compassion in all our censures, for it is my great complaint of the brutish unmercifulness of many parents herein; but I would wish Christians to correct their indiscreet affections herein by heavenly wisdom. Neither am I so stoical as to deny a more mild and affable kind of speech to be both lawfully and conveniently used to children, but yet I wish to be void of all unseemly levity and without all show of foolish, vain, and unnecessary behavior.

To be brief, how needful household government is towards our children may appear by the slender thriving and small profiting of religion and virtue either in the Church or commonwealth. For complain men and preach they never so much abroad, unless they will begin to reform their own houses and give religion a room at home, especially in their own hearts, they shall travail much and profit little. And surely if men were careful to reform themselves first, and then their own families, they should see God's manifold blessings in our land and upon Church and commonwealth. For of particular persons come families; of families, towns; of towns, provinces; of provinces, whole realms. So that conveying God's holy truth in this sort from one to another, in time—and that shortly—it would so spread into all parts of this kingdom. Well, I say, let there be never so good laws in cities, never so pure orders in Church, if there be no practice at home, if fathers of families use not doctrine and discipline in their houses and join their hand to magistrate and minister, they may but most unjustly (as many have done) complain that their children are corrupted abroad, whereas indeed they were before and still are corrupted at home. Alas, if parents to whom the comfort of their children well brought up is a precious crown, will not inform and reform their children in the fear of God, whom it doth chiefly concern, how should hope sustain these men that others will perform this duty to them, for whom the charge doth far less appertain? Lastly, let parents remember that therefore oftentimes they have disordered and disobedient children to themselves because they have been disobedient children to the Lord and disordered to their parents when they were young; wherefore because they have not repented, the Lord punisheth their sins committed against others with the like sin in others against themselves.

William Perkins (1558–1602)

William Perkins was probably the most influential English Puritan, next to Thomas Cartwright. Though some would deny his Puritanism, no one denies his influence. Let Thomas Fuller speak of him:

> Of all the worthies in this learned role,
> Our English Perkins may, without control,
> Challenge a crown of bays to deck his head,
> And second unto none be numbered,
> For's learning, wit, and worthy parts divine,
> Wherein his fame resplendently did shine
> Abroad and eke at home, for's preaching rare
> And learned writings, almost past compare,
> Which were so high esteemed that some of them
> Translated were (as a most precious gem)
> Into the Latin, French, Dutch, Spanish tongue,
> And rarely valued both of old and young,
> And (which was very rare) them all did write
> With his left hand, his right being useless quite;
> Born in the first, dying in the last year,
> Of Queen Eliza, a Princess without peer.

Perkins came fom an important family in Bulkington Parish, not far from Coventry, in Warwick. In 1577 he matriculated at Christ's College, Cambridge, and in Cambridge he remained the rest of his life. He seems to have led less than a pious life, according to legend, until he heard a woman tell her child, "Hold your tongue, or I will give you to drunken Perkins yonder." Before many years, "drunken Perkins" had become "Painful Perkins"—painful in the sense of diligently careful in fulfilling his duties, especially that of preaching. Perhaps Perkins learned to be painful through the teachings of the methodical Laurence Chaderton, under whom he studied.

During his college years he investigated occult studies, especially the art of prognostication. Later in his life he wrote, in his *Resolu-*

tion to the Country-Man Proving it Utterly Unlawful to Buy or Use our Yearly Prognostications:

I have long studied this art, and was never quiet until I had seen all the secrets of the same, but at the length, it pleased God to lay before me the profaneness of it, nay, I dare boldly say, idolatry, although it be covered with fair and golden shows.

While still connected with the University, he took it upon himself to preach to the prisoners at Cambridge Castle every Sunday at the shirehouse near the prison. Townspeople heard about Perkins's expert preaching and went on to listen with the prisoners. Perkins took such an interest in the welfare of the prisoners that he went to their executions. The story is told that one day he noted that the condemned man looked very sad as he climbed the ladder. Perkins shouted to him, "What, man! What is the matter with thee? Art thou afraid of death?" The prisoner confessed that he was less afraid of death than of what he expected would follow it. So Perkins got him down and preached to him till he had converted him and convinced him of his salvation. Then Perkins let him go happily back up the ladder.

Perkins commenced B.A. in 1581 and M.A. in 1584. From the latter year until 1595 he was a fellow of Christ's College, serving for a time as dean. He finally left when he took a wife. Unlike some seventeenth-century Puritans who were criticized for their lack of acquaintance with any but modern theological writings, Perkins became during his student days a profound student of the Fathers of the Church. His studies proved useful for his controversial works, such as his *Problem of the Forged Catholicism*. J. B. Mullinger notes that during the period of his fellowship Perkins did much for the reputation of Christ's College. Among his pupils were William Ames and perhaps John Robinson, both spiritual fathers of the New England Calvinists. When he left, Samuel Ward, later Lady Margaret Professor of Divinity, recorded in his diary his prayer that the college might not now fall into ruin.

In addition to his fellowship Perkins was awarded a lectureship at Great St. Andrew's Church, Cambridge, apparently in the 1580's. He held this position until his death in 1602, and the sermons he delivered there comprise a great portion of his works. For instance, Perkins's commentary on Galatians is, its editor tells us, the substance of the Sunday lectures of three years. Similarly Perkins's famous *Discourse of the Damned Art of Witchcraft* was first preached as sermons.

In his very influential *Art of Prophesying* Perkins sums up his idea of the plan a preacher should follow, and this plan—which Perkins did not invent though he did popularize it—is the basis for all of his sermons. The preacher should plan:

1. To read the text out of the canonical Scriptures.

2. To give the sense and understanding of it being read, by the Scripture itself.

3. To give a few and profitable points of doctrine out of the natural sense.

4. To apply (if he have the gift) the doctrines rightly collected, to the life and manners of men, in a simple and plain speech.

But despite the rigid plan Perkins managed to avoid the tedious sameness which mars so many Puritan sermons. In fact, Perkins cultivated surprises—small ones—almost to a fault. He draws most unlikely doctrines from a text, though with such a display of logic, often even syllogisms, that the reader is almost convinced. Fuller makes a similar point. Perkins, he writes,

so cunningly interweaved terrors and counsels in his sermons that, as a changeable taffeta, where the woof and the warp are of several colors, appears now of one color, now of another, according to the different standing of the beholders; so one and the same sermon of his seemed all Law and all Gospel, all cordials and all corrosives, as the different necessities of people apprehended it.

Especially memorable was the emphasis with which he spoke the word "damn": it "left a doleful echo in his auditors' ears a good while after."

Most of Perkins's sermons were not delivered quite as we have them. Usually his hearers would note the main heads and present them to him with the request that he supply the rest for publication. But the sermons on the Sermon on the Mount were taken down completely by Thomas Pierson, who prepared them for publication after comparing his notes with those of other auditors.

Perkins's sermons were eminently practical, as is illustrated by the names of some of his works: *A Treatise of the Vocations, or Callings of Man; A Treatise of Christian Equity; A Short Survey of the Right Manner of Erecting and Ordering a Family* (also entitled *Christian Economy*). These works, especially the treatise on vocations, reveal that Perkins's attitude towards diligence and thrift is essentially the one that Max Weber ascribed to Puritanism in general, one highly conducive to the development of capitalism. Christopher Hill comments:

> . . . the fundamental concepts of Puritan thought *are* bourgeois. Perkins is the key figure in the systematization of English Puritanism: and the tendency of his thought is towards the exclusion from full membership in the Church, and so from active citizenship, of beggars, and of rentiers and their hangers-on, who take no part in productive activity.

Of Perkins's practical works, probably the most influential was the posthumously published *Whole Treatise of the Cases of Conscience*, which occupies 632 octavo pages, though it is but a fragment. While guides for the handling of moral problems were common in medieval Catholicism, Englishmen of the seventeenth century were even more interested in this matter of casuistry, or cases of conscience. Perkins was the first Protestant to prepare an elaborate casebook on moral problems. Later, his former student William Ames wrote *De Conscientia et Eius Iure, vel Casibus*, Jeremy Taylor wrote a huge *Ductor Dubitantium*, and Richard Baxter compiled *A Christian Directory or Book of Practical Divinity*, a book of nearly a thousand folio pages.

The explanation for such great interest in casuistry in England at this time is, it seems clear, the need felt for moral guides in the midst of overwhelming changes in society, government, and religion. As Protestantism split into a variety of sects, as the middle class came to greater power, as the medieval attitude that this world is a vale of tears was gradually abandoned for the view that the good Christian may, nay, ought, to care about the riches of this world, many Englishmen were deeply confused.

How books such as Perkins's were designed to meet this confusion is suggested by some of the problems dealt with in the *Cases of Conscience*. Can a man in good conscience use "policy" in the affairs of this life? Is it proper for one to defend himself by force? How far may a man desire and seek riches? May one voluntarily give away all, and live upon alms, in fasting and prayer? (Perkins's answer is: generally speaking, no.) May a man give to beggars? (Normally, no.) The sections reproduced here offer in some detail Perkins's attitude towards the vexed question of the proper use of leisure time.

Although the practical works of Perkins were his most popular and are of real interest today because of what they reveal about social conditions and attitudes, it was through his controversial and theological works that he acquired his immense contemporary reputation. Of these one of the most important is *The Reformed Catholic*, which quietly but firmly shows "how near we may come to the present Church of Rome in sundry points of religion and wherein we must forever depart from them." His works of dogmatic theology, such as *De Praedestinationis Modo et Ordine*, won him high honors as an exponent of the Reformed theology. It is interesting to note in this connection that as a theologian he has been studied much more by German scholars than by English, and that the only full-length study of Perkins is in Dutch.

From the time of Whitgift and Bancroft's discovery of the classical movement until the days of Laud, few Puritans had much trouble with the authorities because of their nonconformity. This relative freedom from interference was partly a result of the teachings of Perkins and Greenham, both of whom were more concerned about effectively ministering to their people than with opposing the authorities, who had repeatedly shown the futility of the work of Puritan reformers. It is therefore not surprising to find Perkins's Puritanism causing him very few troubles. In 1587 he was reported to the Vice-Chancellor of Cambridge for having preached, among other things, that ministers should receive Holy Communion from other ministers and that it is better to receive sitting than kneeling. Perkins's reply to the charges is a revealing document. Part of it reads as follows:

I said not that kneeling was idolatrous, anti-Christian, and I do renounce it. My opinion was this, that of the two gestures which are used, sitting and kneeling, sitting is more convenient because Christ sat, the Pope he kneeleth (Jewel *contra* Harding). And in things indifferent, we must go as far as we can from idolatry. This Mr. Calvin taught me in a sermon upon the seventh of Deuteronomy and Bucer, *Censura Super Libro Sacrorum.*

He adds later, "I did not seek the disquiet of this congregation." One suspects that even as early as 1587 Perkins's reputation was such that John Capcot, the Vice-Chancellor, was far from eager to persecute him. He seems to have been satisfied with Perkins's statement, for he left him alone.

In 1589 a number of clergymen interested in the presbyterian movement held a meeting at St. John's College, Cambridge. Among them were Laurence Chaderton, Cartwright, Perkins, and Travers. Two years later Perkins was questioned about the meeting. He confessed that he had been present, but declared that it was the only such meeting that he had attended.

Perkins was greatly loved as a man because of the purity of his life. Fuller says of him, "He lived sermons, and as his preaching was a comment on his text, so his practice was a comment on his preaching." His active but sedentary life was ended by a violent fit of the "stone." At his funeral James Montague, later Bishop of Winchester, preached; Perkins was buried at the expense of Christ's College in the church where he had preached, St. Andrew's.

Concerning recreation

. . . we come to the handling of those questions that concern the moderation of our appetite in the use of pleasures and recreations. And these are specially three.

QUESTION 1. Whether recreation be lawful for a Christian man.

ANSWER: Yea, and that for two causes. First, rest from labor, with the refreshing of body and mind, is necessary, because man's nature is like the bow which, being always bent and used, is soon broken in pieces. Now that which is necessary is lawful. And if

[*The Workes . . . . Newly corrected according to his owne copies* (London, 1613), II, 140–143.]

rest be lawful, then is recreation also lawful. Secondly, by Christian liberty we are allowed to use the creatures of God, not only for our necessity, but also for meet and convenient delight. This is a confessed truth; and therefore to them which shall condemn fit and convenient recreation (as some of the ancient Fathers have done, by name Chrysostom and Ambrose) it may be said, "Be not too righteous; be not too wise" (Ecclesiastes vii.18).

QUESTION 2. What kinds of recreations and sports are lawful and convenient, and what be unlawful and unconvenient?

ANSWER: I will first lay down this ground: that all lawful recreation is only in the use of things indifferent, which are in themselves neither commanded nor forbidden. For by Christian liberty the use of such things for lawful delight and pleasure is permitted unto us. Therefore meet and fit recreations do stand in the use of things indifferent, and not in things either commanded or forbidden. Hence I derive three conclusions that may serve for the better answer of the question.

First, recreation may not be in the use of holy things, that is, in the use of the Word, sacraments, prayer, or in any act of religion. For these things are sacred and divine; they do stand by God's express commandment and may not be applied to any common or vulgar use. For this cause it is well provided that the pageants which have been used in sundry cities of this land are put down, because they were nothing else but either the whole or part of the history of the Bible turned into a play, and therefore the less to be allowed, considering that the more holy the matter is which they represent, the more unholy are the plays themselves. Again, all such jests as are framed out of the phrases and sentences of the Scripture are abuses of holy things, and therefore carefully to be avoided. The common saying may teach us thus much: it is no safe course to play with holy things. Lastly, upon the former conclusion, we are taught that it is not meet, convenient, or laudable for men to move occasion of laughter in sermons.

The second conclusion: recreation may not be made of the sins or offenses of men. They ought to be unto us the matter of sorrow and mourning. David "shed rivers of tears because men broke the commandments of God" (Psalms cxix.136). "The righteous heart of Lot was vexed with hearing the abomination of Sodom" (II Peter ii.8).

Upon this it followeth, first, that common plays which are in use in the world are to be reproved as being not meet and convenient matter of recreation. For they are nothing else but representation of the vices and misdemeanors of men in the world. Now such representations are not to be approved. Paul saith, "Fornication, covetousness, let them not be named among you, as becometh saints" (Ephesians v.3). And if vices of men may not be named, unless the naming of them tend to the reproving and further condemning of them, much less may they be represented for the causing of mirth and pastime. For naming is far less than representing, which is the real acting of the vice. Indeed, magistrates and ministers may name them, but their naming must be to punish and reform them, not otherwise. Again, it is unseemly that a man should put on the person, behavior, and habit of a woman, as it is also for a woman to put on the person, behavior, and habit of a man, though it be but for an hour. The law of God forbids both (Deuteronomy xxii.3). And that law, for equity, is not merely judicial but moral. Nay, it is the law of nature and common honesty.

Here also the dancing used in these days is to be reproved, namely, the mixed dancing of men and women, in number and measure (specially after solemn feasts), with many lascivious gestures accompanying the same, which cannot, nor ought to be justified, but condemned. For it is no better than the very bellows of lust and uncleanness, yea, the cause of much evil. It is condemned in the daughter of Herodias, dancing before Herod (Mark vi.22), and in the Israelites that sat down to eat and drink, "and rose up to play," that is, to dance. We read indeed of a kind of dancing commended in Scripture, that Moses, Aaron, and Miriam used at the Red Sea (Exodus xv.20); and David before the ark (II Samuel vi.14); and the daughters of Israel when David got the victory of

Goliath (I Samuel xviii.7–8). But this dancing was of another kind. For it was not mixed but single, men together and women apart by themselves. They used not in their dancing wanton gestures and amorous songs, but the Psalms of praise and thanksgiving. The cause of their dancing was spiritual joy, and the end of it was praise and thanksgiving.

It may be alleged that Ecclesiastes saith, "There is a time of mourning, and a time of dancing" (Ecclesiastes iii.4). And David saith, "Thou hast turned my joy into dancing" (Psalms xxx.11). And the Lord saith in Jeremiah, "O daughter Sion, thou shalt go forth with the dance of them that rejoice" (Jeremiah xxxi.4). I answer, first, these places speak of the sacred dancing before named, and not of the dancing of our times. Secondly, I say that these places speak not of dancing properly, but of rejoicing signified by dancing, that is to say, a hearty rejoicing or merrymaking. Besides that, the prophet Jeremiah speaks by the way of comparison, as if he should say, "Then shall the Virgin rejoice, as men are wont to do in the dance." And it is sometimes the use of the Scripture to express things lawful by a comparison drawn from things unlawful, as in the parables of the unrighteous judge, the unjust steward, and the thief in the night.

The third conclusion: we may not make recreations of God's judgments, or of the punishments of sin. The Law of God forbids us to lay a stumbling block before the blind, to cause him to fall, though it be not done in earnest, but in sport (Leviticus xix.14). Upon the same ground, we are not to sport ourselves with the folly of the natural fool. For that is the blindness of his mind and the judgment of God upon him. I know it hath been the use of great men to keep fools in their houses. And I dare not condemn the fact, for they may do it to set before their eyes a daily spectacle of God's judgment and to consider how God in like sort might have dealt with them. And this use is Christian. Nevertheless, to place a spiritual recreation in the folly of such persons, and to keep them only for this end, it is not laudable. When David feigned himself to be mad, before Achish the king of Gath, mark what the heathen king could say: "Have I need of madmen, that ye have brought this fellow to play the madman in my presence? Shall he come into my house?" (I Samuel xxi.15)

Again, the baiting of the bear and cockfights are no more recreations. The baiting of the bull hath his use, and therefore it is commanded by civil authority; and so have not these. And the antipathy and cruelty which one beast showeth to another is the fruit of our rebellion against God, and should rather move us to mourn than to rejoice.

The second answer to the former question is this: games may be divided into three sorts: games of wit or industry, games of hazard, and a mixture of both. Games of wit or industry are such as are ordered by the skill and industry of man. Of this sort are shooting in the longbow, shooting in the caliver, running, wrestling, fencing, music, and the games of chess and draughts, the philosopher's game, and such like. These, and all of this kind, wherein the industry of the mind and body hath the chiefest stroke, are very commendable, and not to be disliked. Games of hazard are those in which hazard only bears the sway and orders the game, and not wit; wherein also there is, as we say, chance, yea, mere chance in regard of us. Of this kind is dicing and sundry games at the tables and cards. Now games that are of mere hazard, by the consent of godly divines are unlawful. The reasons are these.

First, games of mere hazard are indeed lots, and the use of a lot is an act of religion, in which we refer unto God the determination of things of moment that can no other way be determined. For in the use of a lot there be four things. The first is a casual act done by us, as the casting of the die. The second is the applying of this act to the determination of some particular controversy, the ending whereof maintains peace, order, and love among men. The third is confession that God is a sovereign judge to end and determine things that can no other way be determined. The fourth is supplication that God would, by the disposition of the lot when it is cast, determine the event. All these actions are enfolded in the use of a lot, and they are expressed [in] Acts i.24,

25, 26. Now then, seeing the use of a lot is a solemn act of religion, it may not be applied to sporting, as I have showed in the first conclusion. Secondly, such games are not recreations, but rather matter of stirring up troublesome passions, as fear, sorrow, etc., and so they distemper the body and mind. Thirdly, covetousness is commonly the ground of them all. Whereupon it is that men usually play for money. And for these causes such plays, by the consent of learned divines, are unlawful.

The third kind of plays are mixed, which stand partly of hazard and partly of wit, and in which hazard begins the game and skill gets the victory, and that which is defective by reason of hazard is corrected by wit. To this kind are referred some games at the cards and tables. Now the common opinion of learned divines is that, as they are not to be commended, so they are not simply to be condemned, and if they be used they must be used very sparingly. Yet there be others that hold these mixed games to be unlawful, and judge the very dealing of the cards to be a lot because it is a mere casual action. But, as I take it, the bare dealing of the cards is no more a lot than the dealing of an alms when the prince's almoner puts his hand into his pocket and gives, for example, to one man sixpence, to another twelvepence, to another twopence, what comes forth without any choice. Now this casual distribution is not a lot but only a casual action. And in a lot there must be two things. The first is a casual act; the second, the applying of the foresaid act to the determination of some particular and uncertain event. Now the dealing of the cards is a casual act, but the determination of the uncertain victory is not from the dealing of the cards in mixed games, but from the wit and skill— at least, from the will—of the players. But in things that are of the nature of a lot, the wit and will of man hath no stroke at all. Nevertheless, though the dealing of the cards and mixed games be no lots, yet it is far safer and better to abstain from them than to use them; and where they are abolished they are not to be restored again, because in common experience many abuses and inconveniences attend upon them; and things unnecessary, when they are much abused, because they are abused they must not be used but rather removed, as the brazen serpent was (II Kings xviii.4).

QUESTION 3: How are we to use recreations?

For answer whereof, we must remember these four special rules.

Rule 1. We are to make choice of recreations that are of least offense and of the best report (Philippians iv.8: "Whatsoever things are of good report, think of them"). The reason is because in all recreations we must take heed of occasions of sin, both in ourselves and others. And this moved Job, while his sons were a-feasting, to offer daily burnt offerings according to the number of them all, because he thought, "It may be my sons have sinned, and blasphemed God in their hearts" (Job i.5). And not only that, but I add further, we must take heed of occasions of offense in others. Upon this ground Paul says that "rather than his eating shall offend his brother, he would eat no meat while the world endured" (I Corinthians viii.13). In this regard it were to be wished that games of wit should be used only, and not games of hazard, because they are more scandalous than the other. Lastly, in things that are lawful in themselves, we are to remember Paul's rule, "All things are lawful, but all things are not expedient" (I Corinthians vi.12).

Rule 2. Our recreations must be profitable to ourselves and others, and they must tend also to the glory of God. Our Savior Christ says that of "every idle word that men shall speak, they shall give an account at the day of judgment" (Matthew xii.36). Where by idle words He meaneth such as bring no profit to men nor honor to God. And if for idle words, then also for idle recreations must we be accountable to Him. Again, St. Paul teacheth that "whether we eat, or drink, or whatsoever we do, we must do all to the glory of God" (I Corinthians x.31). Therefore the scope and end of all recreations is that God may be honored in and by them.

Rule 3. The end of our recreation must be to refresh our bodies and minds. It is then an abuse of recreation when it is used to win other men's money. The gain that comes that way is worse than usury, yea, it is flat theft. For by the law we may recover things stolen, but there is no law to recover things won. And yet, if play be for a small matter, the loss whereof is no hurt to him that loseth it, and if it be applied to a common good, it is lawful; otherwise not.

Rule 4. Recreation must be moderate and sparing, even as the use of meat and drink and rest. Whence it followeth that they which spend their whole life in gaming, as players do, have much to answer for. And the like is to be said of them that have lands and possessions, and spend their time in pleasures and sports, as is the fashion of many gentlemen in these days. Now recreation must be sparing two ways. First, in regard of time. For we must redeem the time, that is, take time while time lasteth, for the procuring of life everlasting (Ephesians v.16). This condemneth the wicked practice of many men that follow this game and that to drive away time, whereas they should employ all the time that they can to do God's will. And indeed it is all too little to do that which we are commanded; and therefore while it is called today, let us make all the haste we can to repent and be reconciled unto God. Secondly, recreation must be sparing in regard of our affection. For we may not set our hearts upon sport, but our affection must be tempered and alloyed with the fear of God. Thus Solomon says that "laughter is madness" (Ecclesiastes ii.2), so far forth as it hath not the fear and reverence of the name of God to restrain it. This was the sin of the Jews reproved by the prophet, that they gave themselves to all manner of pleasure and did not "consider the work of the Lord," that is, His judgments and corrections (Isaiah v.12). And thus if sports and recreations be not ordered and guided according to this and the other rules, we shall make them all not only unprofitable unto us, but utterly unlawful. And so much of the virtue of temperance.

Arthur Dent (*ca.* 1553–1601)

Arthur Dent, famous as the author of the Elizabethan best-seller, *The Plain Man's Pathway to Heaven*, was born in Melton, Leicestershire, about 1553. He was a pensioner at Christ's College, Cambridge, in 1571, and was graduated B.A. in 1576 and M.A. in 1579. He was ordained to the priesthood in 1577 and in 1580 Lord Rich gave him the rectorship at South Shoebury, Essex, on the coast east of London. Here he remained throughout the rest of his life.

He appears to have married a sister of Ezekiel and Samuel Culverwell, both Puritan preachers. Other sisters brought other Puritans into the family circle: one married Laurence Chaderton and another married William Whitaker, a great Puritan scholar and Regius Professor and Master of St. John's College, Cambridge; a third was the mother of William Gouge, who helped prepare the Westminster Confession.

In 1583 Dent's *Sermon of Repentance* was published and immediately became very popular. Twenty-nine separate issues, all published before 1641, are extant. It was because of the success of this work that Dent wrote *The Plain Man's Pathway to Heaven* and presumably his several other works. Extant are three other sermons, the usual commentary on Revelation, two catechisms, and various other works.

Dent's difficulties over nonconformity occurred, as might be expected, soon after Whitgift became Archbishop. Whether or not Dent was silenced is uncertain; we know only that he was one of a number of Essex ministers who protested Whitgift's subscription plans. He is also known to have had trouble with the authorities for omitting the sign of the cross in baptism and for failing to wear the surplice, matters concerning which the Puritans made a protest at the Hampton Court Conference.

Little else is known about Dent's career. He died after a brief illness in 1601, soon after he had prepared *The Plain Man's Pathway* for publication. Since the dedication of this work is dated April

10, 1601, it is doubtful that the second part of *The Plain Man*, first published in 1609, is Dent's work. It is very different in form and style from the first part.

One wonders today why *The Plain Man's Pathway* achieved such great popularity, for although it is in the popular dialogue form, it completely lacks a sense of drama and has no semblance of a plot—ingredients which make the dialogues of Gifford and Udall interesting even today. Dent makes use of four speakers, Theologus, a divine; Philagathus, an honest man; Asunetus, an ignorant man; and Antilegon, a caviler. Their conversation is intended to provide a full treatment of Christian ethics, morality, and theology. Dent's moral strictures on current fashions provide a fair example of his approach:

It was never good world since starching and steeling, busks and whalebones, supporters and rebatos, full moons and hobby horses, painting and dyeing, came into use. For since these came in, covetousness, oppression, and deceit have increased; for how else should pride be maintained? And sure it is, within these thirty years these things were not known, nor heard of. And what say you . . . then to painting of faces, laying open of naked breasts, dyeing of hair, wearing of periwigs and other hair, coronets and top gallants?

For Dent the world is

a sea of glass, a pageant of fond delights, a theatre of variety, a labyrinth of error, a gulf of grief, a sty of filthiness, a vale of misery, a stage of deceit, a cage full of owls, a den of scorpions, a wilderness of wolves, a cabin of bears, a whirlwind of passions, a feigned comedy, a detestable frenzy. . . .

A surprising feature of Dent's dialogue is his use of quotations from classical authors, a practice which most Puritans severely condemn. In *The Plain Man's Pathway* Dent quotes Homer, Hesiod, Aristotle, Sophocles, Euripides, Terence, Herodotus, Theocritus and many other profane writers, as well as St. Augustine, Calvin, and Beza.

The reference to Beza may be considered to indicate that Dent's theology is of the High Calvinist variety. Whereas his contemporary George Gifford maintained predestinarian views but shied away from trying to justify God's ways, Dent discusses in some detail such matters as how one can tell whether he is of the elect. His treatise *The Opening of Heaven's Gates* is especially concerned with these affairs. For instance, Dent provides this analogy to help explain the double decrees of God:

> A king, consulting with himself and purposing to declare his honor and authority, enacteth such laws and statutes as the best industry of his subjects shall not be able to observe, pretending nevertheless, of his own especial grace, to be favorable or merciful to some and upon the remnant of trangressors to execute justice. From this spring (to wit, the honor of the king) do distill two streams, the one for his beloved subjects to drink at and live, the other for the malignant to drown themselves in. . . .

Closely related to his strictly predestinarian views is Dent's conviction that nothing happens in this world except what God wills. This idea was almost universally believed in Dent's day, but few of his contemporaries dwelt on the concept as Dent did. He published one sermon on God's providence and the idea permeates his other sermons, including the one which appears here. One of the most interesting discussions of the relationship of God to external nature occurs rather surprisingly in *A Sermon of Repentance*:

> All the judgments we read of, do see and hear of every day, knock with main strokes, beat down upon our conscience to [cause] repentance. The ugly monsters, strange births, fiery constellations, unknown comets, sudden deaths, marvelous droughts, unwonted snows, horrible inundations, foreign wonders, strange apparitions, threatening of heaven above, with flaming and shooting fire, trembling of the earth under our feet and our houses over our heads, as of late days: what are all these but as it were great cranes with beams and cable-ropes to draw us up to the Lord by repentance?

Most of Dent's thinking, except on strictly theological matters, was conservative. Thus in the sermon reprinted here he offers a traditional view of devils and their work. He was eminently a man of his time, shying away from newfangledness, and this is perhaps the reason for his great popularity. Today his "plain man" quality, a certain hard-headedness, gives his writings a kind of charm. "When any man cometh to a sermon," he preaches, "let him first and foremost make his reckoning to be rebuked, as meet it is, and let him understand that it is for his profit that he is not soothed . . . and let him be content to have his sores rubbed and bewrayed that he may be brought to that which is for his welfare."

Christ's miracles

The third part of this sermon

Now therefore it remaineth to speak of the power of Satan. Certain it is, and we are to believe it by faith, that the power of Satan is not equal to the power of God. It is not so strong, so large, and so wide. It is every way infinitely less. There is no comparison between that which is infinite and that which is finite. If we compare it with good angels, it will be less than some and greater than other some, as afterward we shall more plainly see. But if we compare it with the power of man, it is far greater every way, but yet, we must know, that is a finite and natural power, not supernatural; for then none could be saved. It is mighty, but yet not almighty. But that we may better conceive of it, let us see wherein it lieth.

All the power that Satan hath consisteth in two points: first, in his knowledge or understanding; secondly, in his deed, action, or work. For according as a man's knowledge is, such is his deed. So is Satan's: as his knowledge is great, so also his work [is] great. For his knowledge, it is to be considered whence it ariseth and how he cometh by it; so shall we better judge of the greatness thereof. He hath his knowledge by these means that follow.

First, from his spiritual nature, for by nature he is a spirit and therefore by nature hath the measure of knowledge given by God to a spirit, which is great. We know that there is a greater measure of knowledge in man than is in a brute beast by reason of that nature which the Lord hath given to man above beasts. So the devil is made of a spiritual substance and of that only, so that he hath

[*Christes Miracles, Delivered in a Sermon* (London, 1608), sigs. C2 verso-D3 verso.]

not a body which might hinder him to see into the nature, quality, and operation of a spirit. And therefore, being a spirit, he hath the knowledge of a spirit. In that, therefore, he is a spirit, he hath a greater familiarity with our spirits than otherwise he should have. In regard, therefore, of his nature, his knowledge is great.

Secondarily, the measure of his knowledge may be discerned by his creation. God created him a good angel and gave him the same measure of knowledge that He gave to other angels. Look, therefore, what knowledge is in a good angel by creation, the same knowledge is in Satan by his creation. It may be that he retaineth still that measure of knowledge which he then received, albeit, as it may be thought, that as man by his fall lost a great measure of that knowledge which he had by his creation, so the devil lost a great measure of his knowledge by his apostasy from the Lord. Further, it is to be known that the devil, being now fallen, is not of the consultation of the Lord as the good angels are, for they stand always before His face, ready to do anything that He shall command them for the good of the elect, and therefore they are of the consultations of the Lord, but Satan is not so, and therefore he cannot have so great knowledge as they have, which is a great comfort to those that be the true children of God, that the good angels by the measure of their knowledge are more able to save and defend us than the devil is by the measure of his knowledge to harm us.

Thirdly, the devil since his fall hath increased his knowledge, both on the things on earth and of the ways of God, by long observations and continual experience, who hath always had experimental knowledge of the nature of man, for he is well acquainted with the age of men. He knoweth what be their affections, what is their nature, and what is their disposition; he knoweth what things be offensive to men; he knoweth also what pleaseth them best in their young age, what in their middle age, and what in their old age. And as in these things, so also hath he experience in supernatural things. For he remembereth by whom he hath been resisted and who will not yield to him. This, then, must greatly

amplify his knowledge, seeing he hath always had such long experience of all things that come to pass. As put the case, there
were one man alive which were perfect in sense, in body, in mind,
in reason, and memory, and in all the faculties both of the body
and of the mind, that had lived from the beginning of the world
unto this day and had observed all things that had fallen out heretofore. This man would tell such wonderful things, both past and
to come, by natural causes and continual observation, that I fear
me lest many would worship him as a god. Therefore the devil
must needs have great knowledge, seeing that he hath had all these.
But he knoweth more than any man could have done. For he doth
not only know those among whom he liveth and the things that
falleth out amongst them, but he goeth about into every family
and country, observeth what is done, and is well acquainted with
their conversation.

Fourthly, besides this he hath also another means to increase
his knowledge. When the Lord commandeth him to appear before
Him to render accounts of all the works that he hath done (Job
i.16); when the children of God (that is, the good angels) came
before the Lord, Satan stood amongst them, and the Lord said
unto him, "Whence cometh thou?" and he answered, "From compassing the earth to and fro." And the Lord said, "Hast thou not
considered my servant Job, how there is none like him in the earth,
an upright and just man?" Satan answered, "It is not for nothing
that Job feareth Thee. Hast Thou not made a hedge about him and
his house and about everything which he hath on every side? But
touch all that he hath and then see whether he will not blaspheme
Thee to Thy face." Satan knew well enough that man will make
show of religion in prosperity, but in adversity by impatience
would fall away. For hereupon the Lord gave him liberty to afflict
Job, in visiting his body with sickness, in taking away his children
and his goods. But whence hath he this knowledge? From the revelation of the Lord. He knew that Job should be visited with great
sickness and lose his children and his goods when he heard it from
the Lord, and so he knoweth many other things which are to come

to pass, and after he once knoweth them, he goeth to witches or such like and tells them thereof, who likewise tell others of the same before it comes to pass and so deceive men thereby, making them to think that they know it of themselves, but neither they nor the devil know it of themselves, but by the revelation of the Lord unto Satan.

Fifthly, Satan hath another excellent means to increase his knowledge, which the Lord hath also granted unto men; for they know what is to come by the revelation of the prophets. For if there be any curse belonging to the people, the prophets do denounce the same and make the people to know thereof by the preaching of the Word. Whereas, therefore, the Word is preached, there is Satan present. He observeth the doctrine, whether it be of power to bring men from the kingdom of darkness to the Lord, from sin unto repentance. If it be, then is he most busy, either to stop it from the ear or to pull it out of the heart if they have once received it (as Matthew xiii.19). By this means, therefore, he increaseth his knowledge that he may work more covertly and be the less discerned, for he can turn himself into an angel of light.

Sixthly, he hath yet another means to increase his knowledge, and that is by the observation of natural causes. If you speak of an astronomer, he can tell that best. If you speak of an astrologer, he is most cunning therein. Yea, that which many men guess at and, as it were, grope at in the dark, he beholdeth and knoweth most certainly and can tell anything that is to come to pass by the course of the stars and other natural causes. If we speak of knowledge in the arts, there is none comparable to him, he is most skillful in all the tongues, and there is no time that is hid from him. So that by these means he hath wonderfully increased his knowledge. But some may say, "Hath he knowledge in anything in which the good angels have no knowledge?" No, for they are as diligent for the salvation of the godly as he is for their destruction (Psalm xci.11). God giveth His angels charge to keep Christ and all that are His in all their ways. Nay, they pitch their tents about him that feareth the Lord, to keep him on every side, that no harm befall him any way. And therefore as soon as Satan had left off tempting Christ, the good angels came and ministered unto him all things that were requisite for Him in this life. But doth not Satan's knowledge serve to the working of a miracle? No, for it is a finite knowledge and therefore cannot produce any miracle, for every true miracle is wrought by an omnipotent power.

The second thing wherein Satan's power doth consist is his action or his deed, which, as his knowledge is great, so it is likewise great. Let us therefore see his actions. The deed of persuading is great, for he moved Cain, contrary to his knowledge and contrary to nature, not only to revile his brother but to kill him. He talked not with Cain, but by motions and persuasions in his heart did allure him thereunto. But it appeareth more great in his first action against mankind, as when he came to our first parents in the form of a serpent, which argueth his great power, that he can transform himself into such a creature and abuse the tongue of a serpent to that end. So we read of his actions also in Exodus, when Moses wrought miracles before Pharaoh by the finger of God. Satan also by his enchanters did work the same miracles, yet not true miracles because they did them not by the finger of God but by the power of Satan. So also I Samuel xxviii: Satan comes to a witch and would also tell the witch what success Saul should have in his battle that he took in hand. He came in the shape of Samuel so that Saul thought he had been Samuel. So also would he talk familiarly with men. Therefore, the Lord gave a law that if anyone consulted with a familiar spirit, he should die, which law had been in vain if none had consulted familiarly with him. So he was a liar in the mouth of all the false prophets, although they themselves did not at that time perceive it. So he possessed men's bodies, as in the Gospel, when our Savior had cast him out of a man, he straightway went into a herd of swine, and even so he is able to draw men's bodies after him.

We may also see his power by a comparison with the good angels. II Kings xix: "An angel of the Lord slew 185,000 men of Sennacherib's host in one night." Now the same power is in Satan by his creation, which hereby appeareth to be very great. So when he carried Christ's body up unto a pinnacle of the temple and up unto a mountain to tempt Him. And Acts xvi.19. There were exorcists that would cast forth devils in the name of Jesus, but the evil spirit in the man ran on them and overcame them so that they fled out of the house naked and wounded. It is therefore certain that Satan is of a wonderful power and that the children of God have often-times [been] tried, both in themselves and also in others. Among many others I remember one that is worthy remembrance. There was a man in Geneva who, feeling something to fall out contrary to his mind and for divers causes which is not needful to repeat, blasphemed God and desired that if there were any devils they might come and take him away, who was presently in the air and never heard of after, save only that his cap fell off his head, which showeth that Satan hath great power.

This teacheth us that men must not be careless but must look to themselves. "For Satan is a roaring lion, seeking whom he may soonest devour. Watch, therefore, and pray, lest ye fall into temptation." But if Satan's power be so great, how comes it to pass that many men do so well in this world? I answer, this power is barred and limited by the Lord, and that by two especial limits.

The first limit is his nature, for he is not able to do anything than that which his natural disposition will permit and suffer. The second limit is the will of God, for he can do nothing against the will of God. Except the Lord do either permit him or command him, he is not able to do anything at all. As it is also in other creatures, the waters should by nature overflow the whole earth, yet they do not because it is the will of God. So also is it with Satan, as appeareth when the Lord gave him power of all Job's goods. Beyond the Lord's will he could not go, for the Lord will not suffer him to do anything to His children but only that which shall tend to their good. Art thou in misery or in any dangerous distress wherein thou art most subject to the cruelty of Satan? Be of good comfort; Satan is limited. He cannot do anything to thee but only that which the Lord commandeth him. But may not Satan's knowledge and power be used? I answer, it may. God useth it in punishing, trying, and correcting His children. Again, the apostles used his power, for they have delivered men to Satan as Paul did (I Timothy i.20) Hymenaeus and Alexander, and as he would have done the incestuous Corinthians.

But may not a man use it in familiar sort, in talking, bargaining, and consulting with Satan? No; this is forbidden (Deuteronomy xviii; Leviticus xx); and we are commanded to resist the devil and to fly from him. We must not therefore consult with him. He may oftentimes tell the truth, but we must not accept it. Christ gave us example hereof, for he said that Christ was the Son of God, which was a truth; yet Christ commanded him to be silent, to teach us that the truth is not to be received from him, for he is the father of lies. Here, then, all men are forbidden to seek unto Satan to know any truth whatsoever. And therefore hereby we condemn those that use witchery by the counsel of Satan, and in the former places the very action of consulting with Satan, though no harm come thereby, is flatly death to the party. I would this law were established in all Christian churches. Then there would not be so many witches in that kind as now there are. I confess indeed, there be some which be counted witches which indeed are not, as namely those which hurt cattle, as oxen, horse, swine, or suchlike, or else children, not from the counsel of Satan but by the traditions of other women, by poisoning them, in doing nothing but using the natural causes thereof. Those I would have punished, yet not in the name of witches but in the name of murderers.

Some men think that they may overrule Satan by conjuration in using this preparation which is set down by some of late, that they must make a circle, and in it make triangles, quadrangles, and crosses, and speak certain words, as saying the Pater Noster, and many other suchlike things—that they may call up Satan in what shape they will and he will appear and do for them that which they desire. But is Satan a friend of theirs? Can any such things make him obedient to man? Dost thou think that ye canst overrule him by this means? No, surely, but he rather by this means deceiveth thee and all that are of thine opinion. And thus he deceiveth them that use characters. So there be charms used to get away the headache and toothache. But doth the charm get it away? No, Satan knoweth before that thy headache shall go away, and therefore causeth thee to use that charm and thereby would move thee to ascribe it to the charm.

But when Satan whispereth men in their ears, how shall they know whether it be he or a good angel that speaketh to them? I answer, there be divers manifest tokens whereby thou mayest discern this. First, the Lord doth not now use such means to reveal His will unto men. Thou art therefore always to suspect it to be of Satan. Secondly, if it be a good angel, thou mayest know by this: for if it be a good angel it will tell thee, either at first or at last, what it is and for what it cometh and from whence, as in times past the good angels showed themselves to Abraham and Lot. Thirdly, if it be a good angel, he will allure thee to keep the written Word of God. If he do not, then suspect him.

The use of all this doctrine is to lead us unto God, to acknowledge Him to be our only Lord and Savior, and to embrace the Son of God as our King. In all things, therefore, we must go unto Him.

But whereas it is said, "How can a man that is a sinner do such miracles?" it may be asked whether God's enemies can work any miracles. I answer, he that worketh is not against Christ but with Him; and we see that those which endeavored (Acts xvi) to work a miracle could not.

"And there was a dissension among them."

Herein we see that the Lord doth so work that Christ and His do find favor among their enemies, and that by their dissension among themselves. Here we see that schism is neither a note of a false church nor yet of a true church. Here, it is in a false church. Schism ariseth of the diversity of knowledge and judgment of men, for all men have not one knowledge and judgment and all see not the truth, and if they should, yet all have not the like yielding affection thereunto. We are therefore to prepare ourselves to meet with schisms, for it is necessary that there should be heresies (I Corinthians i.10), and that in the Church of God that those which are approved might be known.

Samuel Hieron (*ca.* 1572–1617)

Samuel Hieron's ministry in the Church was an indirect result of the efforts of John Foxe the martyrologist. Foxe persuaded Hieron's father to abandon school teaching for church preaching. At Epping in Essex, where the senior Hieron was minister, Samuel was born in the early 1570's. In 1590 he went to Cambridge, where he was admitted to King's College. There he commenced bachelor in 1595 and M.A. three years later. At Cambridge he was a student of Thomas Goad, later English representative at the Synod of Dort, and Laurence Chaderton, whose Puritanism he seems to have imbibed. He remained fellow at King's for a short time but spent much more time following his father's example by preaching, in London, where he had been ordained in 1595. The youthful preacher soon achieved a surprising popularity and was sought by several congregations and inns of court. It was doubtless a great compliment to Hieron that he attracted the admiration of Sir Henry Savile, the great classical scholar and Greek tutor to Queen Elizabeth. Savile as provost of Eton awarded Hieron the vicarship of the church at Modbury, near Plymouth in Devonshire, in 1599.

Hieron's Puritanism is apparent in his *Short Dialogue Proving that Ceremonies and Some Other Corruptions Now in Question Are Defended by None Other Arguments than Such as the Papists Have Heretofore Used, and Our Protestant Writers Have Long Since Answered* (1605) and *A Defence of the Ministers' Reasons for Refusal of Subscription to the Book of Common Prayer and of Conformity* (1607). Both were published anonymously, and both attack the formulations of the stringent anti-Puritan Canons of 1604. The story of the publication of the *Defence* is interesting. Printed in Holland, copies were shipped with the goods of a Plymouth merchant, but when no bookseller dared to sell them, the whole edition was given away. Some were sent to the bishops, some to the universities, some left at the door of scholars, and some were dropped in the streets of

London. The secret of the author's name was well kept.

Both the *Dialogue* and the *Defence* are very learned. The dialogue scarcely resembles a conversation, for it is full of references to authorities. Appended to it are forty-five reasons why ministers should not be deprived because of their position on ceremonies and subscription. Hieron argues that though only the use of the sign of the cross in baptism and the wearing of the surplice are now required, they are but an opening wedge, and in time will lead to the requirement of subscription. He is fully aware of the history of the vestment controversy, which he sees as old business, never properly disposed of; he notes that for years the requirement has been forgotten, the bishops suspending or depriving only those who were in their disfavor and leaving untroubled others who were unwilling to use the required ceremonies. "It would be a very strange thing and therefore very scandalous to bring them into use again," declares Hieron.

Besides these anonymous protests, Hieron published in 1604 under his own name *The Preacher's Plea*, wherein he describes the Puritans as those who make conscience of hearing the Word in order to build up their faith. By the end of his life, in 1616, Hieron was reconciled to conformity and speaks not unfavorably of bishops and the Book of Common Prayer. Contrary to his desires, however, he had a popular reputation as a Puritan and felt obliged to protest when serving as a guest preacher that he had not come "to open a pack of Puritanical ware"; and in his last sermon he denounced the practice—which had earlier been his own—of labeling ministers as "Puritans" and "Formalists." Instead, he recommended the encouragement of Christian unity.

Hieron made his mark through his best sellers. *The Doctrine of the Beginning of Christ* appears to have gone through twenty-four editions or printings in the first fifty years of the century. But his great favorite was *A Help Unto Devotion*, which went through about thirty-five editions as a separate publication and as part of Hieron's collected writings. It ranks in popularity with such best-sellers as Arthur Dent's *The Plain Man's Pathway to Heaven*, which had twenty-seven editions to 1650, and Lewis Bayly's *The Practice of Piety*, which had about forty-seven editions to 1650.

Hieron's *A Help Unto Devotion* is a collection of sixty-two prayers, one for just about every imaginable occasion. There is the orphan's lamentation, the captive's prayer, the prayer of the slandered person, a prayer against hypocrisy, a prayer for a malefactor condemned to die, a prayer to be said at the point of death, and a prayer for a childless woman. The longest is an evening prayer of over two thousand words. Many of the known editions of the work are not represented by a single extant copy, a fate not uncommon for devotional books, which frequently were literally worn out. The separate printings were pocket-size duodecimo volumes of about 450 pages. Interestingly, these prayers of Hieron's seem much less dated than most other religious works of the time. They are frequently eloquent, though not flowery, and, if long by modern standards, are not repetitious and wordy. The selection which follows offers insights into the piety of the age, as sermons and treatises seldom do.

Hieron's published works include nearly a hundred sermons, all revealing a nice sense of style. These gave him a sustained reputation as a preacher; he was favorably and frequently cited for his sermons by John Wilkins in his *Ecclesiastes, or A Discourse Concerning the Gift of Preaching* (1646). Hieron also wrote some rather bad poetry. In reponse to a Roman Catholic propaganda poem, he composed *The Papist's Rime, Answered* (1604), of which the following may serve as a sample:

> The faith of Christ may still abide
> Though Rome should into Tiber slide;
> God's spirit is free and is not bound
> Within the limits of Romish ground.
>
> When thou canst prove by Holy writ
> Christ's faith to Rome by charter knit,
> Then shalt thy tale some credit find,
> Where now it turneth all to wind.

By the evidence of Hieron's sermons one can once more see the inaccuracy of most sweeping generalizations about the characteristics of "the Puritan." Tawney believes that "the Puritan . . . sees . . . in riches, not an object of suspicion—though like other gifts they may be abused—but the blessing which rewards the triumph of energy and will." But Hieron's sermon "The Worldling's Downfall" teaches that outward prosperity is no evidence of God's favor: "a man may prosper outwardly, and yet still be hateful and abominable before God." He reminds us that "the Scripture speaketh of some which have their portion only in this life, and yet have no part in Heaven."

Hieron's last years were plagued by what one eulogist calls "the weakness of a sick and crazy body," but this did not "divert or detain him from great painstaking in his study at home and in the church abroad." In June 1617 he died of heart disease, after a month's illness. He left a wife and ten children.

Hieron's active years were not especially significant ones in the history of Puritanism. Facing the new canons and the effective administration of Bancroft and his agents, Puritans were definitely on the defensive. Most of them, like Hieron, found in the parish ministry the chief outlet for their energies.

A help unto devotion

A Prayer Fit for One Whom God Hath Enriched With Outward Things

It hath pleased Thee, O Lord, out of the freedom of Thy bounty, to deal more largely with me than with many of Thy servants, and to furnish me with store of those outward blessings which others every way as good by nature as myself do not enjoy.

My heart is fraught with much corruption, and though riches be in themselves a blessing, yet without Thy especial grace they will be unto me an occasion of many evils. Apt I shall be to lift up my heart, to pride myself in my own conceit, to trust unto my wealth, to despise others, to grow in love with this present world, to become cold and remiss in the best services, to conclude I am highly in Thy favor, because Thou hast enriched me.

These be the diseases which, through the poison of our nature,

[*The Workes* (London [1635]), pp. 744-745, 751-752, 762-763.]

do rise by these outward havings; neither can I say that my heart is clean from these corruptions. Purge them out of me, I beseech Thee, by the fiery power of Thy Spirit. Give me poverty of spirit and humbleness of mind amid this outward fulness with which Thou hast indued me. Make me to remember that, the more I have, the greater shall be mine account and the harder for me to be saved; that by that means my wealth may be so far from puffing me up with secure presumption, that it may move me the rather even with fear and trembling to work out my salvation.

Cause me to think often upon the words of my Savior, that riches are deceitful and of a thorny nature, choking the good seed of the Word and making it to become unfruitful; that so I may learn carefully to handle them and to use them with great heediness and circumspection, lest I should by them gall and wound my conscience or be pierced through with many sorrows.

It is said, O Lord, that these high places of the world are slippery places, in which it is hard to go with a right foot and to keep strait and even steps. Oh, stir me up to so much the more care to ponder my paths and to take diligent heed unto my ways. Suffer me not to justify myself to my own soul, or to make myself believe that I am as I ought to be, because waters of a full cup are wrung unto me. But teach me seriously to consider that, as many of Thy beloved servants do feel the smart of poverty, so even the most wicked and those which rebelliously transgress have a large portion in this life, living, waxing old, and growing in wealth, their goods oftentimes exceeding the very desires of their hearts. Grant, therefore, that I may labor for some better and more certain assurance of Thy grace, not grounding my hope upon my wealth but rejoicing in this, if the due consideration of the danger and vanity of abundance may work by Thy blessing, to the abasing and humbling of my heart.

Oh, let not mine eyes be dazzled, nor my heart bewitched with the glory and sweetness of these worldly treasures, which may be taken from me, or I from them, even in the twinkling of an eye. Draw my affection to the love of that durable riches, and to that fruit of heavenly wisdom which is better than gold, and the revenues whereof do surpass the silver, that my chief care may be to have a soul enriched and furnished with Thy grace, fulfilled with the knowledge of Thy will, in all wisdom and spiritual understanding.

And because, O Lord, in having much, I am but a steward under Thee and a disposer of Thy gifts, enlarge my bowels towards others; make me rich and fruitful in good works, being a father to the poor and causing the heart of the widow to rejoice, warming the loins of the naked with the fleece of my sheep, nor eating my morsels alone, but dealing my bread to the hungry and never hiding myself from mine own flesh.

For why should I make gold my hope? Or wherefore should I strive to lade myself with this thick clay, still plotting to set my nest on high, when all that I have or can have is in a moment turned into vanity? Quicken me up, therefore, to good duties, that the hearts of Thy saints may be comforted by me, and that in the place where I live, I may by my forwardness draw on and provoke others to all the offices of necessary benevolence. Let the bowels of the needy by my treasury, and let it be my desire and care there to lay up in store a good foundation for myself against the time to come, not trusting to be crowned for the worth of my liberality (for what can that be to a weight of glory?), but assuring myself that the mercy showed by me unto others is a beam of that love which shines from Thee upon my soul.

Thus, O Lord, shall I by Thy goodness have the true use of Thy blessings, together with a daily increase of much matter of thanksgiving for Thy great goodness to me, so vile and unworthy, and all for Christ, and in His most glorious and holy name, to Whom, with Thee and Thy Spirit, one true, everlasting, and only wise God, be all praise and power, might, majesty, and dominion, now and evermore. Amen.

The Student's Prayer

O Thou, the Father of lights, from Whom cometh down every good and perfect giving, it is by Thy holy providence that I am here placed in the schools of the prophets, to be trained up in the knowledge of good letters, and it is Thy goodness only which must give a blessing to my labors; otherwise all my studies and undertakings will be in vain.

To Thee, therefore, do I make my prayers; to Thee, O Lord, do I lift up my soul. Thou givest sharpness of wit; knowledge and discretion are Thy bestowing; Thou art the enlightener of the mind; Thou makest to apprehend those things which the shallowness of nature, of itself is unable to conceive. I beseech Thee, therefore, even for His sake Who is Thy wisdom, Whom Thou didst possess in the beginning of Thy way, He being before Thy works of old, that Thou wouldest vouchsafe to furnish me with such a competency of gifts as Thou in the depth of Thy wisdom knowest to be convenient for me. Order my desires; direct my choice; season and sanctify my heart; that I may covet the best gifts, and that my studies may not be led and carried by a vain affectation of knowledge and curious inquiry into hidden sciences for ostentation's sake, that so I may purchase admiration and credit, acuteness and learning before men, but that I may aim at the public good, how I may bring glory to Thy name and comfort to my soul by the promoting of the common benefit of human society.

And because authors are infinite, and much reading is a weariness to the flesh and will soon cause distraction and breed rather variety of endless and unprofitable questions than any soundness of knowledge, for this cause I beseech Thee so to direct me that I may wisely discern whom to follow and whom to avoid, and may constantly apply myself to that course by which I may best attain to my desired end. Preserve Thou me also from the poison of unsound opinions and from the sour leaven of all erroneous fancies, and for that end teach me not to lean to mine own wisdom or to trust to any sufficiency of mine own for the discerning of things that differ, but grant that I may give up myself to be guided by Thy Spirit, which is the alone teacher of that way which we must choose.

And seeing, O Lord, Thy holy Word, which Thou Thyself hast inspired, is the treasury of all true knowledge, where only that wisdom is to be found whose fruit is better than gold, and the revenues whereof do far exceed the finest silver, therefore make me a diligent and a busy searcher of that sacred book, that it may be a familiar unto me and dwell plenteously in my inward parts, and that so I may feel the sweetness of it in my soul.

The times also, O most gracious Father, being so full of peril and so abounding with many dangerous allurements unto evil, partly by wicked company and partly by vain delights, I am an earnest petitioner to Thy goodness to make me wary and circumspect for preventing of these creeping and bewitching mischiefs. Give me wisdom to make choice of the society of those by whose sobriety and gravity and good example I may be bettered, and to have an eye to those who are upright in their way, striving to tread in their steps and to be a follower of their courses.

Cause me to be always even afraid of myself in the use of delights, knowing how hard a thing it is not to exceed and how soon a man's affections shall be ensnared. Let my care, therefore, be to find means rather for redeeming than for passing away my precious time, my thoughts being still busied upon the long journey which I have to go before I can come unto due perfection.

In other things also, O good God, guide me by Thy holy hand, that I may keep myself within the lists of Christianity, being modest in apparel, moderate [in] diet, chaste and temperate in speech, sober in fashion and my ordinary deportment, respective to my superiors, amiable to my equals, without pride and insolency towards those that are below me, courteous and affable and yet without vanity and popularity towards all. Among all let me be ready in my courses, both of scholastical exercise for the polishing of the mind, and of divine and spiritual employments for the adorning and garnishing of the soul, that as I grow in years and standing, so I may also drink in knowledge and grace, and that in Jesus Christ, in Whom only I expect the granting of my requests, Who breathes upon me with His Spirit, making my soul forward and willing to depend upon Thee, and to return unto Thee all due praise and glory, world without end. So be it.

A Prayer before Meat

Sanctify, O Lord, unto us the use of these Thy creatures, of which by our sins we have made ourselves unworthy. Make us sober and thankful partakers of them; grant that the end of our eating and drinking may be to be better enabled to serve Thee in our several places, through Jesus Christ. Amen.

Another

Humble our souls before Thee, O Lord, and cause us to see the smallness of our desert, even in respect of the least of Thy mercies. Make us to hunger after Christ, by Whom only the free use of Thy creatures is restored to us; and give us to enjoy these blessings here provided for us, with that reverence and sobriety as in Thy presence, that, our bodies being refreshed, our souls may praise Thee, Who art the giver of all good, and that in Jesus Christ the righteous. Amen.

A Thanksgiving after Meat

Blessed be Thou, O Lord, for these and for all Thy gifts. Let Thy mercy to our bodies stir up thankfulness in our souls, and let our care to please Thee in our lives be a witness of the feeling we have of Thy rich and abundant mercies towards us. Be gracious to all Thy people through the world; forget not these realms, nor Thine anointed, our sovereign lord and King, the hopeful prince, and the royal progeny. Disappoint the enemies of Thy Gospel, and make it to grow in despite of Satan, to the glory of Thy name and to the rejoicing of the souls of all Thy servants, for Jesus' sake. Amen.

Richard Stock (*ca.* 1569–1627)

Richard Stock is perhaps best known as John Milton's childhood rector. Born about 1569 in York, Stock went up to St. John's College, Cambridge, in 1587. He commenced B.A. in 1590 and M.A. in 1594. While at St. John's, Stock and Thomas Gataker, also represented in this volume, became close friends. Almost forty years later Gataker preached Stock's funeral sermon, a work which provides valuable biographical material. While at Cambridge Stock learned much from William Whitaker, a learned Calvinist divinity professor. Stock was Whitaker's favorite student. In 1606 Stock complimented his master by translating his treatise attacking the Roman Catholics Campion and Dureus.

Not able to become a fellow at St. John's because there were no vacancies, Stock, like his friend Gataker, was chosen to be a fellow of the new Sidney Sussex College, but in 1596 he left Cambridge to become rector of Standlake, Oxfordshire. The first outward evidence of his Puritanism is his subsequent appointment as chaplain to Sir Anthony Cope, the outspoken Puritan M.P. But before long he moved to London, where he served as lecturer and curate at various churches. In 1604 he became curate at the church with which he remained identified till his death, All Hallows', Bread Street, a church on the very street where, four years later, Milton was born. In 1611 Stock became rector at All Hallows'.

Stock's interests are clearly revealed by his sermons and other writings. He seems to have been a modest man who had certain interests which he vigorously pursued. One of these was the Fathers of the Church. His works are full of quotations from Chrysostom, Augustine, and Jerome. Another favorite was Bernard. They are not handled as authorities or as embroidery but rather as if Stock considered them old friends who had the knack of making apt phrases. He defended his use of quotations from the Fathers in his epistle to the reader of *The Doctrine and Use of Repentance*.

This work, published in 1610, was first delivered as sermons.

It reveals another side of Stock's character. He wrote the work, he explains, because he knew of no complete study of repentance. Clearly his was a labor of love. He seems to have left no stone, not even a pebble, unturned in his desire to be thorough. Another striking characteristic of the work is Stock's psychological insight. He is immensely concerned with the danger of hypocritical penitence.

A less attractive aspect of Stock comes out in his Paul's Cross sermon of November 2, 1606, a year after the discovery of the Gunpowder Plot. Stock dedicated the work to the Bishop of Bath and Wells with the recommendation that he use his influence to persuade King James to put down Romanism. The sermon itself combines learning and emotional appeal, both used to attack the Roman Church. Stock cites errors of thirteen popes to counter the belief that the Pope is unable to err: Marcellinus offered sacrifices to idols, Liberius denied the divinity of Christ, Innocent I held baptism and the Eucharist necessary for the salvation of children. He advocates severe treatment of English Catholics on the grounds of love of the true Church, patriotism, the desire for peace, and the need to rescue the souls of the Romanists.

Stock's sermon at the funeral of Lord Harrington (1614) has brought the scholarly attention of Miltonists to Stock's court connections. About 1606 he served as chaplain to William Knollys, a member of the court inner circle. Perhaps through him Stock came to know the Harringtons, especially the promising young lord, who died at the age of twenty-one. Harrington's sister was the well-known Lucy, Countess of Bedford, a patroness of Michael Drayton, Samuel Daniel, Ben Jonson, and others.

Stock's sermon at Lord Harrington's funeral is in two parts. The first part is the customary explication of a Biblical text, with doctrines, reasons, and uses. The principal idea here is that the death of the godly is a punishment of the sins of others. The second part belongs to the category which William Haller calls the spiritual biography. The Puritan equivalent of the medieval Lives of the Saints, the spiritual biographies usually appeared first as lean-tos of funeral sermons, but many were collected later in such volumes as Samuel Clarke's *The Lives of Sundry Eminent Persons* (London, 1683). Most of these books are concerned with preachers' lives, though the laity also are frequently treated. The life of Harrington is of peculiar interest because Stock provides more specific detail than is found in most spiritual biographies.

Stock identified himself with the Puritan movement through his efforts to promote the cause of Sabbatarianism and his work in the non-incorporated self-perpetuating trust which raised funds to buy ecclesiastical impropriations so that more Puritans could preach. Stock was one of the original eight members; the others included the famous London preachers Richard Sibbes and John Davenport, both leading Puritans. This trust, which Laud had dissolved in 1632, began only the year before Stock's death in 1627.

Stock was buried in the church where he had served. The writing of his epitaph was the occasion for a display of wit:

> Thy lifeless trunk, O Reverend Stock,
> Like Aaron's rod sprouts out again,
> And, after two full winters passed,
> Yields blossoms and ripe fruit amain.
> For why? This work of piety,
> Performed by some of thy flock
> To thy dead corpse and sacred urn,
> Is but the fruit of this old stock.

And eleven years later Stock bore fruit again with the publication of *A Stock of Divine Knowledge . . . Description of the Divine Nature* and *A Learned Commentary upon Malachi.*

Stock is less important for what he was than for what he represents. Throughout Elizabeth's and James's reigns London pulpits were occupied by men like Stock. While the London middle class was growing in wealth, power, and prestige, it was encouraged by the example of the likes of Richard Stock, a sober, industrious man, learned in the ways of men and in the ways of God.

The life of John, Lord Harrington

I will . . . speak a few things of this deceased honorable person, the most hopeful gentleman. . . . I say, a few words of his life and death, by your patience, that when we see his worth, we

[*The Church's Lamentation for the Loss of the Godly* (London, 1614), pp. 63–88.]

may conceive of our own loss and be assured of his gain; and so in sorrowing for ourselves, yet we may rejoice over him; in speaking of whom, I fear, as Chrysostom did when he fell occasionally into the commendations of St. Paul: "Lest my speech should rather blemish and diminish the praise of so great a personage than anyways adorn it." I will do what I can, and if I satisfy not men's expectations, as Bernard in another case, "Culpetur sane ingenium, non voluntas"—"Blame my wit and not my will."

.   .   .   .

I will omit to speak of his education and bringing up, which is the honor of his parents, having been so religious and truly Christian as it was. "Non est parvi apud deum meriti bene filios educare." So Jerome: "It is a thing of no small account with God for men to bring up their children well," and in the fear of God, especially men children, which as Chrysostom saith is "a greater burden and more full of fears and cares."

I will not stand upon his natural parts of wit, memory, sweetness of nature, ability of body, all which were in him excellent, but they are common to many others—yet in this different, namely, in the well using and applying of them. "A good wit," saith one, "unsanctified is a prey for the devil." So I may say of the rest; but when it is true of them which Bernard saith, "Grace doth order aright that which creation hath given," then are they honorable and commendable indeed. Such were they in this honorable person, truly sanctified and religiously applied to all good, as shall appear by that which followeth.

For his learning, I must leave it to others to speak that had occasion to confer with him and converse with him in that course; I mean for human knowledge of tongues and arts and the like. I know many, both strangers and Englishmen, speak admirably of him; as some out of certain knowledge testify of him that he had attained four languages very sufficiently, the Greek, Latin, Italian, and French, being able to read Greek authors and to make use of them in their own language. Speaking Latin well and writing a pure and grave style, so also he was able to confer with any stranger readily and laudably in the Italian and the French, as men of best judgment have thought; able also to understand the authors he reads in the Spanish tongue. So for his knowledge in the arts, especially in philosophy and the mathematics: some who are masters of these arts and others of note witness with them that his skill as well in the practic part as contemplative was of that degree towards perfection as that he was not only to have been accounted excellent, in respect he was a gentleman of noble rank and place, but that he might justly be paralleled with most of the best that were renowned in the only professing of the same. For his knowledge in the theory of the art military and navigation, he had made so good a progress therein, as some who understand those arts well do witness, he wanted nothing but the practice to a great perfection in them both. For his understanding in heavenly knowledge and the mysteries of salvation, as his desire was very fervent to it, so was his success very prosperous and happy in it. For he had attained that measure that I never knew in any of what rank soever of his years that did not intend to make it their profession. I have conferred with him many and many times; I never knew the question come in our way which he was not able suddenly and understandingly to speak unto.

But to come to the best and that which is most comfortable, as touching him, and may more make us to bewail our loss: this desire of knowledge was not as Bernard notes of some, who desired to know "For that end only that they might know," which is "turpis curiositas," saith the Father, "a filthy curiosity." Nor as others who desired it "ut sciatur ipsi," "that they might be known," which is "turpis vanitas," "foul vanity"; nor as others, "ut scientiam suam vendant," "that they may make sale of their knowledge," which is "turpis quæstus," "filthy lucre." But it was as he speaketh; others desired knowledge "ut ædificent," "that they might profit others," which was "charitas," "charity," and as others, "ut ædificentur," "that they might be edified," "et prudentia est," "and it is wisdom." Of all these, only the two last are found free from the abuse of knowledge, as who would therefore understand that they might do good. "These two last are not the abuses of knowledge, because they desire to know well what they may do well." Such I assure you was the desire of knowledge in this honorable person, which I manifest thus unto you.

The grace of salvation, that is, this saving knowledge by the Gospel, teacheth not for the speculation, but the practice of it, it being like the voice that bade Lazarus arise, and made him able to rise out of his grave and to walk and work. I say, it teacheth three lessons and enables them that truly apprehend it to work three main things: sobriety, justice, piety. "The grace of God that bringeth salvation unto all men hath appeared and teacheth us that we should live soberly, and righteously, and godly in this present world." How well this noble worthy had both learned and was enabled by the grace of salvation to practice these three, I will manifest to you in few words: of the first two more briefly; of the latter more largely.

For his sobriety, he was a wonderful sober and chaste man in his life. Nay, his lips not heard to utter any unchaste, nay, scarcely unseemly speech, as many report of him with whom haply he would have spoken more liberally and opened himself more freely than with me; which was the more commendable in him because he was, as Jerome speaketh, "in lubrica ætate," "in a slippery age," in the flower of his youth; but yet more because he lived "in lubrico loco," "in a slippery place," the Court; most of all, because he had been a traveler in those places where are schools of uncleanness, whence few ever return such as they went out, but of good and chaste, return unchaste; being unchaste when they went out, they are sevenfold more defiled than before. So was it not with him, but like fishes which retain their fresh taste though they live in salt waters, so in an unchaste age, in unchaste places, he ever kept his chastity; yea, he grew in the love of chastity and hatred of all uncleanness.

And no marvel, for he took the way to it. He avoided the occasions; he spent not his time in courting of young ladies and amorously beholding beautiful women, the bellows of lust and baits of uncleanness, of whom St. Augustine speaketh thus, "To see them hurts the heart; to hear them inflames the mind; to touch them stirs up the flesh; and last of all, all whatsoever is done with women (which are not their lawful wives) is a snare to that man that dealeth with them." But this chaste spouse esteemed his books above their beauty and instead of dalliance with them, his delight was in men of parts and learning, for arts and arms. But besides this, as a special means of chastity, he was temperate in feeding and rare in feasting and frequent in fasting (of which, when I come to his religion). He was, moreover, a great avoider of idleness and sleep, the two nurses of uncleanness; with his will, he ordinarily never slept above six hours, and when he lay awake, he sought to exclude all evil thoughts with meditation upon some heavenly things, as I shall tell you when I come to his piety.

For his justice, he had no public place to show himself in. He was but coming upon the stage and God called him away and suffered him not to manifest what he had gotten by his careful fitting himself for such a place. For his private carriage, I have not heard but that he dealt honorably and honestly with every man that he had to do with. That great and honorable care he had that his father's debts, which were very great by his manifold both private and public occasions, and some few of his own (which I am informed to be no great matter), establishing power in his honorable mother and executress to sell all or any part of the land presently and speedily to pay and discharge all; and when the gentleman who drew the conveyance demanded of him if he approved of that he appointed to be done and confirmed to this purpose, he answered, "Yes, with all my heart, for my honor and my honesty are my nearest heirs." If any think that to impeach his justice, that he left not the land to the heir male to uphold the house, I must tell them that in justice the paying of just debts ought to be preferred before upholding of houses, and will give more comfort at the last. Yea, there can be no true comfort without care of this; and the taille being cut off (as I am informed) by his father in this honorable respect, to pay every man his own, his sisters were nearer to him than his cousin german, both by the law of God and nature, who, being honorable ladies, professors of religion as it lieth in their power and the world looks for it from them, so if they leave no children to inherit, no doubt they will have an honorable care to uphold the house and the name, which I think will be much to their honor.

And now, honorable and beloved, I come to the third branch and the third effect of this saving knowledge, his godliness and his religion, of whom I may say as Salvian saith of one, that "he was noble in that faith which always in all addressings is an ornament, because without this faith there is nothing so specious that can garnish and beautify."

This, this is the temple that sanctifies the gold, this is the altar that sanctifies the offering. By this the sobriety and justice (which in a heathen or civil man, without this, are but glittering sins, as St. Augustine calls them) in him were glorious virtues. For this in general: such was his piety that not I only but many others, better able to judge than myself, will affirm with me that we knew not any of what rank soever in whom we discerned more, nay, so fervent a desire of saving knowledge, so constant a resolution to practice all known good duties, so great tenderness of conscience, and fear to offend God in the least thing which he knew to be sin. How and whereby we discerned this I will discover to you in particular, which when you have heard, I doubt not but you will judge that we conceited not things amiss but as they were.

We discerned this and it did discover itself unto us two ways, by his private and public exercises of piety, which were such, as I say not, were rarely found in a young man, more rarely in a nobleman, most rarely in a young nobleman; but such they were as are rarely found in such measure in any man of what age and condition soever he be. I will first speak of his private course and tell you how he spent one day, and in like manner he spent all the days of the year.

His private exercise and course of piety was on this sort. He usually rose every morning about four or five of the clock, not willingly sleeping above six hours. As soon as ever he was thoroughly awake, he endeavored religiously to set his heart in order and to prepare it for goodness all the day after, offering the first fruits of the day and of his thoughts unto God. Thus having tuned his best instrument, his heart, in the next place he read a chapter of the Holy Scripture. That done, he went to prayers with his servants in his chamber. After this he read some divine treatise to increase his knowledge in spiritual things, and this for the greater part of an hour. He had of latter times read over in this course Calvin's *Institutions*, and was at the time of his sickness reading the works of a reverend man now living, one Master Rogers. And all this he did besides that which was performed with all the family, with whom he joined in the order his honorable father left in the family, namely, reading of the Psalms and a chapter, together with prayer according to the order of our Church, before dinner and supper, and singing of a psalm and prayer after supper.

But to return to his morning business: after he had bestowed the former time in the manner aforesaid, he withdrew himself to his closet, and after his own private prayer disposed himself to some serious study, if some special business interrupted not his course, for the space of three or four hours; after which time he addressed himself, if he had time before dinner, to dispatch business, if any there were required of him, and to converse and confer with his friends, to better them or be bettered by them, or to ride his great horse or walk abroad. But why place I these with his religion? Because hereby he kept himself from idleness and gave no way to the temptations of Satan, knowing well that the flies settle upon the sweetest perfumes, when they are cold, and corrupt them.

Soon after dinner if he had the opportunity he ordinarily withdrew himself for a while to the meditating upon some sermons which he had lately heard, for which use he retained some five or six in his mind. He would not fail, though he was disappointed of that opportunity, to meditate upon them before he slept. Yea, many times travelling by land or water, he performed this duty and then would desire his companions to forbear talk [that] they might think a while. He did ordinarily meditate and call to mind four or five in a day. The rest of his afternoon he gave to business as the occasions were and to study histories and to get instructions from them who were skillful in the discipline of war or in the mathematics and navigation, wherein some report he had made great success for his age and time.

After supper he betook himself to prayer with his servants, and, that which is markable above many other things, after prayers with them he withdrew himself from his servants and friends, and there in a book which he kept for the account of his life he set down what he had done all that day; how he had either offended or done good, and how he was tempted and withstood them, and according to his account he humbled himself. And such was his wisdom that such temptations as were not fit, as I suppose, to come to any man's view but his own and his God's, he writ in a peculiar character known to none. After this, giving himself to his rest, as rising he had care to shut out evil by possessing his heart with good thoughts and the reading of the Holy Scripture, so had he care to shut up his heart against such things, one of his chamber [servants], as he was laying him to rest, reading a chapter or two of the sacred Word of God. And this was not taken up for a fit and as a novelty, but he continued it for the space of four years last past, as some inform me, that is, from January, 1609, to the fifteenth of February, 1613, the day when he took his bed, some twelve days before his death.

And now, honorable and beloved, for his public exercises, which you may well think were carefully and conscionably performed. For he that had such care to approve himself to God in private had no less care to approve himself both to God and man in public. This appeareth in his religious use of the time and means of God's worship and his own edification and salvation.

He was a most religious observer of the Sabbath in public and private duties, professing to affect the public means, if he were where he could enjoy them, before all private, though they were differently performed, and had resolved, though he entertained a household chaplain, yet ever to frequent the public assemblies upon the Sabbath Day, a thing worthy the noting, to the reproof of many of his own, as of inferior, rank, who so much neglect the public assemblies. And for his present practice, he did not miss ordinarily twice a day to hear the Word publicly; no, not when he was a courtier. Yea, he hath ridden four miles to the public worship of God when he could not enjoy it nearer. After he had heard, he usually withdrew himself from company before dinner, if he were so fitted for circumstances, that he might for the space of half an hour meditate upon what he had heard, or for some other private meditations.

After the afternoon's public exercise, two of his servants having written (his memory being such as it exceeded oftentimes all their writings), he repeated with his servants before supper both the sermons and writ them down in his night-book, and after all this he prayed with them, wherein he had a great gift. And that which helped him the better to keep the Sabbath, he was constantly accustomed upon Saturday at night, besides his account for the day, to call himself to a strict account how he had spent the whole week, that according as he found his estate, he might better fit himself to sanctify the Sabbath following. In the morning he repeated to his servants, as he was making ready, those sermons which he had heard the Sabbath before. (Note this, not out of time though somewhat out of place, that a most inward familiar of his hath, since the delivery of this, acquainted me with: that upon the Saturday he took a view of all the week; so upon the month Saturday, he took a view of all the former month to see how he had bettered, as one week more than another, so one month more than another; how he had added and got more grace and strength of piety.)

In the hearing of the Word, he was one of the most attentive and reverend hearers that ever I observed or mine eyes have seen that have seen many thousands, for he well knew that he was before God and that he heard not the words of man but God, and as well did he acknowledge that it is but the error of great men to think they have a privilege to be less reverent and regardful in hearing than the meanest in the congregation. Yea, he knew that kings' scepters are as much inferior to Christ's scepter as he that bears it is inferior to kings. Therefore, when he came to hear, he willingly laid down his honor at Christ's feet.

For the Sacrament, he received it constantly, if by any convenience he could, every first Sunday of the month, and to fit himself to feast at Christ's table, he fasted the Saturday before (besides many other times when he humbled himself), spending the day in prayer, with meditation and examination of himself and his estate; how it was with him since his last receiving, never coming out of his study, unless very importunate occasions pressed him, till towards supper time, nor meddling with any business that day. On the Sunday morning, besides his ordinary preparations, he read the first Epistle to the Corinthians, chapter 11, where the institution of the Supper is set down. And for the space of an hour he read with his servants that should communicate with him a little treatise that is in print, teaching men how to be prepared for worthy receiving. Thus careful was this worthy to be fitly prepared for his Savior's Supper, that he might be a worthy receiver. And all this piety and godliness did this noble heart practice in this age.

Thomas Gataker (1574–1654)

Thomas Gataker combined interestingly the activities of Puritan preacher and humanist scholar. He was born in London in 1574, the son of the rector of St. Edmund's, Lombard Street. He began early the study of literature, which he continued at St. John's College, Cambridge. Among his teachers was John Bois, one of the translators of the authorized version of the Bible. (Gataker attended Bois's extra lecture, delivered at four in the morning from bed.) In 1594 he was awarded the B.A. degree and in 1597 the M.A. When Sidney Sussex College was established, the trustees chose him as a fellow, but he could not commence his duties at once because buildings had first to be constructed. In the interim he served as a family tutor. In this capacity he conducted evening prayers, and during such a service the suffragan bishop of Chichester heard him explicate a portion of St. Paul's Epistle to the Ephesians. Much impressed, the bishop urged him to seek holy orders, and soon he was ordained. When Sidney Sussex was ready, Gataker returned to Cambridge. Though his stay was brief, he established an important friendship with William Bradshaw, later author of the classic congregationalist work *English Puritanism*. Already sympathetic to Puritanism through the influence of college tutors, Gataker now involved himself in a Puritan project, the supplying of preachers in neglected parishes. He preached at Everton, Bedfordshire, where the minister was reported to be one hundred and thirty years old. Soon Gataker felt obliged to adopt the work of the ministry, but, as he tells us in his later *Discourse Apologetical*, he feared he would have difficulty since, for such men as himself, the times proved "more troublesome than formerly they had been." At first he served as a family chaplain in London and preached from time to time at St. Martin's in the Fields. Finally, in 1601, he became preacher at Lincoln's Inn, a post he held for ten years. The Inn had already enjoyed the preaching of the important Puritan William Charke, who had been silenced by Archbishop Whitgift. Later the Inn was to hear the baroque preaching of John Donne from 1616 to 1622, followed by the stern simplicity of John Preston from 1622 till his death in 1628.

Gataker was a man of much influence at the Inns of Court; among those who heard him regularly were Lord Rich and Prince Henry. When he arrived, the only Sunday lecture was given at seven in the morning, most of the rest of the day being devoted by the barristers to conferences with clients. But Gataker soon convinced them that it was as evil to conduct business on the Sabbath as to farm. He then moved the morning lecture to a later hour and the Wednesday lecture to Sunday afternoon. A more nearly Puritan Sabbath was henceforth observed.

Although opportunities to go elsewhere were many, Gataker remained at Lincoln's Inn till 1611, when he chose a position that was scarcely worthy of his talents but would otherwise have fallen into what Gataker felt to be unworthy hands. For forty years he preached at Rotherhithe, near London Bridge, though in his last years his preaching was limited by very bad health.

Although his first book did not appear till he was forty-five, Gataker was an extremely voluminous author; his works are nearly fifty in number. Besides the many separately published sermons, Gataker produced works of other kinds: an elaborate treatise on the name by which God made himself known to Moses and the people of Israel; a work seeking to prove the existence of diphthongs; a book on the nature and use of lots; an attack on astrology (a work which was answered by criticisms of Gataker's life and morals, which Gataker in turn answered with an auto-biographical defense); a discussion of transubstantiation and various other religious matters, mostly in Latin; a life of Bradshaw; and a work for which Gataker was famous for many years: an edition of Marcus Aurelius. Henry Hallam calls it "the earliest edition . . . of any classical writer published in England with original annotations." Gataker worked on this edition for forty years. It was re-published a number of times in the hundred years after it appeared, and a full-dress edition of Gataker's *Opera Critica* was edited by the noted Dutch theologian Witsius. Morhoff, the author of an elaborate survey of classical learning, says of Gataker, "Of all the critics of this age who have employed their pen in illustrating polite learning, there are few, if indeed any, who deserve to be

preferred to Thomas Gataker for diligence and accuracy. . . ."
He corresponded with many scholars, notably Salmasius, Milton's
opponent, and Archbishop Ussher.

Something of Gataker the humanist carried over into his preaching, for his sermons abound in classical echoes, cited properly in
the marginal gloss. Among the authors referred to in the marginal
gloss of *A Good Wife God's Gift* are Petronius, Ovid, Sophocles,
Galen, Menander, Hesiod, Aeschylus, Plutarch, and Erasmus as
well as Lipsius, many Fathers, schoolmen, and Protestant theologians.
Most of the quotations, one of Gataker's admirers explains, were
provided from memory. In this sermon, as well as in three other
marriage sermons, one detects more than reading. As William
Haller has observed, there is in them "something of the quality of
personal confession," revealing "the joys and sorrows of the
godly lover's heart." Since Gataker outlived four wives, he had
reason to know what he was talking about in his marriage sermons.

Gataker's sermon on "A Good Wife" reflects the traditional
Puritan attitude towards woman, much the same attitude which
shocks modern readers of *Paradise Lost*. Milton speaks of Adam
as being created "for God only" and Eve "for God in him,"
and Gataker (in *Marriage Duties Briefly Couched*) warns the wife
that "when the husband admonishes, God admonisheth in him";
"the Christian wife obeyeth her husband for God."

Gataker teaches that a wife's duties are primarily three: the
education of children, caring for food which the husband brings
home, and "a constant and painful endeavour of doing something,
as ability, leisure, and opportunity shall give leave, toward the
raising and advancing of their estate, and the further enlarging of
their means." (One detects in this passage the kind of implication
which has led some scholars to relate closely Puritanism and the
spirit of capitalism.) For Gataker, a wife offers many benefits, for
she brings grace and honor to her husband, serves as a remedy
against incontinence, and offers society, assistance, and solace. But
perhaps most important, says Gataker with feeling, a wife offers
issue, and since the fall of man "want of issue is . . . more uncomfortable when men are subject to mortality than it had been
when man was himself to have lived always" for "by means of

propagation man attaineth a kind of immortality and in posterity surviveth himself."

Throughout his marriage sermons Gataker says little about the duties of the husband. He is to treasure his wife as a gift from God and must do the duty of a husband even to a bad wife; he is required to provide for his wife according to his means. Most of Gataker's advice to men concerns the proper choice of a wife, not the proper treatment of her after marriage.

As a preacher Gataker preserved a pleasing middle course between the plain style and the more elaborate style of the witty preachers. He prepared his sermons carefully, and only occasionally did he fail to speak to his audience's condition. One example of a failure is an interesting betrayal of his erudition:

As a learned man [Joseph Scaliger] said sometime of Rome having been somewhile there, that a man might seek Rome in Rome, and yet not find her there, Rome was so much altered from that it had been; and the orator of Sicily [Cicero], after Verres had governed there, that men sought Sicily in Sicily, it was by him so impoverished; and a reverend prelate of ours [Lancelot Andrewes], of Bellarmine's latter works, that many missed Bellarmine in Bellarmine, they were so much unlike to, and came so far short of his former. So mayest thou find much want and miss of a wife in a wife, if thou makest thy choice amiss.

But even such an entirely uncalled-for display does not bury Gataker's point.

The pleasure he has in playing on words, a feature prominently revealed in *A Good Wife God's Gift*, is also shown in a poem he composed shortly before his death:

> I thirst for thirstiness; I weep for tears;
> Well pleased I am to be displeased thus;
> The only thing I fear is want of fear;
> Suspecting I am not suspicious.
> I cannot choose but live, because I die;
> And, when I am not dead, how glad am I:
> Yet, when I am thus glad for sense of pain,
> And careful am, lest I should careless be;
> Then do I grieve for being glad again,
> And fear lest carelessness take care from me.
> Amid these restless thoughts this rest I find,
> For those who rest not here, there's rest behind.

Besides his preaching, pastoral cares, and writing, Gataker spent much time during his years at Rotherhithe with students who came from abroad as well as from distant parts of England to study and live with him. Perhaps his tour of Holland and Belgium in 1620 to see Protestant churches there was partly responsible for the foreign students' visiting. Such study with a master was a rather common Puritan practice. But Gataker cannot be identified with strict Puritanism, for he was not completely opposed to the episcopal system. He condemned "prelacy" as it existed in James's and Charles's days, but approved "a duly founded and well regulated prelacy joined with a presbytery, wherein one as president . . . hath some preeminence above the rest."

He was an active member of the Westminster Assembly during its first two years, from 1643 to 1645. Gataker petitioned against the execution of King Charles. Till the end of his life he worked hard, leaving three works to be published after his death in 1654.

A good wife God's gift

Proverbs xix.14. "Houses and riches are the inheritance of the fathers, but a prudent wife is of the Lord."

There be two things especially that commend a work, the author and the matter. Both of them conspire to commend this book, as in the title of it they are both expressed: "The Proverbs or parables of Solomon, the son of David, King of Israel." For the author (to omit the principal, God's Spirit, for all Scripture is inspired of God), the penman of it was Solomon, the wisest mere man that ever was in the world since Adam, by the testimony even of wisdom itself. For the matter, it is proverbs or parables (as the word in the original signifieth), master sentences, such as rule or sway and are or may be of principal use in man's life. Now consisting for the most part of such aphorisms and short sentences from the beginning especially of the tenth chapter, it is not necessary that they should

[*A Good Wife Gods Gift: And A Wife Indeed. Two Marriage Sermons* (London, 1624), pp. 1–24.]

have any coherence one with another; neither indeed for the most
part have they. Yet this and the next before it have some connection, the former being of the inconvenience that cometh by a bad
wife, this latter of the benefit that a good wife, that a wise and discreet woman, bringeth with her.

There Solomon compared two grand evils together and made a
bad wife the worse of the twain. Here he compareth two great
benefits together and maketh a good wife the better of the two.
For the former, "A foolish son," saith Solomon, "is his father's sorrow, and a brawling wife is as a continual dropping." "Mala in-
testina gravissima": "Evils are the more grievous, the nearer and
the more inward they are"; as diseases in the entrails. And "mala
domestica," domestical evils, vex a man most when a man's enemies,
as our Savior speaketh, are those of his own house. It is no small
inconvenience to dwell near a bad neighbor. Were such a one
further off us, he would be less troublesome to us. And surely if to
have good neighbors be a matter of no small moment, then somewhat also it must needs be for a man to want such, and much more
for a man to have them that dwell near him evil affected toward
him. An evil at the next door may be bad enough and may prove
over troublesome; an evil within doors, at home, in a man's own
house, much more.

But again within doors there are degrees also. In a man's own
family there are some nearer than others. A son is nearer than a
servant, and a wife than a son. It is a sore cross to be troubled, and
it be but with bad servants. It is no small vexation for a man to find
untoward and unfaithful carriage toward him in those that eat his
bread, that feed at his board; much more to sustain it at the hands
of her that taketh up the same bed with him, that lieth in his bosom.
No evil to a bad bed-fellow, to a bosom-evil, to that evil that lieth
next the heart, either within or about the breast.

Again, though true mercy and compassion in some measure extend itself unto all those whose miseries and calamities we are acquainted with, yet the misfortunes of our dear friends affect us
more than of mere strangers. And the wrongs and injuries offered us

by professed and pretended friends we are wont to take more to heart. "It was not mine enemy," saith David, "that did me this wrong, for then I could have borne it. But it was thou, O man, my companion, my guide, and my familiar friend."

But brethren are nearer than friends. And howsoever Solomon truly saith that "a friend sometime sticketh closer to a man than a brother," yet in nature a brother is nearer than any friend is or can be. There is a civil knot only between friend and friend; there is a natural band between brother and brother. And therefore, "A brother offended is harder to win than a strong city; and their contentions are as bars of brass." It is easier gluing again of boards together that have been unglued than healing up the flesh that is gashed and divided, and the reason is, because there was but an artificial connection before in the one; there was a natural conjunction in the other. So it is easier reconciling of friends than of brethren, there being a civil bond only broken in the disjunction of the one, a natural tie violated in the dissensions of the other. But children—they are yet nearer than either friends or brethren. They are "partes nostri, viscera nostra": they are as our very bowels and part of ourselves. And therefore no marvel if Solomon say that "A foolish son is a sorrow to his father and a heaviness to his mother." And "He that begetteth a fool begetteth himself sorrow, and the father of a fool shall have no joy."

But behold here a further evil than any of the former: an evil wife, a contentious woman, worse than any of them all. Husband and wife are nearer than friends and brethren, or than parents and children; though they spring from their parents, yet they abide not always with them. They are as rivers rising from one head but taking several ways, making several streams, and running apart in several channels. But man and wife must bide by it: they are as two streams that, rising from several heads, fall the one into the other, mingle their waters together, and are not severed again till they are swallowed up in the sea. Children are as branches shooting out of one stem, divided and severed either from other, or as grafts and scions cut off, or boughs and branches slipped off from their native stock, and either planted or ingrafted elsewhere. Man and wife are as the stock and scion, the one ingrafted into the other, and so fastened together that they cannot again be sundered; or as those two pieces in the prophet's hand enclosed in one bark and making both but one branch. And "therefore," saith the Holy Ghost, "shall a man leave father and mother and be glued unto, or cleave fast to his wife; and they two shall be one flesh."

The nearer the bond, then, the greater the evil where it falleth out otherwise than it ought. "A foolish son," saith Solomon, "is the calamity of his father." And how is he his calamity? He is "filius pudefaciens," such a one as shameth his parents and maketh them glad to hide their heads in the house. But an evil wife is as the rain dropping in through the tiles, that maketh him weary of the house, that vexeth him so that it driveth him out of doors.

Yea, as a dropping in a rainy day, when it is foul without and it droppeth within. So that it maketh a man at his wit's end, uncertain whether it be better for him to be abroad in the rain or to bide within doors in the dropping. And for this cause Augustine compareth an evil conscience to a bad wife (and it may seem that he pleased himself somewhat in the similitude, he maketh use so oft of it), which, when a man hath many troubles and afflictions from without, and would look home, hoping for some comfort from within, is much more troublesome to him than any of those his outward crosses are; is as a rock or a shelf to seamen in a storm, where they hoped to have found harbor and shelter against it.

Yea, further, not as a dropping only that driveth a man from his house and home, and that when it raineth, but as a *continual* dropping in such a day, so that a bad wife is worse than a quartan ague, wherein a man hath two good days for one evil. He that hath an evil wife is as one that hath an evil soul, a guilty conscience that evermore sticketh by him, that everywhere accompanieth him, is a continual evil companion with him at bed and board, such as he cannot shift off or shun. And no marvel therefore if it be deemed the greatest temporal evil, because the most continual and the most inward, for a man to be matched with an evil wife or a woman with an evil husband. For what is said of the one is as true of the other, the relation between them being alike.

To draw all to a head then: an unkind neighbor is a cross, but an unfaithful friend is a great cross, an unnatural brother a greater, an ungracious child yet a greater; but a wicked, unquiet, or disloyal wife is the greatest of all and, if we believe Solomon, goeth beyond them all. In regard whereof he also elsewhere pronounceth that "it is better to abide on a corner of the housetop without, than to continue with such a one in a wide house"; yea, that "it is better to live in the wilderness with the wild beasts" than with such.

But to leave this that is without my text, and yet next door to it (so near here do good and bad neighbor together), and to come nearer home: some, it may be, hearing Solomon speak on this manner might say, as our Savior's disciples sometime said, "If the case so stand between man and wife, it is good then not to marry."

Now to such Solomon seemeth to answer in the words of my text, that "it is not evil to marry, but it is good to be wary"; that "it is not the abuse or badness of some that ought to make God's ordinance the less valued or the less esteemed, being in itself and of itself a matter of great benefit"; that "as the inconvenience is great and grievous that a bad wife bringeth with her, so the benefit on the other side is no less that cometh by a good wife, by a wise and a discreet woman," who is therefore here commended as a special gift, as a principal blessing of God, such as goeth beyond any other temporal blessing whatsoever. And surely as there is no greater temporal cross or curse than the one, so is there no greater temporal blessing than the other.

Now this Solomon to show, as before he compared two great evils together and found a bad wife to be the worse, so here he compareth two great benefits together and affirmeth a good wife to be the greater. House and possessions, wealth and riches, land and living is that that most men regard and look after; yea, men are wont to seek wives for wealth. But saith Solomon, "as a good name, so a good wife: a wise and a discreet woman is better than wealth; her price is far above pearls. For house and possessions are

the inheritance of the fathers, but a prudent wife is of the Lord."
Which yet we are not so to understand, neither the former part as
if worldly wealth and riches and possessions were not God's gifts,
for "it is the blessing of God that maketh a man rich; unless He
build the house it will never be built"; and "it is He that giveth men
power to gather wealth together"; nor yet again the latter part as
if parents had no hand, right, or power in disposing of their children, or in advising them and providing in that kind for them.
Samson requireth his parents' consent, And God chargeth His
people not to make matches between their children and the Canaanites, either by giving their daughters unto the sons of the
Canaanites or by taking the Canaanites' daughters unto their sons—
which He would not do, were not they at all to deal in the disposing
of them. And many, no doubt, would they take advice of their
parents and not follow their own fancies and make their wanton
eye or their wandering lust their chooser and counselor in such
cases, might do much better than for want hereof they do. But the
meaning of Solomon is this only, that the one is a more special gift
of God than the other; that there is a more special hand of God in
the one than in the other. As that is a less benefit than this, so that is
in man's power more than this.

So that two points, then, here in Solomon's words offer themselves
unto us: the former, that a good wife is God's gift; the latter, that
God's providence is more special in a wife than in wealth. For the
former, a good wife is God's gift: for "a prudent wife," saith Solomon, "is of the Lord." And "he that findeth a wife"—that is, a good
wife, as "a name" for "a good name," as if an evil wife were no
wife, deserved not the name of a wife—"hath found a good thing,
and hath obtained a special favor from God." It was one of the first
real and royal gifts that God with His own hand bestowed upon
Adam. And it must needs be no small matter that God giveth with
His own hand. The King's almoner may cast small silver about, but
if the King give a man somewhat with his own hand out of his
purse or pocket, it is expected it should be a piece of gold at least.
The woman was God's own gift to Adam. And she was God's gift

bestowed on him to consummate and make up his happiness. Though he were at the first of himself happy, yet not so happy as he might be, until he had one to partake with him in his happiness. It was God that at first gave Adam his wife, and it is God that giveth every man his wife to this day. "God," saith Abraham to his servant, "will send His angel along with thee and will prosper thee in thy journey," when he sent him about a wife for his son Isaac. And "those that God hath joined together," saith our Savior, "let not man sever." As Augustine saith, that "He that at the first created man without man, doth now procreate man by man," so He that gave man a wife at the first immediately doth still give men wives by means: good ones in mercy, evil ones in wrath, the one for solace and comfort, the other for trial, cure, correction, or punishment. No marriages are consummate on earth that were not first concluded and made up in heaven; and none are blest here that were not in mercy made there.

For the latter, there is a more special providence of God in a wife than in wealth: human wisdom and forecast, endeavor and industry may strike a greater stroke and have a more special hand in the one than in the other. Men of wealth may leave their heirs land and living, but they cannot so easily provide fit wives for them. For first, they may be deceived in their choice. Many have good skill in choosing of wares, in valuing of lands, in beating a bargain, in making a purchase, that are yet but blind buzzards in the choice of a wife. Yea, the wisest that are may be soon here overreached, since all is not gold, as we say, that glittereth. "The heart of man," saith the prophet, "is deceitful above all things." And "None can tell what is in man or woman but their own spirit that is within them." Secondly, they cannot link hearts as they list. A father may find out a fit wife and think such a one a meet match for his son, and her parents may be also of the same mind with him, as willing to entertain the motion as he is to make. And yet it may be, when they have done all they can, they cannot fasten their affections. As faith, so "love cannot be constrained." As there is no affection more forcible, so there is none freer from force and compulsion. The very offer of enforcement turneth it oft into hatred. There are secret links of affection that no reason can be rendered of, as there are inbred dislikes that can neither be resolved nor reconciled. When parents have a long time beaten the bush, another oft, as we say, catcheth the bird: affections are set some other way and cannot be removed. And things fall out many times so unexpectedly, such strong liking taken to some suddenly, not once thought on before, and such strange alienation of affections where there hath been much laboring to link them, and that where outward inducements of person, estate, years, etc. have concurred, that even a natural man's dim eye may easily see and discern a more special providence of God oft carrying things in these cases. And the tongues even of such are enforced sometime to confess, as the Egyptian magicians of Moses' miracles, "Digitus Dei hic est," "There is a finger of God here." So with Rebecca's profane friends in such marriage matches: "A Domino factum est istud," "This is even God's own doing"; and there is no contradicting of it.

To make some use of these points. First, is a good wife such a special gift of God? Then is marriage questionless a blessing, and no small one, of itself: one of the greatest outward blessings that in this world man enjoyeth. "Blessed is everyone," saith the Psalmist, "that feareth God and that walketh in His ways. For thou shalt eat of the labor of thine hands. Happy art thou, and it shall go well with thee. Thy wife shall be as the fruitful vine by the sides of thine house, and thy children like the olive plants round about thy table. Lo, thus shall the man be blessed that feareth God." In the first place cometh the wife, as the first and principal blessing, and the children in the next. And surely, to reason backward to that the apostle doth: "If the root," saith he, "be holy, the branches also be holy." And if the branches, say I, be holy, then the root that beareth them much more. So here, if the branches be blessed, the root that beareth them much more. If children be a blessing, then the root whence they spring ought much more to be so esteemed. "Behold, children and the fruit of the womb are the gift of God," saith Solomon. Children are the gift of God, but the wife is a more special gift of God. She cometh in the first place, they in the second. And gifts are usually answerable to the greatness of the giver. It was a witty answer of a great prince, when he was disposed to be rid of a bold begging philosopher: he asked a groat of him, and the king told him it was too little for a prince to give; he requested the king then to give him a talent, and the king told him it was too much for a beggar to crave. And surely God indeed in His special gifts to us is wont to regard not so much what is fit for us to ask or to expect, as what standeth with His goodness and greatness to give.

"God," saith Moses, "looked upon all that He had made, and behold, all was very good." And "Every creature (or ordinance) of God," saith the apostle (and he had spoken of meat and marriage in the words before-going), "is good." All God's creatures and ordinances are good, then, but some are more excellent than others. And marriage being of this latter sort, it is not holy only, but even honorable also. "Marriage," saith the apostle, "is honorable among all men"—and no disgrace then to any man. So are we to esteem of it, and not to condemn what God hath graced, or to dishonor what He hath honored. We shall but wrong the giver in debasing His gift.

Again, is a good wife such a special gift of God? Then if we find in marriage inconveniences, hindrances, distractions, disturbances, let us learn what we are to ascribe it unto: not to God's gift or ordinance, but to man's corruption abusing God's gift, perverting God's ordinance, and turning that to his own evil that God hath given him for his good. For there is nothing but is good as it cometh from God. But as pure water may take a taint from the earth that it runneth by, or the channel that it runneth through, or the pipe that conveyeth it, and the sunbeams receive a tincture from the colored glass that they pass through, so our foul hands and filthy fingers oft soil and sully God's ordinances, and our filth and corruption doth oft so taint and infect them that they lose not only much of their native grace, and are so strangely transformed that God Himself can scarcely discern His own in them, but they miss also of their fruit and efficacy and, of good and commodious, through our own default become evil and incommodious unto us. And as tyranny in government is not the fault of God's ordinance but of man's corruption abusing it, so in these cases the evil and inconvenience is not the fruit of God's ordinance but of man's corruption accompanying it.

If we shall find then in the married estate troubles and distractions, etc. (as the single life is commonly commended for quietness), let us not accuse God, as Adam sometime closely did: "The woman," saith he, "that Thou gavest me, she gave me of the tree, and I ate," as if he had said, "If Thou hadst not given me the woman, she had not given me of the fruit; and if she had not given me it, I had not eaten of it." God's gifts are all good. But let us lay the fault where it is: upon ourselves and our own corruption, that turneth honey into gall, and good nutriment, as the foul stomach, into choler, or as the spider and toad, into venom and poison. Else shall we be like those of whom Solomon saith, "The folly of a man perverteth his way, and his foolish heart fretteth against God."

Secondly, is a good wife God's gift? Then let those that want them learn how and where to seek them. Dost thou want a wife, and wouldst have one, and such a one as thou mayest have comfort in? Seek her of God; seek her with God. Seek her, I say, first at God's hands; seek her where she is to be had. Humble thyself in the sight of God, and betake thyself by prayer and supplication unto God. "Every good gift," saith James, "is of God from above," and to be sought therefore at His hands; and if every good gift, this more especially, that is so special a gift and of so principal use. And "Every creature (or ordinance)," saith Paul, "is to be sanctified by prayer." And if every ordinance of God should be sanctified by prayer and it ought "to usher all our actions," be they civil or sacred, then this also among others, yea, this above and before others, as that which, through the blessing of God upon it, may prove a matter of the greatest benefit unto us, and without it a means of the greatest evil.

Yea, seek her as of God, so with God. Ask counsel at the mouth of God when thou goest about any such business. "The ordinances of God," saith the apostle, "are sanctified unto us," as well "by the Word of God," as "by prayer." Then are they sanctified unto us by prayer when we crave leave for the use of them and a blessing upon the use of them by prayer at God's hands. Then are they sanctified unto us by the Word of God when we have warrant and take direction for what we do in them, out of God's Word, when we ask counsel at God's mouth. Then we seek them with God, when we seek them by good means, when we seek them in due manner.

For when it is said that a good wife is of God, we are not so to conceive it that we are in such cases to use no means at all, but that we are to use none but good and lawful means, such as God hath appointed, either prescribed or permitted. "The wife is bound," saith the apostle, "while her husband liveth; but if her husband be dead, she is at liberty to marry where she will, but yet in Domino, in the Lord."

Wherein they offend, either that go too near, matching within those degrees that God hath inhibited, or that go too far off, matching with such as for matter of religion they are prohibited to marry; and so transgressing those rules and directions that the Word of God giveth. As also those that be under the government of others, or that desire those that be in the power of others to dispose of; they then seek in the Lord when they advise with and are content to be disposed of by those whom God hath given power over them, or when they seek not to them in the first place, but to those by whom God will have them to be disposed. That which not God's people alone, but the heathen also, by the light of nature, saw to be equal and right. When they take other courses, they seek beside God, and cannot hope or expect any blessing from God, Whose order and ordinance therein they break. In a word, wouldst thou be blessed in thy wooing, in thy wiving: take God with thee in wooing; invite Him to thy wedding. He, if He be pleased, will turn thy water into wine; if He be displeased, He will turn thy wine into vinegar.

Thirdly, learn hence what principally to aim at in the choice of a wife: to wit, at virtue and wisdom, discretion and godliness; for that is indeed true wisdom. Solomon saith not, "A fair wife is the gift of God." And yet is beauty God's gift, and a gift of good regard. Neither saith he, "A wealthy wife is the gift of God." And yet is wealth also God's blessing, where it is accompanied with well-doing. But *a discreet or a wise woman is the gift of God.*

Many indeed there are, that choose their wife by the eye. "The sons of God saw the daughters of men to be fair, and they took them wives of them where they liked"—as if they were to buy a picture or an image to hang up in the house, or to stand somewhere for a show. But "Beauty," saith the heathen man, "without virtue is like a bait floating without a hook": it hath a bait to entice, but no hook to hold. And "A fair woman," saith Solomon, "without discretion is like a gold ring in a swine's snout"; "Favor is deceitful and beauty is but vanity, but a woman that feareth God is praiseworthy indeed."

Others again regard wealth only, as if they went about a purchase, as if they were to marry not them but their money, as if they were to wed not the wife but her wealth. But Solomon, when he saith, "Houses and riches are the inheritance of the fathers, but a prudent wife is of the Lord," he implieth that these things may be severed; the one may be without the other. Lands may come by inheritance, when virtue may not. Goods they are wherewith men may do good, but not such as make those good that have them. "Better it is," said the heathen man, "to have a man without money than to have money without a man"—so better it is to have a wife without wealth than to have wealth without a wife. And surely, what comfort can a man have of wealth with such a wife that shall be as a corrosive to his heart, "as corruption and rottenness in his bones"?

Again, let parents learn here what to aim at in the education of their children, whom they desire to dispose of, and to dispose of so as they may be a blessing, not a cross or a curse to those that shall have them: not study only how to provide portions for them, though an honest care also is to be had in that kind ("Parents," saith the Apostle, "ought to lay up for their children"; and "He that provideth not for his issue is worse than an infidel."), nor how to trim them up, and set them out in whorish or garish manner, to make them baits to catch fools with; but labor to train them up in true wisdom and discretion, in the fear of God, and such graces as may make them truly amiable, as well in God's sight as in man's eyes; in housewifery and industry and skill to manage household affairs: that so they may be helpers to their husbands, and not hinderers, as to that end they were made at first.

Yea, hence let the wife learn what she is to strive to and labor for, that she may be indeed a good gift of God, not so much to deck and trick herself up to the eye as to have her inner man adorned with holy skill and discretion, whereby to carry herself wisely and discreetly in that place and condition that God hath called her unto: that she may with the wise woman build up the house and be a crown and a grace to him that hath her; that her husband and children may have cause to bless her, and to bless God for her, and count it a blessed time when they came first together.

Let her consider what a fearful thing it is to be otherwise: for her that was made for a help to prove not a help but a hurt; for her that was given for a blessing to prove a cross and a curse. As one saith of Eve, "reft from Adam as a rib, and shot by Satan at him as a shaft": bestowed on him by God to consummate his felicity, but made by Satan's sleight and her own default the means of his extreme misery.

Fourthly, let men be admonished hence, whom to ascribe it unto if aught have been done in this kind for them: even to God Himself principally, Whose special gift a good wife is. Let us take heed how in this case we "sacrifice to our yarn, or burn incense to our net." Ascribe not what is done for thee to the mediation of friends, or to thine own plots and policies, smoothness of language, fairness of look, or the like. No; acknowledge God to have been the principal agent in the business; regard man and thine own means but as His instruments. "Of Him she is," saith Solomon: not as a creature only made of Him, but as one matched unto thee by Him;

nor as knit to thee by His ordinance, but as assigned thee by His providence. For that is it that Solomon here principally aimeth at.

Yea, let them hence learn what they owe unto God, whom God hath vouchsafed such a blessing unto. Hath God bestowed such a wife on thee, as Solomon here speaketh of? It is a precious jewel, such as thy father could never leave thee. It is a greater treasure than the greatest prince on earth, than the mightiest monarch in the world is able to bequeath to his heir. We see how parents are oft troubled in making search for their sons, and yet when they have done their best endeavor, miss of that they desire. We might here rise by degrees on the better side, as we did before on the worse. As evils, so good things, the more inward the greater. A trusty servant is no small blessing; a kind neighbor is a great one, a faithful friend a greater, a wise son yet a greater, and a prudent wife the greatest of all, a greater blessing than any of the former, that yet for temporal blessings may seem of the greatest. And how do married persons then stand engaged to God above others, whom He hath blessed in their choice? A great measure of thankfulness owe they unto Him, proportionable in some sort to the blessing bestowed on them.

Yea, as there is a greater measure of thankfulness required of them than of others whom God hath not blessed in that manner, so there is a peculiar kind of thankfulness required on their part. All God's favors require thankfulness, and the more favors the more thankfulness; but some special favors require some peculiar kind of acknowledgment proportioned to the quality of the favor received. Children are God's gift, and our thankfulness to Him for them is to be showed in such duties as He requireth of us in the behalf of them, in the careful education and training them up in good courses. In like manner, thy wife thou hast of God's gift, and thy thankfulness to Him for her must be showed in the performance of such duties as He requireth of thee in regard of her, as of love, of kindness, of concord, counsel, contentment, etc.

Fifthly, is the wife given unto her husband by God? Then must she resolve to give herself wholly to him as her owner, on whom

God hath bestowed her, to whom He hath assigned her. When parents have put out their children, the children must be content to be guided by those to whom they commit them. And when God hath given a daughter, she must be content to live with him and be guided by him whom God hath given her unto. Neither is she to forsake him, for they are not to be sundered nor severed, whom God hath conjoined and made one—and there is a foul brand therefore upon her "that forsaketh the guide of her youth and forgetteth the covenant of her God"—nor to refuse to be ruled by him, but submit and subject herself unto him unto whom God hath given her, for that is comely, saith the apostle, in the Lord, and to be embraced therefore of her as her lot by God assigned her.

Yea, is the wife given the husband by God? Then should he esteem her as a gift of God, and live with her as with one given him and bestowed upon him by God. We cannot abide to see anything that we have given another evil used. And it be but a dog, a hound, or a whelp, if we see it neglected where we bestowed it, we are wont to take it evil. But if we should see a jewel of some value bestowed by us on a friend as a token of our love toward him, set at light by him, or should find it cast aside in some corner, would we not much more be grieved at it, and judge that he set as light by our love as he doth by our love-token? And hath not God then just cause to take it evil at thy hands when He shall see His gift abused, evil entertained, and worse used; when He shall see her misused of thee, whom He hath as a special favor bestowed on thee, and hath therefore given thee a special charge well and kindly to use? How are we wont to be grieved when we see matters fall out amiss where we have been means to make the match? If the wife be misused that we have holpen one to, we are wont to count it a wrong to ourselves. And no marvel then, if God Himself take to heart the wrongs done by us to those that He hath joined to us, if He have a quarrel against him that shall transgress against her whom He hath inseparably joined to him, to be "his companion and his wife by a covenant of salt."

Lastly, if a good wife be such a special gift of God, then a good husband is no less. For the husband is as needful for the wife as the wife is for the husband. "Thy desire," saith God, "shall be unto him." And if the husband then be so to esteem of his wife, and to be thankful to God for her, then is the wife no less to esteem so of her husband and to be thankful likewise to God for him.

In a word, let both man and wife so esteem either of other, as joined by God's counsel, as given by God's hand, and so receive either other as from God, be thankful either for other unto God, seek the good either of other in God, and then will God undoubtedly with His blessing accompany His gift to His own glory and their mutual good.

Thomas Hooker (1586–1647)

The only American Puritan represented here is Thomas Hooker, who was a recognized Puritan leader before he left England. The tiny town of Marfield in Leicestershire was his birthplace in 1586. Before he went up to Cambridge in 1604, Hooker attended school at Market Bosworth near his home. At the University he matriculated as a sizar at Queen's College but later transferred to Emmanuel, where he received the bachelor's degree in 1608 and the master's degree in 1611.

Doubtless Hooker's Puritanism was a result of his Emmanuel experiences, for its head, Laurence Chaderton, whom Bishop Bancroft characterized as one of "Cartwright's scholars," was responsible for many a man's being attracted to Puritanism. Hooker was one of thirty-five Emmanuel men who went to New England before 1645; others were John Cotton and John Harvard. Chaderton and Hooker maintained their association for ten years in all, for Hooker served as a Dixie Fellow and dean of the college. Presumably during these years he also came to know William Ames, a Puritan who spent many years on the Continent. Ames's works were of great influence, and Hooker edited one of them after Ames's death.

Hooker's first pastoral responsibility was obtained because he had won a reputation as an "experimental theologian"—that is, he was a specialist in the varieties of religious experience. The wife of a Mr. Francis Drake, who had under his patronage the rectorship of the church at Esher, sixteen miles from London in Surrey, was convinced that she had committed the unpardonable sin. Drake sought aid from Hooker, who, according to Cotton Mather, "now had no superior and scarce any equal for the skill of handling a wounded soul." The outcome of Hooker's efforts are unknown, though it is known that Hooker married Mrs. Drake's maid Susanna.

The church at Esher held fewer than a hundred, and Hooker was destined for greater things. In 1626 he became lecturer in Chelmsford, Essex. The whole county felt his influence, as people went to hear him from considerable distances. But Hooker was a Puritan lecturer, and Laud, Bishop of London, was opposed to Puritans and to the system of using lecturers, who could preach independently of the Book of Common Prayer. Despite the petition of fifty-one Essex ministers in his favor, Hooker was forced to leave his position. After a brief period of teaching at the nearby village of Little Baddow, where his assistant was the later-famous missionary to the Indians, John Eliot, Hooker was cited to appear before the Court of High Commission. Instead, he fled to Holland, where there existed among the English something of a Puritan tradition, stemming from the days of Cartwright and Travers. First at Amsterdam and then at Delft, Hooker ministered to English-speaking congregations. After about two years in Delft he was invited to Rotterdam, where he was associated with William Ames and with Hugh Peter, who was also to go to America.

But Hooker was far from happy in Rotterdam. He was ill for a long time, and he found that the people with whom he dealt managed to "content themselves with very forms" and knew not "the power of godliness." So he reported to his Emmanuel College friend, John Cotton, of Boston in Lincolnshire. Cotton was planning to go to New England, where in 1630 a large body of Puritans had gone. In 1632 a group from the area of Chelmsford went to Massachusetts, where it was known as "Mr. Hooker's Company." Presumably this group had an understanding with Hooker that he would join them when he was well and could travel.

Hooker went back to England to complete plans for the trip, and barely escaped arrest while there. In July 1633 he sailed for New England, with Cotton and Samuel Stone among his companions. Stone had been chosen by the leaders of the Hooker group as a second minister. On their arrival Hooker was ordained pastor and Stone teacher of the church at Newtown, now Cambridge. This ordination by members of the congregation is of course an indication of the congregational form of church government which was in use in both Plymouth and Massachusetts Bay.

Hooker's congregation included at first about a hundred families. It soon prospered and in 1635 was as large as any in the colony.

But its growth caused difficulties, for soon there was felt to be a lack of adequate land for the townspeople. They believed, it seems clear, that they had a destiny apart from that of the other towns nearby. Hooker and the town's leading layman, John Haynes, rivaled in ability the leading men of Boston, just across the river; but Boston, home of John Winthrop and John Cotton, had a natural importance as seat of the General Court of the colony. Furthermore, there is evidence that Hooker had a more liberal policy than Cotton in admitting members to the church and towards civil privileges.

Fortunately, at this time a congregation under the leadership of Thomas Shepard arrived, and the Newtownites took advantage of the opportunity to sell their houses and move from the Boston area. At the end of May 1636 they began a trek to Connecticut, accompanied by 160 cattle. Their departure was less than three years after Hooker's arrival. Mrs. Hooker was carried on a litter because of an infirmity. The group traveled for over a hundred miles to the bank of the Connecticut River, where they settled at what is now Hartford.

Back in England Hooker was not forgotten. In 1629 a fat collection of sermons entitled *The Saint's Cordials* had been published. Included was a sermon by Hooker, probably his first published work. It deals with one of his familiar themes, "the main lets and hindrances which keep men from coming to Christ." In the years that followed many books of sermons by Hooker appeared, nine within the two years 1637–38. Many of these are on the same theme, as is indicated by their titles: *The Soul's Preparation for Christ, The Soul's Vocation, The Soul's Implantation, The Soul's Ingrafting into Christ*, and *The Soul's Possession of Christ*. These sermons date from his days at Chelmsford and were taken down at that time by auditors; Hooker was in no way responsible for their publication. It is from *The Soul's Vocation* that the selection which follows is drawn.

Little is known about Hooker's work in Connecticut, though the fact that the colony thrived is perhaps informative. He played an important role in drawing up the "Fundamental Orders" of Connecticut, and his tendency towards liberalism in government has caused a student of political history to say that he "first planted and nurtured in New England soil the seeds of democracy hidden away in the brittle pod of Puritanism."

In 1643 Hooker served as moderator with Cotton at the very important synod where presbyterianism was condemned. Shortly after, in order to clarify the New England position on church discipline, Hooker wrote *A Survey of the Sum of Church Discipline*. Unfortunately the ship carrying Hooker's manuscript never arrived, and Hooker, now in poor health, reluctantly rewrote it. His "years and infirmities," as he put it, kept him from attending another important New England synod in 1646, and in the following year he died. When a visitor sought to console the dying man with the hopeful comment, "Sir, you are going to receive the reward of your labor," Hooker replied, "Brother, I am going to receive mercy!"

During his New England years Hooker went back to the topic for which he had become famous as a preacher. His sermons on *The Application of Redemption* occupy two large volumes; these he appears to have prepared himself for publication though they did not appear until 1656. Hooker's account of the redemptive process here closely resembles his earlier descriptions.

Hooker's principal techniques throughout his sermons on redemption are the ones which loom largest in the sermon which follows. Hooker takes the point of view of a student of the redemptive process. He offers an analytic description of how God saves men. But the description, because it is a sermon, has the power to save those who hear it if God chooses to use the sermon for that purpose. "When God the Father doth accompany the Gospel," as Hooker says below, "with the powerful operation of the Spirit . . . there the soul learns thoroughly and *effectually* the way of salvation" (italics mine). God works with the preacher, the ordained means of salvation. The preacher, powerless to supply the *sine qua non*, the grace which saves, must nevertheless preach, for the sermon is, in common experience, indispensable. Appropriately, Hooker focuses on what the man does whom God chooses to touch, man's response to God's action, rather than on God's action itself, though he seldom lets us forget that unless God acts, man can do nothing.

Hooker's tough-mindedness and his ability to present a vivid image are two characteristics of his genius which often go hand in hand. In one work he warns the reader:

If we had dropped out of our mother's womb into hell and there been roaring . . . it had been just. . . . Parents, mourn for your children that are natural. When thou lookest upon thy child whom thou dearly lovest, and who perhaps hath good natural parts, and is obedient unto thee in outward respects, when thou beholdest this child of thine, and considerest that he is in a natural estate, then this may pierce thee to the very heart. Then thou mayest burst out and say, woe is me that this child of mine was ever born, for he is in a natural condition, and therefore in a miserable condition. He is a natural child, and therefore a child of the devil.

This passage should be read as an incentive to action, not as a gratuitous insult. It is also interesting to note that New England Puritanism declined because the second and third generations lacked the religious zeal of their fathers.

There is a harshness to much of Hooker's preaching which repels many readers, a harshness by no means common among Puritans. But Hooker does not fit the common misconception of the sour, dour Puritan, for his intelligence and his manliness shine through his writings: what the reader may not find attractive, he still may admire.

The soul's vocation

John vi.45. "Every man therefore that hath heard and hath learned of the Father cometh unto me."

The ingrafting of the humble and broken-hearted sinner into Christ, as we have heard, consists of two particular passages: the first was being put into the stock; secondly, the ingrafting into the same. As in ingrafting naturally, so of implanting spiritually of the soul into Christ. When the soul is brought into this, then a sinner comes to be partaker of all the spiritual benefits: all shall be communicated to us. Now the point at this present to be handled is

[*The Soules Vocation* (London, 1638), pp. 33–48.]

called by the stream of divines *vocation*, and I term it the putting in of the soul when the soul is brought out of the world of sin to lie upon and to close with the Lord Jesus Christ. And this hath two particular passages in it: partly the call on God's part, partly the answer on ours. The call on God's part is this: when the Lord by the call of His Gospel doth so clearly reveal the fullness of mercy and certifies to the soul by the work of His Spirit that the soul humbled returns answer to God's call.

In the first, observe two passages: first, the means whereby God will call the sinner unto Him. The sinner is afraid to appear before God Whom he hath offended, and [who] may therefore proceed in justice against him for those sins which have been committed by him. Now besides the Law which discovers a man's sin unto him, He now prepares another means, the voice of His Gospel. He lets in many sweet inklings into the soul, of His love and kindness, to allure him, to call him and draw him to Himself.

Secondly, the Lord doth not only appoint the means, namely, the ministry of His Gospel, whereby the soul may be brought unto Him and receive communion with Him; but by the work of His Spirit He doth bring all the riches of His grace into the soul truly humbled, so that the heart cannot but receive the same and give answer thereto and give an echo of the subjection of itself to be governed thereby. (That we have finished already.) There must be hearing before coming—not of the Law, to terrify a man—but of the Gospel, to persuade and allure a man to come unto the Lord and receive mercy and kindness from Him. The Gospel is the means ordained by God to call home the soul unto Him. But this will not do the deed. There must be something else or the sinner will be at a stand and cannot come on cheerfully and receive the grace offered him. Therefore besides the means, we have the special cause expressed, which is the Lord. For when a man hath heard, that is one thing; but that is not all, for the principal cause is the Lord. God the Father alone can buckle the heart to receive the grace appointed and the mercy offered to the soul; and without the principal cause, all other means, I mean the ministers of the Gospel, although it be "a savor of life unto life," yet it may be "a savor of death unto death," unless the Spirit of the Lord goes with it. For when the Gospel is only revealed to the understanding, and that only conceives of the letter thereof, and it soaks not and sinks not into the heart—this we call an outward calling; that is the phrase of divines. When some light flash is imparted and communicated into the soul and is not set on sufficiently, that is an outward calling. But when God the Father doth accompany the dispensation of the Gospel with the powerful operation of the Spirit, and it puts its hand to the key of the Gospel and unlocks a blind mind and a hard heart, there the soul learns thoroughly and effectually the way of salvation. The text saith, there must not only be hearing, but learning of the Father, else the soul will not, nor cannot come. Now before I can collect the several passages out of the words, there is some difficulty and obscurity in the phrase. Therefore give me leave, as I am able, to discover the meaning and sense of the words, and then the collection will be clear.

First for the explication of the phrase, and I will discourse four questions unto you, which will be useful for the clear explication of the text: first, what the lesson is that a man must learn before he come; secondly, why the Father is said to teach, and not the Son, nor the Holy Ghost; thirdly, what is the manner how the Father doth teach the soul when He will call it home to Himself; fourthly, what is the frame and disposition of the soul, how doth the heart behave itself when it hath in truth learned the lesson. When the Lord will propound unto and learn the souls of His that belong to Him, you must not think the truth tedious, because they will give us light into all the truth that shall be hereafter discussed out of the Word.

He that hath heard and learned of the Father, what is the lesson that he must learn before he can come? That after he hath learned this lesson he may be able to see the path of salvation as propounded to him, so also near at hand that he might walk therein and receive comfort thereby.

For answer hereunto, the lesson that the soul must learn is this,

namely, the fullness of the mercy and grace and salvation that
God the Father hath provided and also offered to the poor humbled
sinner in and through the Lord Jesus Christ, which indeed is able to
do that for a poor sinner which all the means and things in the
world could not do and yet notwithstanding he needs. I have heretofore discussed the poor miserable plight which a sinner hath
brought himself into by his manifold rebellions. There is no help,
no hope of himself in what he hath or doth to relieve and succor
himself, and therefore he falls flat at the footstool of the Almighty
and is content to be at His disposing. Now the lesson that the soul
must learn is the fullness, greatness, and freeness of the perfect
salvation which is brought unto us through the Lord Jesus Christ.
And that we may not learn this lesson by halves but fully and perfectly, and that your minds may conceive of the same, give me
leave to lay it out fully, because it will be profitable for our ensuing
discourse; and this lesson discovers itself in three things, as in three
lines, as I may so term it.

The first is this, that the soul may learn there is enough sufficiency in the mercy of God to fill up all the empty chinks of the
soul and supply all the wants that a sinner hath and relieve him in
all those necessities that either do or can befall him. This is the condition of every son of man since the fall of Adam, that there is not
only a great deal of weakness in the soul, but there is a great deal
of wants and emptiness in the soul.

Now this is the fullness of the mercy of God, that whatsoever
our weaknesses, wants, or necessities be, there is full sufficiency
enough in that mass to fill up all and to give the soul full content in
every particular. Hence the phrase of Scripture runs thus: when
God propounds the fullness of mercy in Jesus Christ, He calls it a
treasury, and all the treasures of wisdom and holiness are in
Christ; not one treasure, but all treasures; not some treasures, but
all treasures (Isaiah lxi). When the Gospel was professed, there was
a fullness of mercy, and there we shall see a kind of meeting and
concurrency of all blessings together. So that where the Gospel
comes, there is joy for the sorrowful, peace for the troubled,

strength for the weak. Be your miseries what they can be, here is relief seasonable and suitable to all your wants, miseries, and necessities. Nay, this is not only for the present necessity. Mercy is not only able to relieve your present necessity but your future also. It is not with mercy as with the widow of Sarepta, who thought when the meal in the barrel, and the oil in the cruse was spent, she should then surely perish. No, it is not so in the fullness and sufficiency of this mercy; it hath not only enough to do you good for the present and to succor you in all present wants; but what miseries soever shall befall thee, or what troubles shall betide thee for future times, the fullness of God's mercy lays in provision against such necessities and times of miseries and vexations. For a poor sinner may be driven to a stand after this manner: "It is true," saith the sinner, "I have therefore committed many sins. God hath sealed up the pardon of them unto me, and those sins which have heretofore pleased me, God hath given me a sight of them in some power and measure against them. But what if more sins, if more temptations, if more corruptions, if more guilt, if more horror seize upon my heart, how then shall I succor myself?" But now this is the fullness and sufficiency of mercy: it doth not only ease a man in regard of present necessity, but lays provision for all future wants and calamities that can befall the soul (Psalm cxxx.7).

The text saith, "Let Israel hope in the Lord; there is mercy, and with Him is plenteous redemption." The word in the original is, "there is multiplying redemption," or redemption increasing. If misery, sorrow, and anguish be multiplied, there is multiplied redemption also. Then know it, if you know your own souls. You see it, if you see your own lives, that it is new sins, new corruptions prevailing with you. But here is the comfort of the soul: as sin increaseth, so mercy increaseth; as corruption multiplies, so redemption multiplies. Therefore He is called the "Father of mercy," as who should say, He begets mercy, even a generation of mercies, from day to day; and it is a large generation of new mercies framed and made to encourage poor souls. Therefore it is said, "With the Lord there is a fountain of life." Look, as it is with a fountain—

there is not only water in it for the present, but it feeds several cocks
and conduits and, though it runs out daily, it enlargeth itself daily—
so with the Lord there is a fountain of life. If there be a fountain of
death in thy soul, in regard of thy sins to kill thee; so a fountain in
God to quicken thee. Hence it comes to pass that the Lord, speaking
of His mercy, calls it "the exceeding riches of His mercy" (Ephesians ii.7). I say, the Lord hath not only fullness of mercy, but He
is rich in all His fullness. Nay, He exceeds in all the riches of the
fullness of His mercy. So that, be we never so poor and beggarly,
these sins increase, and those miseries increase.

Why yet, though thou be a bankrupt in grace, yet the Lord is
full of goodness, full of mercy. Yea, He exceeds in His fullness, to
succor thy heart in all necessities. Nay, our miseries and wants be
great, yet haply thy fear is greater than all the rest. Thy soul is
troubled many times more with the fear of what will be than with
the feeling of what is already befallen thee. But now, however thy
miseries be great and thy fear exceeds all misery that can betide,
yet mercy will remove and prevent those fears, and Christ will do
more for thee than thou canst fear will fall upon thee. Nay, a man
doth not fear what misery can befall upon him, but his heart may
imagine more than he doth fear. But here is the fullness of mercy,
mercy full to the brim and running over. Mercy is able to do more
for thee than thou canst fear or conceive shall come upon thee.
Ephesians iii.20: then saith the Lord, exceeding excess, "abundantly
above that we can ask or think." So then the words run thus, then
wind up the point: thou seest, thou findest, thou feelest many sorrows now assailing thee; thou expectest more trouble to befall thee,
and thou dost conceive more than thou dost fear. Thy sorrows
outbid thy heart, thy fears outbid thy sorrows, and thy thoughts
go beyond thy fears; and yet here is the comfort of a poor soul: in
all his misery and wretchedness, the mercy of the Lord outbids all
these, whatsoever may, can, or shall befall thee.

Gather, then, up briefly and shut up this first passage. Many
are the sorrows of the righteous guilt of sin perplexing the sinner,
and filthiness of sins tyrannizing and domineering over the soul;

nay, many fears and cares for future times. For a sinner saith, "Sometimes my condition is marvelous poor, my estate marvelous miserable. What if small temptations, what if small corruptions, what if such a fall should betide me, what then shall become of my soul?" Nay, a man's imagination exceeds all fears. The soul thinks with itself, "Should the Lord deal in justice, and should my sins get the victory over me, which I hope will never be, what shall I then do for succor?" Yet this is the comfort of a poor soul; let it read this lesson: the Lord is able, and mercy can do excessive, exceeding abundantly above all. Thy sorrows are abundant; thy fears are very abundant; thy imaginations are excessive, exceeding abundant, exceeding above all present sorrows, above all future fear, and above the course of all imaginations. This discourse shall serve for the first passage.

We will now add the second. The soul is not yet fully satisfied, but replies, "It is true, 'there is bread enough in my Father's house'; that I yield, and that I confess. There is abundance of mercy in God, a world of mercy that pardoned Manasses and saved Saul, but what is that to me if there be bread enough in my Father's house, and I starve for hunger and get no benefit by this mercy of God?" But how shall a man starve in this mercy? If a way can be conceived and a means can be propounded for another supply to the soul to fill up the necessity of it, this will be seen in the next particular. I say herein appears more fullness of mercy.

It is not only sufficient to relieve a man in all the miseries that can befall him, but this is another thing considered: mercy is able to make thee partake in the same mercy. God doth not leave thee to thyself that thou shouldst buy it and purchase it, and buy it and procure it, but mercy is able to suffice thy soul that thou mayest be refreshed thereby. This is the tenor of mercy: God requires of a man that he should believe; now mercy doth help to perform the duty commanded. The Lord, as He requires the condition of thee, so He worketh the condition in thee. He makes thee believe that thou shalt be saved as there is fullness of grace in Himself to do thee good if thou dost receive the same. This is the difference between the two covenants, the Covenant of Works and the Covenant of Grace. The first covenant runs, "Adam shall do and live." Now it stood upon the use and abuse of his free will, either to do the will of God, and be blessed; or to break the law, and be cursed. It was in his power to receive the life, and thus either by breach or not doing the condition required, Adam must perform. But it is not so here. The Lord indeed requires a condition: "No man can be saved but he must believe"; but here is the privilege: that the Lord as He makes this condition with the soul, so also He keepeth us in performing the condition, for the Lord requires that the soul should rest upon Him, and He makes him also to do it; He requires the soul to cleave unto Him. There is the tenor of this covenant: "A new heart will I give you, and a new spirit I will put within you, and I will take away your stony heart and give you a heart of flesh, and I will put my spirit within you and cause you to walk in my statutes" (Ezekiel xxxvi.26–27). Or if thou wilt walk in my ways, out of thine own power, then I will vouchsafe this mercy and favor. Now the Lord requires this condition and works it also in His children; He requires this of them, and He works this in them, for their everlasting good. The Lord saith, "This is the covenant I will make with the House of Israel; I write my laws in their hearts, and they shall not need to be taught" (Hebrews viii.9). Men must know God and believe in the Lord. Now as the Lord requires this as the condition of the covenant, so the Lord will work this in them, as He requires this of them. John i.12 saith, "To them that believe, He gave them power to be the sons of God." Now if a man will believe, he shall be saved. Now then He makes a man believe that he may be a son—this is the second passage whereby the soul of a sinner comes to be cheered—or that there is not only abundance of sufficiency in the Lord Jesus Christ, but that mercy, as it is able to do him good, so it will make him partaker of the good.

The third particular is this: that as mercy hath all good and will make us partakers of what it hath, so also it will dispose of us and of that it bestoweth upon us. Mercy will not only have a sinner, but it will rule and order that grace it hath bestowed upon the soul. For if mercy purchase a soul at so high a rate as the blood of the Lord Jesus, it is right that the soul purchased by grace and supplied with grace—that mercy should dispose it for the honor of God. "You are not your own," saith the apostle, "but bought with a price." Therefore you must glorify the Lord in body and soul. Nay, it is not only right that mercy should do it, but reason, and beneficial to the soul that mercy should do thus. Nay, I say, unless that mercy should rule a man, he had not been able to give full content to the soul. If the Lord should leave any poor soul to the destiny of his own heart and the malice of Satan, he would run to ruin presently. He is not able to supply his own wants and to dispose of his own spirit and employ aright his own soul. For if Adam in his innocency had a stock in his own hands, fell and perished; then if mercy should put a man into the same estate that Adam was, a man should bring himself into the same misery that Adam was brought into. But there is that fullness of that mercy that is in Christ, that it will bestow all good needful for me; so also, it will dispose of that good in me so that Satan shall never prevail, the world shall never overcome, nor my corruptions bear sway in me; but the Lord shall rule me forever. And this is the fullness of God's mercy. Gather up the point, then, that we may see what we must learn. There is sufficiency in mercy to supply all wants. Nay, there is ability in mercy to communicate that it hath and we stand in need of. Nay, mercy will preserve us; and that it giveth to us against all oppositions that can befall thee. This is the lesson that the soul must learn that it may be able in some measure to see the way and learn the path that leadeth to everlasting happiness. This is the first lesson that the soul must learn of God the Father.

[Now] for the use of this. Is this the lesson the soul must learn? Then look wisely upon it, and when this comes upon thee, and sorrow assails thee heavily, do not look into the black book of conscience and think there to find supply. Neither look into the book of the privileges and performances and think to find power out of thy own sufficiency. Look not on thy sins to pore upon them, whereby thou shalt be discouraged; neither look into thy own sufficiency, thinking thereby to procure anything to thyself. These are but lessons of the lower form. It is true, thou must see thy sins and sorrow for them; but this is for the lower form, and thou must get this lesson beforehand. And when thou hast gotten this lesson of contrition and humiliation, look only to God's mercy, and the riches of His grace; and be sure as you take out this lesson, take it not out by halves, for then you wrong mercy, and yourselves too, if you think that bare works will serve, and that is all. No, no, mercy will rule you. Therefore take all the lesson out, and then the heart will be cheered, and thy soul in some measure enabled to come on to the Lord and will see some glimpses of consolation from the Spirit.

We see the lesson, what must be learned. Now we must see the reason why the Lord must teach this lesson. I answer, it is not appropriated to the Father alone, for the Father teaches not alone; but the Son and the Holy Ghost teach too. But why then doth the text give it to the Father? Here I answer directly, because the Father was directly offended with the sin of man. "If we sin, we have an advocate with the Father" (I John i.7), namely the Lord Jesus Christ, to plead for us with the Father. He doth not say, "We take an advocate with an advocate, that doth plead with himself." The reason is, God the Father was directly offended. Though all the persons in the Trinity were offended, yet the Father more directly. Now he that is directly offended, favor and mercy must come from him to the party that doth offend. And that is the reason why Christ especially cast this upon the Father. Take a creditor that hath money, and debtors that are bankrupts. Now there is no means to help and succor these men, but it lieth upon the creditor that owneth the debt, for he only it is must come to forgive the debts. It is here God the Father, being directly offended by the son of man. Therefore from Him in the first place must proceed the pardon and mercy to the son of man. Hence it comes to pass that the text saith, the Father must teach this lesson.

The next question is this: after what manner doth the Lord teach the soul? Christ speaks now of the work of the Spirit; and that you may not be mistaken, know this, that the work of the Spirit doth always go with and is communicated by the Word. Therefore if the question be, after what manner doth God teach the soul to spell out this lecture of mercy and pardon? I answer briefly: the Lord teacheth the soul by His Spirit. I told you before that not only the Father, but the Son and Holy Ghost also teacheth, the Father from Himself, the Son from the Father, and the Holy Ghost from both. Therefore understand what I say. The Spirit of the Lord doth not only in the general make known God's mercy, but doth in particular, with strength of evidence, present to the broken-hearted sinner the right of the freeness of God's grace to the soul. Nay, it holds those special considerations to the heart and presenteth the heart with them. Not only so, but in the second place, the Spirit doth forcibly soak in the relish of that grace into the heart, and by the over-piercing work doth leave some dint of supernatural and spiritual virtue on the heart. The Spirit doth not only with truth bring home the evidence to the heart, but it is still whispering, and calling, and making known the same, and forcibly soaketh in the relish of the freeness of God's grace, and leaveth a dint of supernatural virtue upon the soul. We will express the points because it is somewhat difficult and is the scope of that place, II Timothy i.7: "The Lord hath not given you the spirit of fear, but of a sound mind." The spirit of fear is the spirit of bondage, in humiliation and contrition. When the spirit showeth a man his sins and showeth him that he is in bondage and in fetters, lets him get out how he can: this is the spirit of fear and of bondage. In the second place, there is the spirit of power. But what is this spirit of power? You must imagine this spirit of power doth not intimate any particular grace, but [is] as it were the sinews and strength of the work of the Spirit, conveying itself through the frame of the heart. And this I term to be the effectual work of the Spirit of God. When the soul is humbled, the Lord sweetly communicates into the soul a supernatural and spiritual virtue. Lastly, as it is in nature: take a knife, if it be rubbed on a lodestone, it will draw iron unto it. Now it cannot do that because it is a knife, but because it is rubbed on a stone and receives virtue therefrom. So it is with a heart humbled: it is a fit subject for the grace of God to work upon. The love of God is like the lodestone, and if the heart be rubbed thereupon and affected with the sweetness thereof, it will be able to close with that mercy and come to that mercy and go to God from whence that mercy comes.

What is the behavior of the soul, when it hath learned this lesson from the Lord? I answer, when these two things meet together in the soul, then it hath learned two lessons. The first is this: when the soul, having heard of the plentiful redemption that is in Christ, as also having apprehended the revelation thereof, it cometh to close with the work of the Spirit, revealing, presenting, and offering grace to the heart. Nay, it comes to give entertainment to the riches of that mercy revealed to the soul. There is in the mercy of God, and in the blessed truth of the promises, a great excellency. Now when this is so plentifully brought home to the heart that it breaks through all oppositions which may hinder the work of the Spirit upon the soul, when it is brought home by the Spirit of God, and the heart gives way and closes with it, so that there is nothing between that and the soul—this I take to be the first frame of the soul that begins to learn this lesson. It begins to close to the truth, to give way to the sweetness that is in it, and bids adieu to all delight and sins and whatsoever may be a hindrance unto it from receiving of this grace into the soul. This is the first passage.

The second, with which I will conclude, is this, that as the soul closeth with that mercy and welcometh it, and the heart is content to take up mercy upon those terms, so in the second place there is an impression and disposition left upon the soul that it is framed and disposed. There is a kind of print which the soul hath with it, so that as the mercy of God is revealed to the soul and communicated to the soul, so there is a kind of impression, frame, and print, which the heart retaineth and hath wrought upon it by this grace and free favor of God made known. Therefore that phrase at Romans vi.17 is a marvelous pattern to our purpose. The text saith, "They were delivered to this form of doctrine." Look as it is with a seal: if the seal be set to the wax and leave an impression, just so many letters upon the wax as in the seal, then it is wholly sealed. So the Spirit of God through Christ in the promises doth reveal all the freeness and grace of mercy in Christ. Now when the Spirit doth leave an impression on the soul, that man is delivered into the truth. I conclude all in Acts xxvi.18. When Saul was sent to preach to the Gentiles, the text saith, he was but "to bring them out of darkness into light." Mark, when the Lord doth come to work effectually upon the soul, He brings men from under the power of darkness. Whereas the understanding was dark and blinded, when the Spirit comes it turns it from the darkness and power of sin, unto the power of light and grace.

Lastly, the power of the heart doth these two things: for since not only some of the heart must be brought to God, but the whole heart, therefore in the precious promises of grace and salvation there is fullness of all good to draw all the faculties of the soul unto the Lord. And therefore the faithfulness and the truth of God is mainly revealed in the promises. Now that fits the understanding and makes it look to God for pardon, for power, and mercy.

John Preston (1587–1628)

John Preston's early death probably changed the course of English Puritanism in a significant way, but his importance has only recently been recognized. Preston is the subject of Irvonwy Morgan's thoroughly interesting *Prince Charles's Puritan Chaplain*. Another study of value is the brief masterpiece which Thomas Ball wrote of his teacher's life.

Preston was born at Heyford, Northamptonshire, on October 27, 1587, into a family of modest circumstances. Although he was left fatherless at the age of twelve, his great-uncle, onetime mayor of Northampton, saw to it that he received a good education. Preston went up to King's College, Cambridge, in 1604, but two years later moved to Queen's. His original plans were to seek a position at court, and he went so far as to arrange to study French fashions and the French language at Paris. When these arrangements were frustrated, he settled down to the study of natural philosophy. He settled down with a vengeance, for as Ball tells us, studying was more precious to him than sleep; "he would let the bed clothes hang down, that in the night they might fall off, and so the cold awaken him." Ball also tells of Preston's reading in the barber's chair, blowing the hairs off the page as they fell.

In 1609 Preston became a fellow of Queen's and Prebendary of Lincoln Cathedral, but he had no intention of remaining at Cambridge or taking holy orders. Instead, he seems to have been biding his time until something came his way which really interested him. For a while he thought this might be medicine, which he studied for a time in Kent. In this connection he even spent some time studying astrology. But one day Preston heard John Cotton preach at St. Mary's in Cambridge. This was Cotton the famous Puritan, who was several times arrested for nonconformity. He caused Preston to question his low opinion of the ministry and preaching and his high opinion of "State Employments." The result was that Preston attacked the study of divinity, just as he had earlier attacked philosophy and medicine. He started with an intensive study of the schoolmen, especially Duns Scotus, Occam, and Thomas Aquinas, seeking out for each the first or oldest available edition. Finding Aristotle's name often cited delighted him.

Because he was one of the University's most noted scholars, Preston was chosen to be Opponent when a Philosophy Act was planned for the entertainment of the visiting King James. The subject was much to James's taste: Whether dogs can make syllogisms. Preston argued that enthymemes are proper syllogisms, and dogs can make them. A hound, argued Preston, has the major proposition in mind, namely, the hare is gone either this way, or that. He smells out the minor with his nose, namely, she is not gone that way, and follows the conclusion, *ergo,* this way, with open mouth. King James soon became involved in the discussion, so that the Answerer had to protest that "His Majesty's dogs were always to be excepted, who hunted not by common law but by prerogative."

As a result of this occasion, many courtiers, seeing that Preston had attracted James's eye, promised him assistance in obtaining a position at court. Sir Fulke Greville even went so far as to settle a stipend of fifty pounds per annum on him. However, Preston did not take advantage of his chance, probably because at this time he had just decided that his career lay in the Church.

An important result of Preston's growing reputation was that he became known to John Dod and Arthur Hildersam. Dod—Decalogue Dod, he was called—was a kind of spiritual father to most of great Puritans of his time, partly because, since he lived to be nearly a hundred, he knew Elizabethan Puritanism, and thus was able to help seventeenth-century Puritans see their position in perspective. With Hildersam, Dod took charge of Thomas Cartwright's papers after his death.

Because of his connection with leading Puritans, Preston drew many pupils to his tutelage, sixteen in one year. He was careful to choose eldest sons, whose influence might help Puritanism later. His influence at court was such that he was able to get his candidate chosen master of Queen's. But at almost this same time he was beginning to labor under the disadvantages which went with his Puritan associations. While Dean and Catechist at Queen's his

sermons—which were intended to be a complete survey of theology—attracted scholars from other colleges and townspeople
as well. But because he was considered a Puritan, the University
authorities ruled that the services should be limited to Queen's men.
Other difficulties which Preston encountered made it plain that
one of his enemies was Bishop Lancelot Andrewes and that Andrewes was seeking to embarrass him. Preston's success in avoiding
a serious conflict with the authorities was the result of his keen
intelligence and his ability to sense just how far he could go.

But at this point in his career Preston established two very
important connections. First the Duke of Buckingham, then nearly
at the height of his power, made friends with Preston in order to
strengthen his position should the Puritans come into power. Second, he became a chaplain to Prince Charles. These associations
were important to different people for different reasons: to Preston
and the Puritans because he hoped through his influence with
Buckingham to establish within the court a significant pro-Puritan
force; to King James because he hoped to win over to his side the
man who was coming to have great influence in the Puritan party.

Among Preston's services to the court was a journey abroad,
ostensibly made to improve his Latin style, but in fact probably
a diplomatic errand. Preston visited the Queen of Bohemia to obtain
information necessary for the negotiations then going on with
Spain in preparation for Prince Charles's marriage.

Two additional important honors came to Preston in 1622.
First he was made Preacher at Lincoln's Inn, a highly influential
position. Here he succeeded John Donne, who had just been
made Dean of St. Paul's. Since Donne's pulpit style was highly
ornate and Preston's as plain as any Puritan style to be met with
anywhere, it is interesting to note that the men of Lincoln, perhaps as intelligent an audience as could be found in England,
greatly preferred Preston to Donne, for though Donne's departure
was considered by the Society as a great loss, the chapel had to
be enlarged to hold the overflowing congregation less than a year
from Preston's appointment. Preston's Puritanism presumably was
considered more attractive than Donne's Anglo-Catholicism, but
it is hard not to believe that an even more influential factor was
that Donne's style demanded too much of his hearers. The style

of the Preston sermon included in this volume may be compared with this passage from a Lincoln's Inn sermon by John Donne, delivered the Sunday after Trinity, 1621:

. . . He that was God *the Lord* became *Christ*, a man, and He that was *Christ*, became *Jesus*, no man, a dead man, to save man: to save man, all ways, in all his parts, and to save all men, in all parts of the world; to save his soul from hell, where we should have felt pains, and yet been dead, then when we felt them; and seen horrid spectacles, and yet been in darkness and blindness, then when we saw them; and suffered unsufferable torments, and yet have told over innumerable ages in suffering them: to save this soul from that hell, and to fill that capacity which it hath, and give it a capacity which it hath not, to comprehend the joys and glory of Heaven, this *Christ* became *Jesus*.

Another important position proved less significant because Preston's other duties caused him to neglect it. This was the mastership of Emmanuel College, Cambridge, to which he was elected to succeed the longtime master Laurence Chaderton, then seventy-six but still active. Preston's election seems to have been the result of the fellows' search for a Puritan with court connections who might help protect the college. A great deal of skilful maneuvering by Preston and the fellows preceded the election. The fellows did not, however, benefit greatly from their selection, for the changes in the statutes which they hoped for were not obtained.

Preston continued to accumulate power through the influence of Sir Arthur Chichester, Lord Belfast, a member of James's Privy Council. Cambridge University conferred the Doctorate of Divinity on Preston in 1623. The following year, after elaborate efforts, Preston won the most influential preaching post in Cambridge, the lectureship at Trinity Church, originally established for Richard Sibbes, like Preston a plain-style Puritan preacher. It appears that Preston's influence was so great that he won the lectureship against the opposition of the King, who was so unwilling to see him have the post that he arranged for Preston to be made Bishop of Gloucester. Preston's perseverance in seeking the Cambridge post did him no good politically.

Preston's efforts now were directed at winning the currently very popular Buckingham over to the Puritans. These Puritan diplomatic overtures have recently been characterized by J. F.

MacLean as confirming "the suspicion, already suggested by the Hampton Court Conference in 1604, that until very late many Puritans were willing to work with any agency—crown as well as parliament—that promised to implement a reformation."

Finding Buckingham in need of money to pay the King's debts and otherwise to further his plans, Preston suggested to the Duke a plan for raising money. According to John Hacket, he told the Duke to

become a warm and zealous Christian, that would employ his best strenuously to lop off from this half-reformed Church the superfluous branches of Romish superstition that much disfigured it . . . the choir service of cathedral and collegiate churches, with the appendages, which were maintained with vast wealth and lands of excessive commodity, feed fat, lazy, and unprofitable drones. And yet all that chanting and pomp hindered the Heavenly Power and simplicity of prayer and furthered not the preaching of the Gospel. . . . The land of those chapters, escheats to the Crown, by the dissolution of their foundation will pay the King's debts.

Preston's proposal was an old pet project of Puritans; for cathedrals retained more ceremonial after the reformation than did parish churches. The expedient Buckingham was not unwilling to consider the proposal. But John Williams, Lord Keeper of the Seal and later Archbishop of York, persuaded him that the move would hurt him politically.

Despite this incident, Preston's standing in court circles continued to improve, although the death of James in reality doomed Puritan chances of winning concessions from the court. Buckingham's power was never greater than it was in the early days of Charles's reign, before the King revealed that he favored High Churchmen. The change in the relationship between Buckingham and the Puritans appears to have come when the King challenged Buckingham to use his influence with the Puritan leaders in the House of Commons to supply much-needed funds. When this effort failed, the Duke attempted to separate Preston from the Puritan party, perhaps by offering him the post of Lord Keeper of the Seal; but Preston declined.

A crucial incident further separated Buckingham from the Puritans. The writings of Richard Montague, especially his *Appello*

Caesarem, offended many Puritans because of their Arminianism. After much ado, in a formal debate over Montague's doctrines Thomas Morton, Bishop of Coventry and Lichfield, blundered so completely in his attempt to defend the Calvinist points that Preston, who was present, and the other defenders of the teachings of the Synod of Dort lost face with the Duke, who had called the conference.

Preston now joined those Puritans who had never been convinced that Buckingham was a man they should support. Unfortunately a letter from Preston explaining his new attitude toward Buckingham fell into the hands of the Duke himself. On learning of this, Preston realized the uncertainty of his position and devised a plan to leave England for Basel should the need arise.

Throughout the time that he was cultivating his relationship with Buckingham, Preston was leading an important group of Puritan lawyers and clergymen in London, and this organization, which continued after Preston's death, was responsible for that fusing of Puritan and parliamentary interests which led to triumphs for the united cause in the 1640's. Among those who felt Preston's influence were William Prynne, Lord Saye and Sele, the second Lord Brooke, and the Earl of Lincoln. Preston's effort with this group was thus much more successful than his efforts with Buckingham, though he did not live to see them bear fruit.

It seems to have been at the time of the break with Buckingham that Preston was delivering the series of sermons of which the first is printed here. Preston was considered to excel among those Puritan preachers who used a rational approach, and these sermons are probably the best example of Preston's brand of reasoning. They were published posthumously, as were nearly all of Preston's sermons, constituting more than twenty-five separate publications.

Perhaps because Buckingham was in the midst of important State business, he did not disturb Preston, even though some of Preston's sermons referred obliquely to the Duke's affairs. Preston's health, never good, suddenly failed in 1628. Through bad medical attention he became worse, and in July he died while visiting John Dod at Fawsley. Dod preached his funeral sermon, and he was buried in Fawsley Church.

That God is

Hebrews xi.6. "He that cometh to God must believe that God is and that He is a rewarder of them that seek Him."

Having undertaken to go through the whole body of theology, I will first give you a brief definition of the thing itself which we call divinity. It is this: it is that heavenly wisdom or form of wholesome words, revealed by the Holy Ghost in the Scripture, touching the knowledge of God and of ourselves, whereby we are taught the way to eternal life.

I call it "heavenly wisdom" for so it is called (I Corinthians ii.13): "The wisdom which we teach is not in the words which man's wisdom teacheth, but which the Holy Ghost teacheth." So likewise the apostle in another place calls it "the form of wholesome words"—that is, that system or comprehension of wholesome doctrine delivered in the Scripture.

Now it differs from other systems and bodies of science, first, because it is revealed from above; all other knowledge is gathered from things below; second, again, all other sciences are taught by men, but this is taught by the Holy Ghost; third, all other knowledge is delivered in the writings of men, but this is revealed to us in the holy Word of God, which was written by God Himself, though men were the mediate penmen of it; therefore I add, to distinguish it from all other sciences, that it is not revealed by men but by the Holy Ghost, not in books written by men but in the Holy Scriptures.

In the next place I add the object about which this wisdom is conversant; it is "the knowledge of God and of ourselves," and so it is likewise distinguished from all other knowledge, which hath some other objects. It is the knowledge of God, that is, of *God*, not simply considered, or absolutely in His essence, but as He is in reference and relation to us.

[*Life Eternall or, A Treatise of the knowledge of the Divine Essence and Attributes. Delivered in XVIII. Sermons* (London, 1631), pp. 1–13.]

And again, it is not simply the knowledge of ourselves (for many things in us belong to other arts and sciences), but as we stand in reference to God; so that these are the two parts of it: the knowledge of God in reference to us, and of ourselves in reference to Him.

Last of all, it is distinguished by the end to which it tends, which it aims at, which is to "teach us the way to eternal life." And therein it differs from all other sciences whatsoever, for they only help some defects of understanding here in this present life, for where there is some failing or defect which common reason doth not help, there arts are invented to supply and rectify those defects; but this doth somewhat more: it leads us the way to eternal life; for, as it hath in it a principle above all others, so it hath a higher end than others; for as the well-head is higher, so the streams ascend higher than others. And so much for this description, what this sum of the doctrine of theology is.

The parts of it are two: (*1*) concerning God, (*2*) concerning ourselves. Now concerning God, two things are to be known: (*1*) that He is, (*2*) what He is. Both these are set down in the text.

First, that God is, we shall find that there are two ways to prove it, or to make it good to us: (*1*) by the strength of natural reason, (*2*) by faith. That we do not deliver this without ground, look into Romans i.20, "For the invisible things of Him, that is, His eternal power and Godhead, are seen by the creation of the world being considered in His works, so that they are without excuse." So likewise, Acts xvii.27–28, you shall see there what the apostle saith, that they should "seek after the Lord, if happily they might grope after Him, and find Him, for He is not far from every one of us, for in Him we live, move, and have our being." That is, by the very things that we handle and touch, we may know that there is a God; and also, by our own life, motion, and being, we may learn that there is a Deity, from whence these proceed. For the apostle speaketh this to them that had no Scripture to teach them. So likewise, Acts xiv.17, "Nevertheless, He hath not left Himself without witness, in giving us fruitful seasons," as if those did bear witness of Him, that is, those works of His in the creatures. So that you see, there are two ways to come to the knowledge of this—that God is: one, I say, is by natural reason; or else, to make it more plain, we shall see this in these two things. First, there is enough in the very creation of the world to declare Him unto us. Second, there is a light of the understanding or reason put into us, whereby we are able to discern those characters of God stamped in the creatures, whereby we may discern the invisible things of God, His infinite power and wisdom; and when these are put together, that which is written in the creature, there are arguments enough in them, there is reason enough to see the force of those arguments, and thence we may conclude that there is a God, besides the arguments of Scripture that we have to reveal it. For though I said before that divinity was revealed by the Holy Ghost, yet there is this difference in the points of theology: some truths are wholly revealed and have no footsteps in the creatures, no prints in the creation, or in the works of God, to discern them by; and such are all the mysteries of the Gospel and of the Trinity. Other truths there are that have some *vestigia*, some characters stamped upon the creature, whereby we may discern them, and such is this which we now have in hand, that there is a God.

Therefore we will show you these two things: first, how it is manifest from the creation; second, how this point is evident to you by faith. A third thing I will add, that this God Whom we worship is the only true God. Now for the first, to explicate this, that the power and Godhead is seen in the creation of the world. Besides those demonstrations elsewhere handled, drawn from the creation in general, as from: (*1*) the sweet consent and harmony the creatures have among themselves, (*2*) the fitness and proportion of one unto another, (*3*) from the reasonable actions of creatures in themselves unreasonable, (*4*) the great and orderly provision that is made for all things, (*5*) the combination and dependence that is among them, (*6*) the impressions of skill and workmanship that is upon the creatures; all which argue that there is a God.

There remain three other principal arguments to demonstrate

this. First, the consideration of the original of all things, which argues that they must needs be made by God, the maker of heaven and earth; which we will make good to you by these three particulars. If man was made by Him for whom all things are made, then it is certain that they are made also. For the argument holds, if the best things in the world must have a beginning, then surely those things that are subserving and subordinate to them must much more have a beginning. Now that man was made by Him, consider but this reason. The father that begets knows not the making of him; the mother that conceives knows it not; neither doth the formative virtue, as we call it, that is, that vigor that is in the materials, that shapes and fashions and articulates the body in the womb; that knows not what it does. Now it is certain that he that makes anything must needs know it perfectly and all the parts of it, though the stander-by may be ignorant of it. As, for example, he that makes a statue knows how every particle is made; he that makes a watch or any ordinary work of art, he knows all the junctures, all the wheels and commissures of it, or else it is impossible that he should make it. Now all these that have a hand in making of man know not the making of him, not the father, nor the mother, nor that which we call the formative virtue, that is, that vigor which is in the materials, which works and fashions the body as the workman doth a statue, and gives several limbs to it; all these know it not. Therefore he must needs be made by God and not by man, and therefore see how the wise man reasons, Psalm xciv.9, "He that made the eye, shall he not see? He that made the ear, shall not he hear?" etc. That is, He that is the maker of the engines or organs or senses or limbs of the body, or He that is maker of the soul and faculties of it, it is certain that He must know, though others do not, the making of the body and soul, the turnings of the will, and the windings of the understanding. None of those three know it, neither the father nor mother nor that formative virtue, for they are but as pencils in the hand of Him that doth all. The pencil knows not what it doth, though it draws all. It is guided by the hand of a skillful painter; else it could do nothing; the painter only knoweth what he doth. So that formative virtue, that vigor that forms the body of a man—that knows no more what it doth than the pencil doth, but He in Whose hands it is, Who sets it on work, it is He that gives vigor and virtue to that seed in the womb from whence the body is raised; it is He that knows it, for it is He that makes it. And this is the first particular by which we prove that things were made, and had not their original from themselves.

The second is: if things were not made, then it is certain that they must have a being from themselves. Now to have a being from itself is nothing else but to be God, for it is an inseparable property of God to have His being from Himself. Now if you will acknowledge that the creatures had a being of themselves, they must needs be gods; for it belongs to Him alone to have a being of Himself and from Himself.

The third follows, which I would have you chiefly to mark. If things have a being from themselves, it is certain then that they are without causes, as for example that which hath no efficient cause, that is, no maker—that hath no end. Look upon all the works made by man, that we may express it to you; take a house or any work or instrument that man makes. Therefore it hath an end, because he that made it propounded such an end to himself, but if it have no maker it can have no end, for the end of anything is that which the maker aims at. Now if things have no end, they could have no form, for the form and fashion of everything ariseth only from the end which the maker propounds to himself; as, for example, the reason why a knife hath such a fashion is because it was the end of the maker to have it an instrument to cut with. The reason why an axe or hatchet hath another fashion is because it might be an instrument to chop with; and the reason why a key hath another fashion different from these is because the maker propounded to himself another end in making of it, namely, to open locks with. These are all made of the same matter, that is, of iron, but they have divers fashions because they have several ends which the maker propounds to himself. So that, if there be no ends of things, there is no form nor fashion of them, because the ground of all their fashions is their several ends. So then we will put them all together; if there be no efficient, no maker of them, then there is no end, and if there be no end, then there is no form nor fashion; and if there be no form, then there is no matter and so consequently they have no cause; and that which is without any cause must needs be God; which I am sure none dares to affirm, and therefore they have not their being of themselves.

But besides that negative argument, by bringing it to an impossibility that the creatures should be gods, we will make it plain by an affirmative argument that all the creatures have an end. For look upon all the creatures and we shall see that they have an end; the end of the sun, moon, and stars is to serve the earth; and the end of the earth is to bring forth plants, and the end of plants is to feed the beasts, and so if you look to all particular things else you shall see that they have an end, and if they have an end it is certain there is one did aim at it and did give those creatures those several fashions which those several ends did require. As, for example, what is the reason why a horse hath one fashion, a dog another, sheep another, and oxen another? The reason is plain: a horse was made to run and to carry men, the oxen to plow, a dog to hunt, and so of the rest. Now this cannot be without an author, without a maker, from whom they have their beginning. So likewise this is plain by the effects, for this is a sure rule: whatsoever it is that hath no end but itself—*that* seeks to provide for its own happiness in looking no further than itself; and this is only in God, blessed forever. He hath no end but Himself, no cause above Himself; therefore He looks only to Himself and therein doth His happiness consist. Take anything that will not go out of its own sphere but dwells within its own compass, stands upon its own bottom to seek its happiness, that thing destroys itself. Look to any of the creatures, and let them not stir out of their own shell—they perish there. So, take a man that hath no further end than himself; let him seek himself, make himself his end in all things he doth, look only to his own profit and commodity. Such a man destroys himself, for he is made to serve God and men, and therein doth his happiness consist, because that he is made for such an end. Take those that have been serviceable to God and men, that have spent themselves in serving God with a perfect heart; we see that such men are happy men; and do we not find it by experience that those that have gone a contrary way have destroyed themselves? And this is the third particular.

If things had no beginning, if the world was from eternity, what is the reason there are no monuments of more ancient times than there are? For, if we consider what eternity is and what the vastness of it is, that when you have thought of millions of millions of years, yet still there is more beyond; if the world hath been of so long continuance, what is the reason that things are but, as it were, newly ripened? What is the reason that things are of no greater antiquity than they are? Take all the writers that ever wrote (besides the Scripture), and they all exceed not above four thousand years; for they almost all agree in this, that the first man that had ever any history written of him was Ninus, who lived about Abraham's time or a little before; Trogus Pompeius and Diodorus Siculus agree in this. Plutarch saith that Theseus was the first; before him there was no history of truth, nothing credible; and this is his expression: take the histories of times before Theseus, and you shall find them to be like skirts in the maps, wherein you shall find nothing but vast seas. Varro, one of the most learned of their writers, professeth that before the kingdom of the Sicyonians, which began after Ninus's time, that before that time nothing was certain, and the beginning of that was doubtful and uncertain. And their usual division of all history into fabulous and certain by historians is well known to those that are conversant in them, and yet the historians that are of any truth began long after the captivity in Babylon; for Herodotus, that lived after Esther's time, is counted the first that ever wrote in prose, and he was above eight hundred years after Moses's time. For conclusion of this we will only say that which one of the ancientest of the Roman poets, drawing this conclusion from the argument we have in hand, saith. If things were from eternity and had not a beginning,

> Cur supra bellum Thebanum et funera Trojae
> Non alias alii quoque res cecinere poetae?

"If things were from eternity, what is the reason that before the Theban and Trojan war, all the ancient poets and ancient writers did not make mention of anything?" Do you think, if things had been from eternity, there would be no monuments of them? If you consider the vastness of eternity, what it is? So likewise for the beginning of arts and sciences: what is the reason that the original of them is known? Why were they no sooner found out? Why are they not sooner perfected? Printing, you know, is a late invention; and so is the invention of letters. Take all sciences, the ancientest, as astrology and philosophy, as well as the mathematics; why are their authors yet known, and we see them in the blade and in the fruit? So for the genealogies of men (for that I touch because it is an argument insinuated by Paul, when he disputed with the heathens, Acts xvii.26, "that God hath made of one blood all mankind"), you see evidently how one man begets another and he another, etc., and so go and take all the genealogies in the Scripture and in all other historiographers. We shall see that they all come to one well-head. Now I ask, if the world was from eternity, what is the reason that there is but one fountain, one blood whereof we are all made? Why should they not be made all together? Why was not the earth peopled together and in every land a multitude of inhabitants together, if they had been from eternity and had no beginning?

The second principal head by which we will make this good to you, that *there is a God* that made heaven and earth, is the testimony of God Himself. There is a double testimony; one is the written testimony, which we have in the Scripture; the other is that testimony which is written in the hearts of men.

Now, you know that all nations do acknowledge a God (this we take for granted), yea, even those that have been lately discovered, that live, as it were, disjoined from the rest of the world, yet they all have and worship a God. Those nations discovered lately by the Spaniards in the West Indies and those that have been discovered since, all of them without exception have it written in their hearts that *there is a God.*

John Bastwick (1593–1654)

Though many laymen had been actively identified with the Puritan cause since the days of Hooper, most of them took a part in Puritan reform efforts only by supporting Puritan clergymen or by working in Parliament for the further reform of religion. But by the 1630's two laymen were leaders of Puritanism. One, William Prynne, is well known to students of English history; the other, John Bastwick, deserves to be better known to students of English literature, for his *Letany* calls to mind the days of Martin Marprelate. It is a notable example of Puritan satire.

Bastwick was born in Essex in 1593. He entered Emmanuel College in 1614, but remained at Cambridge only briefly. After a time on the Continent, perhaps as a soldier in the Dutch army, he studied medicine at Padua and was awarded an M.D. degree. Thereupon he took up residence in Colchester, Essex, as a physician, in 1623.

Bastwick was the master of a classical Latin style, which he put to use in 1624 in writing *Elenchus Religionis Papisticae,* an attack on the Mass and the supremacy of the Pope. Nine years later he and William Prynne prepared *Flagellum Pontificis,* a Dutch publication. It argues for presbyterianism and the parity of bishops and presbyters. For this Bastwick was arrested and tried before the High Commission. He was fined and imprisoned till he should retract his views. He thereupon attacked the High Commission in a book, perhaps published in London, entitled *Prazin ton Episkopon, sive Apologeticus ad Praesules Anglicanos.*

In prison Bastwick was permitted guests, among whom was a cheerful old man who urged him to write an attack on the bishops in English. Bastwick obliged, and the result so delighted the old gentleman that he brought others, among whom was John Lilburne, later active as a Leveller. Lilburne saw to it that Bastwick's piece was printed. The title-page is also a table of contents: *The Letany of John Bastwick, Doctor of Physics, being now full of devotion, as well in respect of the common calamities of plague and pestilence* [note the echo of the Anglican litany]; *as also of his own particular misery: lying at this instant in* Limbo Patrum. *Set down in two letters to Mr. Aquila Wykes, keeper of the Gatehouse, his good angel. In which there is a universal challenge to the whole World, to prove the parity of Ministers, to be* jure divino. *Also a full demonstration that the bishops are neither Christ's nor the apostles' successors, but enemies of Christ and His kingdom, and of the King's most excellent majesty's prerogative royal. All which he undertakes to make good before King and Council, with the hazard of otherwise being made a prey to their insatiable indignation. A book very useful and profitable for all good Christians to read, for the stirring up of devotion in them likewise.* 1637.

The bitterness of this very angry book can be explained by a consideration of autobiographical sections of its sequels. According to Bastwick, he originally became involved in controversy when his Protestantism was challenged repeatedly by a Roman Catholic physician in his neighborhood. One of the questions his opponent proposed was, Are Roman Catholic bishops true bishops? Bastwick took the position, he relates, that he was not concerned with Anglican bishops, whose authority came from the King. But at this time English bishops asserted that they held their positions by divine law, not by statute. Because Bastwick denied the divine foundation of episcopacy, he was imprisoned. What he felt to be the injustice of his case enraged him. He considered Laud to be especially at fault and said of him that he "hath a long time been nibbling at my ears. I marvel what he will say or do to them now, for this work." (Prynne had lost most of his ears in 1634.)

The bishops' power is Bastwick's theme in the original *Letany* and its four sequels. At meals, Bastwick reports, servants precede the bishops' platters and call, "Be uncovered; my lord's meat is coming up." In an ugly touch he alleges that some of Laud's servants carry his tail, "for the better breaking and venting of his wind and ease of his holy body (for it is full of holes)." Having made this scurrilous remark, Bastwick then charges that the bishops' officers are guilty of "swearing, ribaldry, scurrility, bawdy, corrupt speeches, and filthy communication (such as chaste ears cannot hear). . . ."

Bastwick accounts for his Puritanism in the *Letany*. He explains how he absorbed the prejudice against Puritans which prevailed in his home area, though many of the Puritan charges against the Church could have been verified there. Only twice a year could a sermon be heard, and that usually one read from a book devoted largely to attacking the Puritans. He changed his views when he learned that those who attacked Puritanism most commonly on their deathbeds chose Puritans, not relatives, as guardians of their children and their estates. By the time he wrote the *Letany* he had concluded that there are "none in life and death happy and truly comfortable but those that are branded with the name of Puritan."

He is willing to suffer for his Puritanism, he jestingly admits:

Calves you know in old time were good sacrifices, and well accepted of, and I doubt not they may yet be well pleasing. Now I am an Essex calf, and the prelates have made me one, and pent me up in a coop a-fatting. If they shall in fine and after all this sacrifice me upon the altar of the pillory, I will so bleat out their episcopal knaveries as the odor and sweet smelling savor of that oblation, I hope, shall make a propitiation for the good of this land and kingdom, as the King himself and all loyal subjects shall fare the better for it.

The first pages of the *Letany*, which immediately precede the section reprinted below, have a more humble tone. Here Bastwick complains to his jailer that the authorities had not meant that he should be completely without liberty. Since his wife is with child and the plague is raging, he must find a place for her and help those who need the services of a physician. Priests, Jesuits, and other Catholics, he observes, though sentenced to prison, are permitted the measure of liberty which he seeks.

In June 1637 Bastwick was one of three tried in the Star Chamber for libel. The others were Prynne, charged for his attack on Bishop Wren and other bishops in *News from Ipswich*, and Henry Burton, a clergyman who had preached and published two sermons attacking what he considered to be innovations: altars with crucifixes, and bowing towards the East. Nothing like a fair trial took place; Chief Justice Finch sneered at Prynne when he took his place at the bar. Because of unavoidable delay in preparing replies to questions put to them before the trial, the three were considered guilty *pro confessio,* and were sentenced to lose their ears (Prynne had stubs left) in the palace yard of Westminster, be fined five thousand pounds each, and be perpetually imprisoned in remote places of the kingdom.

Public reaction to the judgment was great. The lawyers and physicians were especially resentful, for Prynne's and Bastwick's membership in the learned professions should, they felt, have shielded them from such shameful treatment. A huge crowd was present to witness the mutilation. The three made the best of the occasion to arouse public opinion. They congratulated one another, and Bastwick's wife kissed his ears. On their way to prison a month later, multitudes cheered them. Those who were not present at these events could soon read of them in a pamphlet which claimed to reproduce even the speeches of the three at Westminster.

Bastwick was imprisoned at first in Cornwall. Later, because his prison was not considered sufficiently remote, he was transferred to a fort in the Scilly Isles, and his wife was not permitted to land on the island.

At the beginning of the Long Parliament, the House of Commons resolved to erase the infamy, and the three were sent for to plead their cause before an investigating committee, which appears to have freed them and returned their fine money. In 1642 Bastwick was made a captain in the Leicester trained bands. In the very early stages of the Civil War he was captured briefly. Little more is heard from him. He published in 1643 another sharp attack on the bishops, *A Declaration Demonstrating . . . that all Malignants, Whether they be Prelates, &c. Are Enemies to God and the Church,* and two lesser works in 1648. In 1654 he died.

Bastwick is by no means an entirely admirable man. His skill in vituperation played an important part in the propaganda campaign against the episcopal Establishment. The more restrained Puritan clergy furnished the ideals; Bastwick and Prynne were among those who fired the Puritan party to action.

The prelates' practices

I am resolved, therefore, to put a few nettles under Antichrist's tail, and to make him frisk a little, before I fly.

After I have done that, and my method of physic for the care of the Whore of Babylon, which I am now about (for, the prelates having taken away my practice and not suffering me any longer to cure men, I was willing to try if I could heal beasts, and among other that scarlet harlot and all those that commit fornication with her, that brutish crew), and that work being finished, I will then so anatomize the prelates' theory as the whole macrocosm shall see the depth of Satan in the ventricles of their hearts. And I will make it appear that there is as little need of their government in King Charles's dominions as was of Samson's foxes with firebrands in their tails in the Philistines' corn. And after I have put an end to that volume, I will then write the practical part of the prelates; I mean their lives and morals, and the acts and monuments of their wicked courts. And if two or three drops of my iatral [i.e., medical] rhetoric, which I let fall only upon the beast, did so much displease them, what will they say or do, think you, when I open the cataracts of all my Greek and Roman oratory upon them? I doubt not but by the torrent of that to carry their wickedness to the extremest parts of the earth, and out of the confines of the Christian world, that the very pagans and barbarians may blush at their impiety and cruelty, and that they may be spewed out at aliens and strangers from the commonwealth of all learning and goodness among all such as call upon the name of God in sincerity.

They pretend indeed, and would fain have the world believe, that they are the successors of Christ and His apostles. And as you yourself think, they verily are. But I pray compare Christ and His apostles and the prelates and priests of our age together. Christ was humble and meek; they are proud and arrogant. No sooner was Malchus's ear cut off but Christ put it on again; and they cut off men's ears. Christ went about preaching and teaching, healing and

[*The Letany* . . . (1637), pp. 14-15.]

doing good wherever He came; they neither preach nor teach nor cure; neither will they suffer others to do either, by their good wills or that which is good anywhere. But if I should run through all disparities I might make a mighty volume. I beseech you now, compare them and the apostles together a little. And for example let us look upon Paul and Barnabas at Lystra. You shall see them so full of piety, pity, compassion, goodness, and humanity that the inhabitants and men of Lystra concluded that gods were come down among them in human shape. But if we look upon the lives, actions, and manners of the priests and prelates of our age and see their pride, fast [i.e., arrogance], impudency, inmanity, profaneness, unmercifulness, ungodliness, etc., one would think that hell were broke loose and that the devils, in surplices, in hoods, in copes, in rochets, and in foursquare cowturds upon their heads, were come among us and had beshit us all—foo, how they stink! For they open the very schools to ungodliness and unrighteousness, impiety and all manner of licentiousness, not only teaching men to be wicked and rejoicing in it but constraining them thereto.

And in times of greatest calamities, when fasting, humiliation, and mourning is called for, and when ministers ought most of all to cry aloud and to lift up their vocies like a trumpet and to stir up and awaken the people to humble themselves under the mighty hand of God, in that His plagues and judgments are gone out among us and His hand of displeasure lifted up, readier deeply to wound, then do they take this occasion to put down both teaching and preaching.

And as the hypocrites in Christ's time under the pretense of long prayers devoured widows' houses, so the prelates under the show of advancing their common prayers and devised service, they murder and devour preaching, and hinder the publishing of the Gospel, by which men should be instructed rightly to pray and orderly to live and learn their duty towards God and men.

Neither do they only suppress preaching, but they make it a crime and matter of punishment and vexation for Christians to discourse about points of religion and confer and talk together of Holy

Scripture and their most sacred faith and profession, and for them privately among themselves, by reasoning and arguing, to find out the meaning of the Word of God, which Christ notwithstanding commands and the Holy Ghost commends everywhere, and which is and hath been to Christians a great and excellent means of instruction and information, and of no small comfort. This also, so holy, so divine a duty, so useful and profitable an exercitation, is by the prelates counted a heinous offense and in their courts punished and branded by the name of Puritanism and profanation of the Scriptures.

And, which is yet more, all private Christian meetings for the invocation of the name of God and for the mutual edification of each other in their most holy faith and for the humbling of their souls before God, under His heavy displeasure for their own sins and for the abominations of the times, by which they might divert judgments and procure blessings to the Church and land, and mutually benefit and profit one another—these likewise are by the prelates adjudged criminal, and severely punished by them through the whole kingdom under the name of schismatical meetings and conventicles, when notwithstanding the Lord Himself highly commendeth and commandeth these endeavors and promiseth a special blessing unto them. Yea, the apostles themselves are precedents, to Christians, of them, who testify that from house to house, night and day, they did not cease to admonish Christians and to preach unto them, and commanded the ministers of the Word to follow their example in so doing, and this in the most profound peace of the Church, when they had the free liberty of their public meetings. And yet then, I say, the apostles did honor with their presence and applause these private assemblings of themselves together for holy purposes, and earnestly in all their epistles exhorted all the saints of God to those holy duties and excited them in all places and everywhere to lift up pure hands and hearts, and counted it a great sin to forsake the assemblies of the saints. And Christ Jesus, the Lord of life, hath also graciously promised that wheresoever two or three are gathered together in His name, there He will be with them. And for that purpose He consecrated all places before, in the Fourth of John, to make them fit for all holy Christian employments.

These pious exercises, howsoever thus renowned by the apostles, are by the prelates condemned amongst abominable things and worthy of extreme punishment, and are matter everywhere of presentment and great severity and trouble to poor Christians. I pray therefore, once again let me entreat you to behold how little they resemble the apostles. The apostles in all things endeavored to conform themselves to the image of Christ and to His blessed will, and to have a uniformity with Him in life and sufferings. The prelates, they labor all they can to be like Antichrist, and seek a conformity with him in life and pleasures, and in persecuting and afflicting the dearest servants of God. Are these successors then of Christ and His apostles, think you? I trow not.

William Whately (1583–1639)

William Whately was identified throughout his life with Oxford-shire, although his university was Cambridge. He was born at Banbury, in 1583, the son of a justice of the peace and two-term mayor. After study near Banbury he went up to Christ's College at the age of fourteen, having already learned well Latin, Greek, and Hebrew. There he heard Chaderton and Perkins preach regularly. Because of his masterful memory, he remembered their sermons perfectly and could repeat them afterwards to his college tutor. Soon after he commenced bachelor in 1601, he married, and at the behest of his father-in-law, a clergyman, decided to enter the ministry. He went up to Oxford for the M.A., which he received in 1604.

In 1605 he became lecturer at Banbury, and held the post till his death. Banbury, twenty-three miles from Oxford and inhabited by about sixteen hundred people, was famous for its piety, as indicated by the expression "Banbury is famous for cakes, cheese, and zeal." By the time Ben Jonson wrote *Bartholomew Fair* Banbury was so famous for its Puritanism that Zeal-of-the-Land Busy, Jonson's satirical portrait of a Puritan, is listed simply as "a Banbury Man." A favorite Sunday exercise of Oxford students was to make the trip to Banbury to hear the famous "Roaring Willy." His friend Robert Harris preached at nearby Hanwell.

Whately's tremendous strong voice and his great memory made him an effective preacher. One who heard him calls him "that famous and perfect preacher, and that not only *ad populum*, as some great wits have liberally acknowledged, who would often step out of Oxford on purpose to hear him, and came at first with prejudice enough." He was noted for his "great solidity of reason and embroidery of rhetoric." Anthony à Wood describes him as "an excellent preacher, a person of good parts, well versed in the original text both Hebrew and Greek . . . a Calvinist . . . much frequented by precise and busy people there." And Thomas Fuller calls him "a good linguist, philosopher, divine."

Whately obtained a degree of notoriety in 1621 as the result of the delivery and publication of a sermon called "A Bride Bush," in which he taught that adultery "doth untie the knot of marriage and annihilate the covenant first made by so palpable a breaking of it, so that the party wronged is free from the law of his husband or wife." Also he taught that "it is lawful for any . . . causelessly or wrongfully forsaken or put away by the yoke-fellow, to marry another." Although called before the High Commission, Whately was released when he retracted his opinions.

Whately tells us that one memorable Sunday while services were being held,

the cry of fire, fire, came flying in at the church doors even in that instant when we had begun to celebrate the Lord's Supper; when some had received that holy Sacrament and the greater number were to receive, then did God pull us from His table, and thrust us out of His house by force; then was I compelled to request all . . . (that had strength and ability to do service there) to make all haste to the place of danger, and the rest (that could have but troubled others with their presence and outcries) to stay still at church.

The fire consumed 103 dwelling houses and cost twenty thousand pounds. As a result of this calamity, Whately preached and published a sermon on John v.14: "Sin no more lest a worse thing come unto thee."

Whately's troubles over Puritanism came not in Banbury, where for some reason he was out of the jurisdiction of the diocesan authorities, but at Stratford, a center of Puritanism since Cartwright had preached there in Elizabeth's reign. (Stage plays were prohibited in Shakespeare's home town in 1602!) In 1623 an alderman left a sum of five pounds a year for weekly lectures. The post so established was filled by Robert Harris from 1629 to 1631 and then by Whately till 1637. The details of Whately's troubles are unfortunately not known. However, we do have Archbishop Laud's report to King Charles in 1637: "My Lord the Bishop certifies that he is less troubled with nonconformists since Mr. Whately of Banbury gave over his lecture at Stratford within that diocese."

Of the many collections of sermons which Whately wrote, decidedly the most interesting is *Prototypes, or the Primary Precedent Presidents out of the Book of Genesis* (1640). The sermons in this volume appear to be the last that Whately delivered; the editor tells us that Whately would have completed, had he lived, his study of the characters of the Old Testament and of what we can learn from them. The sermons are almost uniformly interesting; they reveal a rather vivid imagination and the wisdom which comes with full maturity. The style is simple but not flat: Whately had a better ear for prose rhythm than most Puritan preachers. His theological assumptions are clear, but the sermons are less theoretic than practical. The sermon which follows is especially interesting because its theme is Milton's: man's first disobedience.

Henry Scudder, Whately's friend and biographer, tells how Whately prepared his sermons. First he read the text in the language in which it was written, analyzing with the help of rhetoric the tropes and figures used. Then he would carefully consider the context. He would next discover what doctrine his text taught, so that "the truth observed in the text should be the argument or middle term, whereby in a simple syllogism he could conclude his doctrine." Then he sought out proofs from Scripture to appeal to reason in supporting his doctrine. These proofs were likewise used as middle terms in a syllogism. In applying the doctrine also he used the syllogistic method, with the doctrine as the middle term.

A glance at Whately's use of the syllogism is helpful. Preaching on the text "He that giveth unto the poor shall not lack, but he that hideth his eyes shall have many a curse" (Proverbs xxviii.27), Whately argues, "What is commended to men with a gracious promise and whose contrary is threatened with a curse, must be a duty sure, as all will yield; now so is this work of giving to the poor, as you see with your eyes." So Whately concludes with the doctrine "Giving to the poor is a necessary duty" (*The Poor Man's Advocate*, 1637).

In the sermons of *Prototypes*, however, he was much less systematic and logical, though still methodical. He seems to have been willing to be a bit casual. There is less appeal to the reason, none to the imagination. But moral earnestness is still there. Whately addresses the rich:

Do you not count these poor snakes almost nothing? the mud, the scum, three-half-penny creatures, less than dust almost to you, mushrooms, shrubs; verily, these thoughts proclaim you to be monstrous proud. . . . 'Tis pride of heart we seek for, and 'tis nothing but pride that sets up these bustling thoughts in you.

The sermons of *Prototypes* are all typological; that is, they assume that the unity of the Old and New Testaments is such that the crucial events of the New Testment are foreshadowed in the Old. Typology, an ancient way of reading the Old Testament, continued to be popular through the seventeenth century.

Whately died in 1639, on the eve of the Civil War. His epitaph reads in part as follows:

Whatso'er thou'lt say who passest by,
Why here's enshrined celestial dust,
His bones, whose fame and name can't die;
These stones as feoffees weep in trust;
It's William Whately that here lies,
Who swam to's tomb in's people's eyes.

The example of Adam and Eve

As all other knowledges are conveniently taught by precepts and examples, so is that best of knowledges, the art of living holily. Hence it is that as I have instructed you to my poor ability in the Law and the precepts of good life, so I do now intend to set before your eyes the examples recorded in Scripture of men both good and bad, that by observing the swervings of the one, and the right walking of others, you may better keep your own feet in the straightest paths. Only concerning examples, you must know this in general, that no example at all hath the force of a precept either to bind the consciences of men to anything as a duty, or to restrain from anything as a sin, because the knowledge of sin is from the Law, and where there is no law there is no transgression, and our care must be to walk in God's ways, not in the ways of any man

[*Prototypes, or the Primary Precedent Presidents out of the Book of Genesis* (London, 1640), pp. 1–13.]

whatsoever. But example prevaileth alone to persuade the will as a fit argument of exhortation or dehortation, not as an argument to prove a thing needful or sinful. Seeing then my duty is to persuade you to all goodness, and to dissuade you from all evil, and the examples of Scripture are undoubted and certain, and they offer themselves as it were unto the senses, and so more work on the will to allure or deter: I think it a convenient means of helping you in all righteousness and against the contrary, to make a collection of those examples of good or bad things which are left us upon record by a divine pen. I will range these examples according to the order of time wherein they lived, so far as I can inform myself thereof by the Word of God. And I will begin with Adam and Eve, and put them both together, because their good and evil was put together in practice thereof.

The method I intend to take in each person is this: I will consider his birth, life, and death, and in his life I will look to his carriage and behavior in respect of the deeds he did, good, bad, indifferent, and doubtful, and the things that befell him, either prosperously or adversely, in benefits or afflictions.

Now for Adam and Eve, because they were the first fountains of mankind, and therefore could not be born in the same manner as others be (for he that is born must have a parent, and he that hath a parent was not the first man or woman, because his parent was before him), therefore I cannot tell you anything of their birth, but of their entering into the world by another way, which was to them the same in effect that our begetting and birth is to us. I will inform you according to the Scriptures, for it much concerns us to understand our original and to know certainly how mankind came into the world. Know then, in sum, that God made man of the dust of the earth and breathed into him the breath of life, and man became a living soul. Here is in brief the creation of Adam (now Adam signifieth red earth, because his body was made of such kind of earth), and concerning woman it is noted that God caused a deep sleep to fall upon Adam, and then took one of his ribs, closing the flesh instead of it, and framed it into the body of a woman, in which also he placed a reasonable soul.

Concerning this creation of man, you must first inform yourselves of the necessity of it. It must needs be granted by force of reason that there must be some first man, seeing otherwise there must be infinite men, because a number without beginning must be also without end, inasmuch as there is the same reason of both. That which caused men without beginning did cause them necessarily, and therefore it must cause them forever. Now all reason agrees to this truth, that there cannot be an infinite number, seeing to a number still one at least may be added. I mean it of actual numbers and actual infiniteness, so we reason thus: either an infinite number of men, or some first man and woman; not the former, therefore the latter. And if there must be a first man and woman, either they came by chance and without any maker, which is so absurd that no man can choose but hiss it out, or else they were made by some agent or matter that had a being before them. If so, then either as heathen theology tells, they grew out of the mud as frogs do in some countries, or else were formed by God as our theology teacheth. Let every man that hath his right wits about him, judge in himself whether of these twain is more agreeable to reason and more likely to be true.

So man was created by God. Now about his creation, the time and matter of it is to be noted. For first, man was not created till the sixth day, when a fit place for him to dwell in, and all necessary furniture for the place, and all needful servants and attendants were before provided for his use. God saw it not fit to bring man into the world before it was garnished and stored with all contents useful for him. And then, man was made in the first place and woman after him, to show that man is the superior in nature; woman was made for man and not man for woman; therefore was man made first and woman after. So doth the apostle reason in two places where he handles the difference of sexes, I Corinthians xi.8–9, and I Timothy ii.13. So you have this cleared, how man came into the world, and how woman; but you must observe more particularly the different matter of which they were made and the parts of which they consist.

Man had a body and that was made of the dust of the earth to teach him humility, but he had also a soul and that was breathed into his nostrils, that is, infused by God, wonderfully and immediately put into man's body. It is called a breath of life, and after, a soul of life, that is, a soul which procured breathing and living. Nothing is harder for a man to conceive of than the nature of his own soul; next, the nature of God and angels, for the former is much more hard to comprehend, the latter equally difficult at least. It should be unto us a matter of great abasement that we cannot tell what to make of ourselves, that is, of our souls. That is, we know by the effects it works in the body, and the absence of these effects and the following of contrary effects when it is departed from the body, and this is all we know in a manner, only we may gather by discourse that it is a substance incorporeal, because itself doth inform the body, and one body cannot in reason be fit to inform another.

The Scripture also tells us certainly that it is an immortal substance which must return to God that gave it, and reason subscribes to this truth, because, finding the soul a thing simple, it cannot conceive how it should be corrupted. Oh, how ignorant are we and what cause have we to be puffed up with conceit of our knowledge, seeing so much blindness doth now possess our minds that in a manner all we have to say of our own souls and spirits, the best part of us, is this, that we cannot tell what to say.

As for Evah, she also consisted of a body, and that was made not of earth, but of a bone of her husband, to instruct her and him both of their duty, that she should acknowledge her subjection unto him as being taken out of him, and helpful to him as being made of a rib, a helpful bone in his side; and to instruct him that he should account her dear unto him and make precious reckoning of her, using her as in a manner his equal, as being a piece of himself and extracted from his own side. Now a woman also hath a soul, an immortal spirit to make her a living and a reasonable creature; for where sin is found there is a reasonable soul, because none other is capable of knowing and consequently transgressing a law made by God. But woman was in the transgression, that is, she sinned, and sinned first before Adam; therefore she had a soul and a reasonable soul; and they seem to have been wilfully blind that, whether out of the silence of God in not mentioning the breathing of a soul into Evah, or upon what other mad conceit, would needs make themselves and others believe that women had no souls. I conceive it was the device of some brutish and sensual man that, by instilling this most absurd conceit into that sex, would fain draw them to commit all licentiousness with boldness, for if they have no soul it could be no fault in them more than in the brute creatures to give over themselves to all sensuality and libidinousness.

You have heard man's beginning; know now his life, and herein consider his behavior and the things that befell him—his behavior bad, good, indifferent, doubtful.

Their bad carriage stands in two things: their first sin whereby they fell, and their following sins which they added after their fall. The first sin was the eating of the forbidden fruit; for you shall have it recorded that the Lord, having placed Adam in a garden to dress and keep it, spake to him in this wise, "Of all the trees of the garden thou mayest eating eat"—that is, thou mayest lawfully and with mine allowance eat. It was at his choice to eat of what kind he pleased, and if it seemed good unto him to forbear eating of any he might forbear. Then follows a prohibition of one kind of fruit, viz., "Of the tree of knowledge of good and evil which in the midst of the garden thou mayest not eat"—that is, you shall not lawfully do it. In regard of natural power he had ability to eat and not eat of that as of any other, but God did take away from him the moral liberty of eating of it, and by His authority saw good to abridge his liberty, and this alone to make it appear to Adam that He was an absolute and a sovereign Lord over him, and had full power and authority to forbid him what He saw good to forbid, and to command what He saw good to command. So the Lord did here call Adam to a profession of his absolute subjection to God his maker, and of God's absolute right to himself and all other creatures. And to this prohibition He subjoins a threat of death, "In the day that thou eatest it thou shalt certainly die"—in dying thou shalt die. Doubtless the Lord meant this of both deaths natural and spiritual, and it is to be interpreted, thou shalt become subject to a natural and to an eternal death; thy body and soul both shall be made in their kind mortal, thy body subject to such putrefaction and distemper as shall cause it to be an unfit receptacle for the soul, and thy soul subject to such sinfulness and distemper in its kind as shall make it unfit to hold any fellowship with God. And so thy soul shall be separated from thy body, and both from God the life of thy life. In this same phrase is the wicked man threatened by the prophet at God's appointment, "O wicked man, thou shalt die the death," that is, "most surely die and be damned." The Lord did not mean that natural and eternal death should instantly follow upon their eating, but obnoxiousness to both and some degrees of both should follow instantly, and at last the consummation of both, with an implicit exception of His grace in Christ in pardoning him.

Lo, now Adam had from God's own mouth an express and plain commandment, wherein he was directly forbidden one and but one tree, with warrant for the use of all the rest, and a plain and express threat of death to begin to ensue immediately upon his eating. And this commandment either God Himself or else Adam had made known to Evah, for you to hear that she doth both allege it and oppose it to the serpent's temptation at the first. Now this commandment so plain, so easy, so equal that he could not be ignorant of it nor incur any inconvenience by yielding to it, nor pick any exception against it—this commandment which both of them knew full well did they transgress, and that very speedily. How long they continued free from the sin I know not, because I find it not revealed and will not conjecture, because the not revealing it by God makes me think it is not to much purpose to know. If the first act of eating were that of the forbidden fruit, it is a great aggravation of their sin that they transgressed God's law in a manner afore they did any other thing; if they stood any while it is a great aggravation that after much experience of God's bounty they would be bold to offend Him and taste of the forbidden fruit after the feeling of the sweetness and goodness of other fruits. But it was not long afore they did eat, and it was likewise done upon a poor motive, the temptation of a base worm, and it was yielded unto without much resistance, for not many words passed them before Eve had condescended. You have the story of this sin in Genesis iii.1 etc., where is first the tempter, a serpent, the most naked or subtilest of all beasts, then the temptation in the matter of it and the success: the matter, "The serpent said to the woman, 'Hath God indeed said you shall not eat of every tree of the garden?'" in which he would make Eve either doubt of God's commandment, or else be discontent with it, as if He had dealt niggardly with them in not permitting them to eat of every tree, or as if the forbidding of this were as much as if He had prohibited them all the trees, intimating that this was as good as all the rest, and the not giving them this as much as the denial of all the rest; then the woman's answer, telling him that He had allowed them all the rest and forbidden this alone, and that on pain of death; then the serpent's reply, in which he contradicteth God's threat, that the woman might not give credit unto it. For he tells Evah that they should not certainly die, yea, not only so, but that God knew well enough how eating of that tree would procure to them an increase of knowledge. Then the success of the tempter is that she, believing the serpent and conceiving that she should gain knowledge by the eating and considering the beauty and pleasantness of the fruit, did not alone eat of it herself but also gave her husband, persuading him also to feed of it, which he at her persuasion did.

Thus was the first commandment utterly transgressed, which so soon as it was done they began to have sense of their nakedness, and sewed fig leaves together to make them aprons for the covering of their nakedness, which now began to appear shameful unto them.

This was their first sin; upon this followed divers other sins, viz.

their running away from God and hiding themselves among the trees, as if it had been possible for them so to have escaped His sight, and then excusing their fault, he by laying the fault partly on Eve which gave him, and partly upon God which gave her to him, and she upon the serpent which had seduced and beguiled her. So they had done evil and sought to hide their sin instead of confessing it and humbling themselves, for so sin blinds the mind, hardens the heart, drives a man from God, and sets all the mind out of frame, estranging the soul from God and causing a man to be filled with slavish fear that makes him fly from His presence. This sin brought terror of conscience, from whence of necessity followed sinfulness and mortality. This is their bad carriage.

Doubtful and indifferent may seem to have been their making for them aprons of leaves, for that showed some shame and desire to hide their shame.

Now follow the things that were good in them, viz. their embracing of God's goodness and turning to Him by faith and repentance after the promise intimated in the giving Eve the name of Evah or Mother of all living, as much as if he had said, "Though we be all dead by this sin, yet we shall live by the promised Seed which Evah shall bring forth." And then Evah giveth the name of Cain to her first son, saying, "I have obtained a son the Lord, or of the Lord," perhaps expressing her hope that Cain was that son the Lord which should bruise the serpent's head; and after calling the second son by the name of Abel, to signify their submitting themselves to the crosses and miseries which they felt, and after bringing up their sons in a calling, the one a shepherd, the other a husbandman, and in teaching them to worship God and to bring gifts and sacrifices to Him, the one of his sheep, the other of the fruits which the land did afford.

Now consider we the benefits God had bestowed upon them before their fall, the making of them after His own image, in knowledge, righteousness, and true holiness, with a most beautiful, strong, swift, healthy, and comely body, free from all danger of sickness, death, or other misery; giving them dominion over all creatures, planting so excellent a place for them as Paradise, and granting them the use of all the trees, and that of life, and putting on them so pleasant a service as that of dressing and keeping the garden, besides the hope and assurance of eternal life upon condition of their obedience, of which Paradise itself and the tree of life were signs unto them. For if we should live the life of glory by obeying the Law, so should they have done, seeing they also were under the same Covenant of Works that we be under.

Now after their sin God bestowed divers benefits on them. The chief was the promise of a Savior, viz. the Seed of the woman to tread on the serpent's head, that is, to destroy the devil and the works of the devil and to deliver them from the mischief which Satan sought to bring upon them—by which words He did make the Covenant of Grace with them and their posterity, providing a remedy equal to the disease and the means of revealing it to all, in that He manifested it to them that they might teach it to their children, and so one to another till all knew it; and then making them breeches and continuing their life and granting them children. These be the benefits.

The miseries they felt were: pronouncing a curse upon them, adjudging them to an unavoidable necessity of natural death, to much sorrow in their life, he by tilling the ground (which should bring forth ill things to him), and that with sweat and labor, and she by bearing children in sorrow and by being compelled by subjection to her husband; then by casting them out of Paradise, debarring them the tree of life, and giving Cain over to kill his brother better than himself, which must needs be a heavy cross to them, which God did somewhat mitigate by giving them another godly son, even Seth. This is their life; their death follows.

Adam lived nine hundred years, and for Eve's death, it is not mentioned how long she lived, for God hath not thought it fit to tell us the length of the life of any woman except Sarah in Scripture, upon what consideration it is hard to guess, but sure it is to humble womankind, that, because they were first in bringing in death, deserved not to have the continuance of their lives recorded by God's pen. So have I briefly run over the first man and the first woman. And now I will make use of all.

First, from their creation and the benefits bestowed upon them in and after their creation, let us learn to acknowledge God to be our creator, the fountain of our being, and to submit ourselves wholly to Him in all things, seeing we have received our being from Him. For in making them He made us in them, and whatsoever benefits He gave him in Creation, He gave them to us in him, seeing if he had not cast them away we should not have wanted them. We must not less praise God and be less thankful for that happy estate because Adam forfeited it, for his naughtiness in sinning cannot diminish the goodness of God in granting to him and his so great a heap of pleasures here with certainty of eternal life after. Do you not see that God made us all to happiness and life in our first parents, fitting all things so that he might have stood against God for the punishment justly inflicted upon us in them, and delivered over all those benefits unto us? Let us not murmur and on them for the sin committed by them. Especially we must praise God for the promise of the Seed of the woman which now God hath performed to us, by Whom salvation and life was offered and tendered to all, so that by the second Adam all might have received happiness as they lost it by the first, if the fault had not been and were not merely in themselves, that have been and are careless of God's goodness, neglecting to consider of His mercy, to believe in Him, and to turn to Him.

Secondly, in Adam's sin let us all see our own sinfulness, and our mortality and misery in his misery, "for by one man sin came into the world, and by sin death, and so death passed over all." This sin is our sin after a sort; we must lament it and bewail it, and be humbled for it, and in the sense of our wretchedness run to the promised Seed to deliver us from sin and death, and to repair the image of God in us by the mighty work of His Spirit, which is as easy for Him to do as to create us just at the first, and which He will as certainly perform for us if we seek it as He did then in our first making.

Again, let us learn to hate and loathe sin and Satan, not to hearken to his suggestions, but to believe God's threats and submit to His commandments. Let the husband resolve not to obey the voice of his wife against God; let the wife take heed of drawing her husband to sin; let the husband rather reform her than be corrupted by her. Oh, beware of thinking to get anything by doing wickedness; disobedience will bring nothing in conclusion but misery and unhappiness.

Let us take heed of flying from God and of excusing our faults and casting the blame upon others, chiefly upon God Himself, as Adam did, but let us rather confess, lament, and trust in His mercy, and implore it, than daub and dissemble and think to escape by frivolous shifts and extenuations. And especially learn not to be proud of apparel, which is no better than a badge of our wicked rebellion and of our shameful nakedness. Let us be the better for the things we know concerning Adam and Eve, our first parents.

Again, let us be careful to follow them in all good deeds which they did. Oh, let us repent and believe in Christ, hoping for life by Him according to the Covenant of Grace, as they did when they had broken the Covenant of Works. For by trusting in Christ we shall go to heaven in the way of evangelical obedience, standing in a resolution and endeavor not to sin, and a careful humbling ourselves and seeking pardon when we fail, as sure as they or we should have done in the way of legal obedience, if they and we had remained innocent. And God will surely enable us to this evangelical obedience, if we seek to Him for grace and the renewing of His image in us, as He had enabled him to legal and exact obedience. In truth Christ hath made the way to life eternal as easy to us in the path of the Gospel as it was to him in the path of the Law, for we have grace to keep us from loving and serving sin as sure as he had power to abstain from committing sin. Say to yourselves, "Adam's sin shall not damn me, if in sense of the misery which it brought upon me I can fully seek to Christ, the promised Seed."

Further, let us follow him and her in what was good in both.

How did Adam accept his wife? Saying, "This is flesh of my flesh, and she shall be called Evah," and "A man shall forsake father and mother and cleave to his wife." O you husbands, love your wives as your own flesh, cleave to them above all, and forsaking all other, keep you only to them. You wives, be content to be subject to your husbands, as it is sure Evah was before her fall at least, and probable after too, for we read of no brawls betwixt them. Oh, join together to bring up your children well, first in some honest calling, then in the knowledge of the true God and care of worshipping Him. I say, teach your sons and daughters things necessary for their profitable and holy living in the world; bring them not up in idleness and ignorance, but so carry yourselves to them that it may not be imputed to you if they prove wicked; and be thankful to God for your children and learn to rejoice especially in their goodness, as Adam and Evah did in Seth's. Learn of your first parents to be good parents, and follow all the things that were good and commendable in them.

Again, from their afflictions learn to prepare for afflictions and to make a good use of them when they come. If you think to live in this world without briers and thorns, without sweat and labor, you are much deceived. Crosses are assigned to us as just chastisements for our sin. We must to dust; let us expect misery and death, and labor to make ourselves fit for crosses. It was God's great goodness that He would not suffer Adam to remain in Paradise and to enjoy the tree of life. For had he lived in so much pleasure as that place would have afforded, and had he found all the creatures as good and comfortable to him now after his fall when his nature was made sinful, as when it was sinless, oh, how greatly would his sin have grown through the fatness of that over-delightful estate, even as weeds do in a rich and unmanured soil. Sure, had not God sent a curse on the earth, and inflicted grief and misery upon man, he would never have repented, never have conceived of his spiritual misery, never have turned to God and sought God; so that, as it is a mercy in the physician to make the patient sick with a medicine, so it was in God to send these afflictions on us. Let us not, therefore, flatter ourselves in vain conceits of living merrily, but let us prepare for afflictions, which all must in some degree meet withal in their several callings. It was the voice of an epicure in the rich man that said, "Eat and drink and take thine ease." We should say to ourselves rather, "Sin hath made me subject to divers crosses, and I will labor to receive them patiently from God's almighty hand, if He think it fit to exercise me with them."

Especially you that are parents of children, look for crosses in your children; think this boy may prove not an Abel, not a Seth, but a Cain, a wicked and a sinful Cain, a hater of goodness and fugitive from God. Let me take heed therefore that I do not over-love him, that I do not cocker him, and as it were mar and kill his soul by over-cherishing his body. If we find ourselves apt to over-prize and over-love our children, we must moderate those passions by such meditations, and if we find ourselves apt to over-grieve for their death, we must tell ourselves, "Ah, might not their lives have proved much more bitter to me than their death can?" Who would not rather bury a son young than live to see him prove a Cain, and who can tell but his son, for whose death he takes on with so much excessive sorrow, may not fall out to be as wicked as Cain? If any say, "I hope not so," I answer him, where be the grounds of his hope? Did not our first parents hope as much, think you? Sure Evah giving Cain a name showed that she had good hopes of him when he was born. Yea, those that have good and godly children must prepare to be crossed in their afflictions. Hast thou an Abel, a godly child? Oh, make thine heart ready to hear that some wicked hand hath knocked him on the head, perhaps his own brother, that some violent death hath seized upon him and taken him away before his time; and labor to be willing to yield to God's hand if He will so cross thee, for why shouldst not thou stoop to as heavy a burden as that which Adam and Eve did bear in the beginning of the world? For the death of good children, yea, their miserable and untimely death, and for the wickedness, yea, the notorious and unnatural wickedness of other children, let every man prepare himself by looking upon the example of Adam and Eve, that suffered these crosses. Yea, let every godly man learn to prepare for persecution from all Cains; but that we shall treat on when we come to Abel's example.

But brethren, we must not only prepare for crosses of this kind, but we must also make a good use of them when they come. That is, we must turn them into medicines as physicians do some poisons, causing the sorrow which they will work in us to become a medicine against our sins, of which they be the proper and natural effects. When you meet with crosses and calamities, say, "Now I see God's justice and God's truth; now I see the hatefulness and hurtfulness of sin; and therefore now I will mourn, not because I am crossed, but because I have deserved this cross, and a worse too," and so frame to confess and bemoan the sin and to supplicate for pardon and help at the hand of God in the name of Christ. Especially look to those sins to which your crosses have some reference and respect. Are you crossed in your goods? Think if you did not over-love them and get them unjustly, or if in your children, see if you did not over-love them and cocker them, and so in all things of like kind. In what God smites you, see if you have not in that sinned against Him, and so frame to lament your sins and to seek help against them. This will help to make your cross easy and quickly to remove it; this will cause that you shall be gainers even by crosses. When we see the ill deservings of sin and the perfect righteousness, yea, the goodness of God in calling thus to repentance: happy are they that be so afflicted and so taught in God's ways.

And brethren, let me yet make one use of Adam and Eve's great sin, to warn you that you take heed of presuming of your own strength, and of boasting that you will never commit such and such a sin, for if these two in their innocency could not escape when they neglected to sue to God for strength, oh, how much more shall not we stand if we adventure to brag and boast and promise much of ourselves? But when sin begins to gather upon you, and Satan to tempt, then fly to prayers and to requests and to the threats and commandments, and apply those threats and pray God to enable you to keep the commandments. Then shall you do so well as you wish, else large promises will bring forth nothing but sorry performances. Thus should Eve have done, and then she should have had her prayers granted and her faith stablished and escaped the fault. And as I think, the first of all the faults of Evah was that she was led away by the wary speeches of the serpent (by which he sought by step and step to descend to this solicitation) that then she did not revive in her mind the consideration of God's presence and of her dependence upon Him and of His readiness to give her help on her seeking it and of her own imbecility, as being a creature, to stand without continual support from Him. For sure the moral law lay upon Adam and Evah as well as upon us, and they ought thus to have behaved themselves in temptation; here therefore, I say, was her first failing. For we must not think that there was no sin precedent to the actual eating of the forbidden fruit; yea, her being enticed and drawn away to distrust God's truth, to deny His threats, to affect knowledge against God's allowance, and to be bold to sin when she conceived that no danger would grow from it but much benefit: all these were faults and preparations to the great actual fault. Indeed, it is probable that if she had taken herself in these slips and set herself and graces on work to have resisted them before they had come to such a head, that then she should not have been corrupted by them, so as to fall into sinfulness and mortality, because the Lord had limited the threat of death to actual eating. But howsoever, these things were faults in Eve, and now we must learn therefore not to presume anything of ourselves, but to confess that if we do not seek to God for His sustentation and so obtain the same from Him, we shall surely be overcome to commit any sin though never so grievous.

But again, we must be encouraged to repent of sin and to crave pardon of it, any greatness of it notwithstanding, for even this sin of our first parents is to them pardoned. This first and grand sin, the sin of sins, that did enwrap in it all the blasphemies and idolatries, etc. of all aftertimes, and was, as I may so speak, in power all sin—even this sin is forgiven. Adam, which cast all into sin out of Paradise and out of heaven, that in him lay—even this Adam is in heaven himself. Yea, Eve, that drew Adam to it and persuaded her husband to the committing of so monstrous a trespass, to the poisoning of him and all his—she is pardoned, she is in heaven. As God set forth the riches of His mercy in pardoning so vile and capital a sinner as Paul was, that in him He might show an example of all long-suffering, so hath He set forth the abundance of His grace in Christ by remitting the fault and saving the souls of these and these sinners, which did not what they did in false zeal as Paul, but in wilful unbelief and rebellion. Wherefore let no man doubt of obtaining pardon by the grace of God in Christ because of the greatness of his sin. For if by the offense of one many be dead, much more shall the grace of gift, and the gift by grace abound unto mercy; and if in Adam all die, that is, be made subject to death, so in Christ much more shall all be made alive if they trust in Him and turn. If death reigned by the first Adam, much more shall grace reign by the second Adam. If by one man's disobedience many were made sinners, much more by one man's obedience shall many be made righteous.

It is an extreme disvaluing of Christ's righteousness and underprizing of God's mercies in Christ if any greatness of sin hinder from seeking to God for pardon and trusting to find it. If we should be appointed to deserve remission of our own sins, every man for himself, then a man might hope to get out of little sins but not out of great, and so greatness of sin might dishearten him. But seeing it is Christ, the Son of God as well as man, that hath satisfied at once for the sins of all, by being a propitiation for the sins of the whole world, now it is too, too great a weakness, and too, too palpable an ignorance of Christ and disparagement to Him to doubt of pardon because of the greatness of sin. And that we may assure ourselves, lo Adam and Eve saved, a couple that let in the floodgates to all sin and that in committing so great a disobedience did commit at once all the sins of all the world. There cannot be thought any offense greater, for the time, place, persons sinning, occasions of sinning, helps against sin, commandment transgressed, no, nor the matter of the sin neither. For though the thing materially considered were but eating an apple, a plum, or whatsoever fruit it might be, yet that apple was as it were a sacrament, a visible profession of their care to forbear all sin by forbearing it. And so the taking of that was a worse sin than if it had been very actual adultery or murder, as, if a man should take the Sacramental bread and give it to a dog, or cast it into the fire, or trample it under feet, knowing it to be the Sacrament, sure he were as vile and far more vile an offender than if he should lie in wait at his neighbor's door to deflower his wife or to murder himself or any of his household. Now therefore take heart to run to God penitently for pardon in Christ, and be sure of success. And if greatness and multitude of sin offer itself to discourage you and to damp your hopes, refer yourselves to Adam and Eve and say, "Their one sin was more in badness than all my sins, and yet they were pardoned upon their repentance, and so shall I." And then even violently breaking through all objections, give over thyself to sorrowful confessions and supplications and thou shalt be pardoned.

If any say, "My sin was worse than Adam's, for I have sinned against the Holy Ghost," I answer, if thou hast sinned against the Holy Ghost, repent and thou shalt be pardoned, for the cause why that sin cannot be forgiven is not want of mercy in God or merits in Christ, but such abundance of hardness in them, that they will not seek to God for pardon or for grace to repent. Wherefore I say again, look on thy first parents, that, how bad soever thou beest, were causes of thy being so bad, and promise thyself pardon upon repentance, because they are pardoned, and hope to be pentitent if thou endeavor and seek it, because they were helped which were as vile sinners as thyself.

John Milton (1608–1674)

The thoroughly individualistic Milton reveals the inadequacy of labels, but to say that Milton was a Puritan is to recognize a dominant force in his life. He was an idealist, and from its earliest years Puritanism had always made an appeal to idealists, who found in Anglicanism just what Elizabeth had intended, the middle way of compromise. Milton's eventual disenchantment with one variety of Puritanism, presbyterianism, did not prevent him from later throwing in his lot with Cromwell and another variety. But since the Puritanism of the 1640's and '50's is a very different thing from the Puritanism which we have been considering, here we can examine Milton's identification with Puritanism only through his publications in 1641 and 1642, though we shall not deny ourselves some glimpses of Milton's later Puritanism.

John Milton was born on December 9, 1608, in Broad Street, Cheapside, London. His father was a scrivener, one of the industrious sort of people to whom Puritanism especially appealed, though there is no evidence that John Milton the elder devoted himself in any way to the reform of the Church. The poet's nephew, Edward Phillips, has it that Milton's grandfather was a Roman Catholic who disowned Milton's father for his Protestantism; such an event would do much to link the poet with a militantly Protestant position. Perhaps a more important source of his Puritanism was Richard Stock, to whom an earlier section of this study is devoted. Other Puritan preachers of note were nearby: John Preston at Lincoln's Inn, less than a mile away, and Thomas Gataker, Stock's friend, across London Bridge at Rotherhithe.

A great influence on Milton's youth was his tutor, Thomas Young, who had established his Puritanism before Milton came to know him. In his fourth elegy, written at the age of eighteen, Milton celebrates Young and characterizes him as a pastor famous for his piety, one to whom he is much indebted. More important, in a letter he tells Young that he considers him his father, perhaps because through Young he first achieved a Christian faith. Milton's first attack on episcopacy may have resulted from his devotion to Young.

Though Saint Paul's School, where Milton studied for about four years, was by no means a Puritan institution, Cambridge, where Milton was enrolled in 1625, had a long tradition of Puritanism, as we have seen. By the year of his enrollment, however, Puritanism was being successfully stifled. Whereas only a dozen years earlier Thomas Goodwin had found six Puritan tutors in Milton's own college, Christ's, no really great Puritan leader was then connected with the University except Goodwin himself. This repression of Puritanism may have inclined Milton to abandon his original plans for a career in the Church, "to whose service by the intentions of my parents and friends," he writes in *The Reason of Church-Government* (1642), "I was destined of a child, and in mine own resolutions, till coming to some maturity of years. . . ."

As late as July 2, 1628, Milton still planned to enter the priesthood, or so a letter to Alexander Gill, Jr., a teacher at Saint Paul's School, seems to indicate. (The letter may even have been written in 1631.) But, Milton complains,

Among us there are only two or three, who without any acquaintance with criticism or philosophy, do engage with raw and untutored judgment in the study of theology; and of this they acquire only a slender smattering, not more than sufficient to enable them to patch together a sermon with scraps pilfered, with little discrimination, from this author or that.

Religion was from an early age only one of Milton's commanding interests. Poetry and humanistic learning were of nearly as much concern. A successful fusion of these three is to be found in "On the Morning of Christ's Nativity," written when Milton was twenty-one. In this poem Pan and Christ are identified, and Christ's purity causes Nature "To hide her guilty front with innocent snow."

Milton's idealistic devotion to the cause of purity did not endear him to his fellows at Cambridge. He was called "The Lady," perhaps because, he wrote in his sixth academic prolusion (1628), he had not proved his manhood by debauchery. He consoled himself, he writes, with the thought that what then caused him taunts would lead to honor. In the later seventh prolusion, Milton praises purity at length. He argues that no man can be happy "without upright-

ness of life and blamelessness of character"; "by spending our
life modestly and temperately, we prefer to subdue the primary
impulses of the ungovernable age through reason and constant
zeal in studies, preserving the heavenly vigor of the mind pure and
unharmed from all contagion and defilement."

Milton's studies continued after his seven years at Cambridge, and
his "constant zeal in studies" at his father's estates at Hammersmith
and Horton led to further praise of purity in the masque which
he wrote in 1634 for presentation at Ludlow Castle. The masque
is a tribute to chastity, as well as a study of temptation. One
critic has called it a Puritan sermon. The Elder Brother's famous
speech suggests Milton's approach to his theme:

> 'Tis chastity, my brother, chastity;
> She that has that, is clad in complete steel,
> And like a quivered nymph with arrows keen
> May trace huge forests, and sandy perilous wilds,
> Where through the sacred rays of chastity,
> No savage fierce, bandit, or mountaineer
> Will dare to soil her virgin purity.

Milton alludes to his plans to enter the Church in an undated
letter from his Horton years, in which he also writes of "a desire
of honor and repute and immortal fame." The great work of the
Horton years, "Lycidas" (1637), seems to indicate that he had
finally decided against a Church career in favor of poetry. The
explanation is in part dissatisfaction with the clergy, who "for
their bellies' sake, / Creep and intrude, and climb into the fold,"
in part a recognition of his developing talent. Later, in *The Reason
of Church-Government*, Milton argues that he did not abandon
his plans to enter the ministry; he was denied the opportunity to
serve the Church, for he perceived that "he who would take
orders must subscribe slave, and take an oath withall, which unless
he took with a conscience that would retch, he must either perjure
or split his faith. . . ." Milton "thought it better to prefer a
blameless silence before the sacred office of speaking bought. . . ."
Thus he was "church-outed by the prelates."

During his Horton years Milton read widely in early Christian
church history, the writings of the Church Fathers, and English
history. These studies, combined with his immense literary talent

and his conviction that the bishops were responsible for the corrupt state of the Church, made him a very effective spokesman for the Puritan cause.

Why Milton was at this time a presbyterian is not difficult to surmise. Thomas Young, his former tutor, was a presbyterian. Milton was an advocate of the simple life; the bishops' wealth and luxurious living infuriated him. (Later he singled out Archbishop Mountain, whom he attacked for his "canary-sucking and swan-eating.") He was an advocate of that liberty which is necessary for human dignity; the power of Church officials denied this liberty and was unwarranted by Scripture. The obvious alternative was presbyterianism, which seemed to Milton to have the support of Scripture and to lead to the kind of liberty he sought for England.

Milton's dedication to his country is closely related to his Puritanism. Before the Puritan Revolution developed, he had planned to celebrate his native land in a poem on the kings of ancient Britain. In *Areopagitica* (1644) Milton was to declare that when God reveals himself to his servants, "his manner is, first to his Englishmen." He foresaw then a glorious day, for he pictured "a noble and puissant nation, rousing herself like a strong man after sleep, and shaking her invincible locks." He gloried in the task of defending the English people to Europe in his position as Secretary for Foreign Tongues in Cromwell's government.

Therefore we can well believe that he found exciting the news in early 1639 of resistance to the bishops' efforts to force a Book of Common Prayer on the Scottish Church, prelude to the Bishops' Wars. (Since the wars caused Charles such financial embarrassment that he was forced to call for a parliament, they were indeed crucial.) Milton was in Italy at the time, completing his formal education by visiting the humanist centers there. In England again in August 1639, he at first found little to contribute to the cause of reform. But with the summoning of the Long Parliament in October 1640, following a second attempt to subdue the Scots, the growing dissatisfaction with the Church leaders, the king, and his government found a means of expression. In December Parliament was petitioned to eliminate episcopacy; in March 1641 Milton urged the case against the bishops in *Of Reformation and the Causes which hitherto have hindred it*. Milton's reasons for writing this work and the four which followed it in the next thirteen months are explained in his Latin *Second Defense*, published in 1654:

When I discovered that much-sought true way towards liberty, towards the freeing of the whole life of man from servitude (since church discipline may influence the customs and manners of the state), I proceeded straightway. I could not help knowing above all things the difference between divine and human law, since I had prepared myself with studies from adolescence. I could not in this crisis fail my fatherland (yea, indeed, the Church and my brothers) in the cause of the Gospel, since I had so trained myself that I could never be considered really useful if now I paid heed to other things. Since in this opportunity I had to prove useful, I determined to transfer all my strength and all my talent to this project. First of all, therefore, I wrote to a certain friend two books concerning the reformation of the Anglican Church. (My translation.)

The learning displayed in *Of Reformation* was the fruit of Milton's years of reading at Cambridge and Horton. The work is far from being a dispassionate piece of scholarship, however. With a rich vocabulary and a striking vigor Milton gives us a work that makes use of many techniques of earlier Puritans. Here are the learning of the most learned of them—Cartwright, Travers, and Perkins—and the wit and scorn of Martin Marprelate and John Bastwick.

The work has at best a loose kind of organization. Milton begins with a description of the degeneracy of Christianity during the Middle Ages. (Laud's emphasis on decency in God's worship is, Milton implies, really a return to this degeneracy.) Next Milton turns to the Reformation in England and the forces which frustrated Puritanism. He then attends to matters closer to hand—the objections to Puritan reforms in his own time. He first considers those who favor episcopacy on the grounds of its antiquity. He notes the major differences between the functions and prerogatives of primitive bishops and contemporary English bishops. In particular he examines the changes wrought in the Church by Constantine: he it was who first gave wealth and power to the bishops. Milton also criticizes the Church Fathers, whom he finds wrongheaded and even heretical.

The third major concern of Milton's work is to compare the advantages and disadvantages of presbyterianism and episcopacy to the state. The portion of *Of Reformation* reproduced here is designed to show the dangers of the bishops' growing power and to contrast to them the glories that will come about if presbyterianism is adopted. After answering objections to his position, Milton ends with a powerful peroration, a prayer that God will reform the Church and a curse on the opponents of Puritanism. The prayer opens in this fashion:

Thou therefore that sitst in light and glory unapproachable, Parent of angels and men! next Thee I implore, omnipotent King, Redeemer of that lost remnant whose nature Thou didst assume, ineffable and everlasting Love! And Thou the third subsistence of divine infinitude, illuminating Spirit, the joy and solace of created things! one tri-personal Godhead! Look upon this Thy poor and almost spent and expiring Church; leave her not thus a prey to these importunate wolves that wait and think long till they devour Thy tender flock, these wild boars that have broke into Thy vineyard, and left the print of their polluting hoofs on the souls of Thy servants.

With the answering of his prayer Milton expects "this great and warlike nation, instructed and inured to the fervent and continual practice of truth and righteousness," to "press on hard to that high and happy emulation to be found the soberest, wisest, and most Christian people of that day when Thou, the eternal and shortly-expected King, shall open the clouds to judge the kingdom of the world. . . ."

In 1641 and 1642 Milton clearly believed that a Puritan Holy Commonwealth was about to be established. *Animadversions*, his third attack on the bishops, identifies clearly the basis of his position: the Bible, "the just and adequate measure of truth, fitted and proportioned to the diligent study, memory, and use of every faithful man." He declares that the Bible teaches that bishops and presbyters are two names for the same position.

In *The Reason of Church-Government*, the fourth of these prose works, Milton writes of himself as now devoted to poetry; he describes poetic genius as "of a power beside the office of a pulpit." Like the preacher, the poet seeks "to inbreed and cherish in a great people the seeds of virtue and public civility, to allay the perturbations of the mind and set the affections in right tune. . . ."

In time Milton abandoned presbyterianism. One reason was
the denunciation by leading presbyterians, such as Prynne, of
his liberal position on divorce. Another was his discovery that
presbyterianism was not so different from episcopacy as he had
expected. By 1644 he wrote, in *Areopagitica*, ". . . the episcopal
arts begin to bud again," for the Long Parliament had established
censorship of the press. Some two and a half years later Milton
denounced presbyterians with great vigor.

> . . . you have thrown off your prelate lord
> And with stiff vows renounced his liturgy
> To seize the widowed whore plurality
> From them whose sin ye invied, not abhorred,
>
> . . . .
> New presbyter is but old priest writ large.

Milton's utopianism also faded. In *Tetrachordon* (1645) he ac-
knowledges that the Gospel "aimed at the restorement of all things
as they were in the beginning before Adam's fall. . . . But who
will be the man shall introduce this kind of commonwealth, as
Christianity now goes?"

In *Samson Agonistes*, which modern scholarship has suggested
may be from the years 1646–48 (though revised later), Milton's
continuing dislike of ceremonial worship is suggested in his comments on the Philistines' idolatrous worship of Dagon. More
interesting to students of Puritanism is a passage in *The Tenure of
Kings and Magistrates* (1649), which defends the death penalty
for Charles and attacks those who opposed the sentence. Milton
here contrasts the older Puritanism, the subject of this study, with
the Puritanism of the presbyterians of the 1640's. The earlier
Puritans

for so many years laboring under prelacy, through all storm and
persecutions, kept religion from extinguishing, and delivered it pure
to us, till there arose a covetous and ambitious generation of divines
(for divines they call themselves), who, feigning of a sudden to be
new converts and proselytes from episcopacy, under which they had
long temporised, opened their mouths at length, in show against
pluralities and prelacy, but with intent to swallow them down both;
gorging like harpies those simonous places and preferments of their
outed predecessors, as the quarry for which they hunted, not to

plurality only but to multiplicity, for possessing which they had accused them, their brethren, and aspiring to the same authority and usurpation over the consciences of all men.

Milton's appointment as Secretary for Foreign Tongues to the Council of State in 1649 is a clear indication of his devotion to the variety of Puritanism with which Oliver Cromwell was identified. Milton believed that at last the saints were in power, and that Cromwell, a Seeker, was not interested in ruling men's consciences. These years must have been rewarding ones for Milton, even though he was now blind. When after Cromwell's death most of England was ready to restore the monarchy, Milton looked back at the events of the previous years with considerable satisfaction. He dreaded the idea of a return to anything like the days before 1640. In *The Ready and Easy Way to Establish a Free Commonwealth*, published just before the return of Charles, he declares that to restore monarchy and then to see the restoration as an error will mean that

we may be forced perhaps to fight over again all that we have spent, but are never like to attain thus far as we are now advanced to the recovery of our freedom, never to have it in possession as we now have it, never to be vouchsafed hereafter the like mercies and signal assistances from Heaven in our cause, if by our ungrateful backsliding we make these fruitless . . . .

The freedom which Milton so cherishes he identifies as "this liberty of conscience, which above all other things ought to be to all men dearest and most precious."

One clear indication of Milton's continuing identifications with Puritan ideals is his attitude towards the Bible. In *The Ready and Easy Way* and in *A Treatise of Civil Power* (1659) he argues that liberty of conscience is necessary since the sole rule in matters of religion is the Bible as interpreted by the Bible itself, with the Holy Spirit illuminating each man. It is to the teachings of the Bible that Milton turned in the long work of the 1650's, *De Doctrina Christiana*. Though in many ways this work is peculiarly Miltonic, it was intended to create an ecumenical movement. Addressing himself to "all the churches of Christ and to all who profess the Christian faith throughout all the world," Milton goes back to what he conceives to be the Christian faith before the time of the creeds and sets forth a theology which he argues is wholly Biblical.

The Puritanism of *Paradise Lost* is a topic too big to be dealt with adequately here. One notes the emphasis on the dignity of labor in Adam's lecture to Eve in Book IV, where we also read that Adam and Eve stood to pray to God, "other rites/Observing none, but adoration pure/Which God likes best. . . ." Perhaps one can detect in Book V a kind of attack on the Book of Common Prayer in the comment that Adam and Eve's prayers were "In various style, for neither various style/Nor holy rapture wanted they to praise/Their maker. . . ."

Milton's experiences in the 1640's and '50's demonstrate that the break-up of Puritanism into varieties, some organized, some parties of one (such as Milton's finally was), makes it all but meaningless to refer to Puritanism after 1640; the word has no clear referent.

Milton lived on for fourteen years after the end of the Puritan experiment, and the years were fruitful ones for his work as a poet. His continuing interest in reforming religion is seen in a pamphlet of 1673, *Of True Religion;* here he speaks again as the Puritan when he denounces "the pride, luxury, drunkenness, whoredom, cursing, swearing, bold and open atheism" which he sees "everywhere abounding." Milton remained a reformer to the last.

Of reformation

I proceed within my own bounds to show you next what good agents they [the bishops] are about the revenues and riches of the kingdom, which declares of what moment they are to monarchy, or what avail. Two leeches they have that still suck and suck the kingdom: their ceremonies and their courts. If any man will contend that ceremonies be lawful under the Gospel, he may be answered otherwise. This doubtless that they ought to be many and over-costly, no true Protestant will affirm. Now I appeal to all

[*Of Reformation in England And the Cawses that hitherto have hindred it* (London, 1641), pp. 61–70.]

wise men, what an excessive waste of treasury hath been within these few years in this land, not in the expedient but in the idolatrous erection of temples beautified exquisitely to out-vie the Papists, the costly and dear-bought scandals, and snares of images, pictures, rich copes, gorgeous altar clothes; and by the courses they took and the opinions they held, it was not likely any stay would be, or any end of their madness, where a pious pretext is so ready at hand to cover their insatiate desires. What can we suppose this will come to? What other materials than these have built up the spiritual Babel to the height of abominations? Believe it, sir, right truly it may be said that Antichrist is Mammon's son. The sour leaven of human traditions mixed in one putrified mass with the poisonous dregs of hypocrisy in the hearts of prelates that lie basking in the sunny warmth of wealth and promotion is the serpent's egg that will hatch an Antichrist wheresoever, and engender the same monster as big or as little as the lump is which breeds him. If the splendor of gold or silver begin to lord it once again in the Church of England, we shall see Antichrist shortly wallow here, though his chief kennel be at Rome.

If they had one thought upon God's glory and the advancement of Christian faith, they would be a means that with these expenses thus profusely thrown away in trash, rather churches and schools might be built where they cry for want, and more added where too few are, a moderate maintenance distributed to every painful minister that now scarce sustains his family with bread, while the prelates revel like Belshazzar with full carouses in goblets and vessels of gold snatched from God's temple; which I hope the worthy men of our land will consider.

Now then for their courts, what a mass of money is drawn from the veins into the ulcers of the kingdom this way, their extortions, their open corruptions, the multitude of hungry and ravenous harpies that swarm about their offices declare sufficiently. And what though all this go not oversea? 'Twere better it did, better a penurious kingdom than where excessive wealth flows into the graceless and injurious hands of common sponges to the impoverishing of good and loyal men, and that by such execrable, such irreligious courses.

If the sacred and dreadful works of holy discipline, censure, penance, excommunication, and absolution, where no profane thing ought to have access, nothing to be assistant but sage and Christianly admonition, brotherly love, flaming charity, and zeal, and then according to the effects, paternal sorrow or paternal joy, mild severity or melting compassion—if such divine ministries as these, wherein the angel of the Church represents the person of Christ Jesus, must lie prostitute to sordid fees and not pass to and fro between our Savior that of free grace redeemed us and the submissive penitent, without the truckage of perishing coin and the butcherly execution of tormentors, rooks, and rakeshames sold to lucre, then have the Babylonish merchants of souls just excuse.

Hitherto, sir, you have heard how the prelates have weakened and withdrawn the external accomplishments of kingly prosperity, the love of the people, their multitude, their valor, their wealth, mining and sapping the out-works and redoubts of monarchy. Now hear how they strike at the very heart and vitals.

We know that monarchy is made up of two parts, the liberty of the subject and the supremacy of the king. I begin at the root. See what gentle and benign fathers they have been to our liberty. Their trade being, by the same alchemy that the Pope uses, to extract heaps of gold and silver out of the drossy bullion of the people's sins, and justly fearing that the quick-sighted Protestant's eye, cleared in great part from the mist of superstition, may at one time or other look with a good judgment into these their deceitful peddleries, to gain as many associates of guiltiness as they can and to infect the temporal magistrate with the like lawless though not sacrilegious extortion, see a while what they do. They engage themselves to preach and persuade an assertion for truth the most false and to this monarchy the most pernicious and destructive that could be chosen. What more baneful to monarchy than a popular commotion, for the dissolution of monarchy slides aptest into a democraty, and what stirs the Englishman, as our wisest writers have observed, sooner to rebellion than violent and heavy hands upon their goods and purses? Yet these devout prelates, spite of our great charter and the souls of our progenitors that wrested their liberties out of the Norman grip with their dearest blood and highest prowess, for these many years have not ceased in their pulpits wrenching and spraining the text to set at nought and trample underfoot all the most sacred and life-blood laws, statutes, and acts of Parliament that are the holy covenant of union and marriage between the king and his realm, by proscribing and confiscating from us all the right we have to our own bodies, goods, and liberties. What is this but to blow a trumpet and proclaim a fire-cross [a sign used to call men to war] to a hereditary and perpetual civil war?

Thus much against the subject's liberty hath been assaulted by them. Now how they have spared supremacy or likely are hereafter to submit to it remains lastly to be considered.

The emulation that under the old Law was in the king toward the priest is now so come about in the Gospel that all the danger is to be feared from the priest to the king. Whilst the priest's office in the Law was set out with an exterior lustre of pomp and glory, kings were ambitious to be priests. Now priests, not perceiving the heavenly brightness and inward splendor of their more glorious evangelic ministry, with as great ambition affect to be kings, as in all courses is easy to be observed. Their eyes ever imminent upon worldly matters, their desires ever thirsting after worldly employments, instead of diligent and fervent study in the Bible, they covet to be expert in canons and decretals, which may enable them to judge and interpose in temporal causes, however pretended ecclesiastical.

Do they not hoard up pelf, seek to be potent in secular strength, in state affairs, in lands, lordships, and demesnes, to sway and carry all before them in high courts and privy councils, to bring into their grasp the high and principal offices of the kingdom? Have they not been bold of late to check the common law, to slight and brave the indiminishable majesty of our highest court, the law-giving and sacred Parliament? Do they not plainly labor to exempt churchmen from the magistrate? Yea, so presumptuously as to question and menace officers that represent the king's person for using their authority against drunken priests? The cause of protecting murderous clergymen was the first heart-burning that swelled up the audacious Becket to the pestilent and odious vexation of Henry II. Nay, more, have not some of their devoted scholars begun, I need not say to nibble, but openly to argue against the king's supremacy? Is not the chief of them [Archbishop Laud] accused out of his own book and his late canons to affect a certain unquestionable patriarchate, independent and unsubordinate to the crown? From whence having first brought us to a servile estate of religion and manhood, and having predisposed his conditions with the Pope that lays claim to this land, or some Pepin of his own creating, it were all as likely for him to aspire to the monarchy among us as that the Pope could find means so on the sudden both to bereave the emperor of the Roman territory with the favor of Italy and by an unexpected friend out of France, while he was in danger to lose his new-got purchase, beyond hope to leap into the fair exarchate of Ravenna.

A good while the Pope subtly acted the lamb, writing to the emperor, "My Lord Tiberius," "My Lord Mauritius," but no sooner did this lord pluck at the images and idols but he threw off his sheep's clothing and started up a wolf, laying his paws upon the emperor's right, as forfeited to Peter. Why may not we as well, having been forewarned at home by our renowned Chaucer and from abroad by the great and learned Padre Paolo [Sarpi], from the like beginnings (as we see they are) fear the like events? Certainly a wise and provident king ought to suspect a hierarchy in his realm, being ever attended, as it is, by two such greedy purveyors, ambition and usurpation. I say he ought to suspect a hierarchy to be as dangerous and derogatory from his crown as a tetrarchy or a heptarchy. Yet now that the prelates had almost attained to what their insolent and unbridled minds had hurried them —to thrust the laity under the despotical rule of the monarch that they themselves might confine the monarch to a kind of pupilage under their hierarchy—observe but how their own principles combat one another and supplant each one his fellow.

Having fitted us only for peace, and that a servile peace, by lessening our numbers, draining our estates, enfeebling our bodies, cowing our free spirits by those ways as you have heard, their impotent actions cannot sustain themselves the least moment unless they rouse us up to a war fit for Cain to be the leader of, an abhorred, a cursed, a fraternal war. England and Scotland, dearest brothers both in nature and in Christ, must be set to wade in one another's blood, and Ireland, our free denizen, upon the back of both, as occasion should serve—a piece of service that the Pope and all his factors have been compassing to do ever since the Reformation.

But ever blessed be He and ever glorified that from his high watch-tower in the heavens, discerning the crooked ways of perverse and cruel men, hath hitherto maimed and infatuated all their damnable inventions and deluded their great wizards with a delusion fit for fools and children. Had God been so minded he could have sent a spirit of mutiny amongst us, as he did between Abimelech and the Sechemites, to have made our funerals and slain heaps more in number than the miserable surviving remnant, but He, when we least deserved, sent out a gentle gale and message of peace from the wings of those his cherubins that fan his mercy-seat. [See Numbers vii.89.]

Nor shall the wisdom, the moderation, the Christian piety, the constancy of our nobility and commons of England be ever forgotten, whose calm and temperate connivance could sit still and smile out the stormy bluster of men more audacious and precipitant than of solid and deep reach, till their own fury had run itself out of breath, assailing, by rash and heady approaches, the impregnable situation of our liberty and safety that laughed such weak enginery to scorn, such poor drifts to make a national war of a surplice brabble, a tippet-scuffle, and engage the unattainted honor of English knighthood to unfurl the streaming red cross or to rear the horrid standard of those fatal guly [red] dragons for so unworthy a purpose as to force upon their fellow subjects that which themselves are weary of, the skeleton of a mass-book. Nor must the patience, the fortitude, the firm obedience of the nobles and people of Scotland, striving against manifold provocations, nor must their sincere and moderate proceedings hitherto be unremembered, to the shameful conviction of their detractors.

Go on, both hand in hand, O nations, never to be disunited; be the praise and the heroic song of all posterity. Merit this, but seek only virtue, not to extend your limits. For what needs? [Not] to win a fading triumphant laurel out of the tears of wretched men, but to settle the pure worship of God in His Church, and justice in the state. Then shall the hardest difficulties smooth out themselves before ye; envy shall sink to hell, craft and malice be confounded, whether it be homebred mischief or outlandish cunning. Yea, other nations will then covet to serve ye, for lordship and victory are but the pages of justice and virtue. Commit securely to true wisdom the vanquishing and uncasing of craft and subtlety, which are but her two runagates. Join your invincible might to do worthy and godlike deeds, and then he that seeks to break your union, a cleaving curse be his inheritance to all generations.

Sources

Part One: General Introduction

Ames, William. *Conscience, With the Power and Cases Thereof.* N. p., 1639.

_____. *The Marrow of Sacred Divinity.* London, *ca.* 1638.

Bancroft, Richard. *A Survay of the Pretended Holy Discipline.* London, 1593.

Bibby, Edna. "The Puritan Classical Movement of Elizabeth's Reign." Unpublished M.A. thesis, University of Manchester, 1929.

Black, J. B. *The Reign of Elizabeth, 1558–1603.* 2nd ed. Oxford, 1959.

Babbage, Stuart Barton. *Puritanism and Richard Bancroft.* Naperville, Ill., 1962.

Blench, J. W. *Preaching in England in the Late Fifteenth and Sixteenth Centuries.* New York, 1964.

Brook, V. J. K. *A Life of Archbishop Parker.* Oxford, 1962.

Calder, Isabel. *Activities of the Puritan Faction of the Church of England, 1625–1633.* London, 1957.

Cardwell, Edward, ed. *Documentary Annals of the Reformed Church of England.* Oxford, 1844. 2 vols.

_____, ed. *A History of Conferences.* 3rd ed. Oxford, 1849.

Cartwright, Thomas. *A Commentary Upon the Epistle of Sainte Paule Written to the Colossians.* London, 1612.

Chaderton, Laurence. *An Excellent and Godly Sermon . . . Preached at Paules Crosse the XXIV daye of October, An 1578.* London, n.d.

Collinson, Patrick. "John Field and Elizabethan Puritanism," in *Elizabethan Government and Society*, ed. S. T. Bindoff, et al. London, 1961.

_____, ed. *Letters of Thomas Wood, Puritan, 1566–1577.* London, 1960.

Curtis, Mark H. "Hampton Court Conference and Its Aftermath," *History*, XLVI (1961), 1–16.

_____. *Oxford and Cambridge in Transition, 1558–1642.* Oxford, 1959.

Davies, Godfrey. "Arminian versus Puritan in England, ca. 1620–1640," *Huntington Library Bulletin*, V (1934), 157–179.

_____. *The Early Stuarts, 1603–1660*. Oxford, 1937.

Dawley, Powel Mills. *John Whitgift and the English Reformation*. New York, 1954.

Dickens, A. G. *Lollards and Protestants in the Diocese of York, 1509–1558*. London, 1959.

_____. *The English Reformation*. London, 1964.

A Directory of the Publique Worship of God. London, 1644.

Dixon, Richard W. *History of the Church of England from the Abolition of the Roman Jurisdiction to 1570*. 3rd ed. Oxford, 1895–1902. 6 vols.

Dodwell, C. R. *The English Church and the Continent*. London, 1959.

Eusden, John D. *Puritans, Lawyers, and Politics in Early Seventeenth-Century England*. New Haven, 1958.

Fisch, Harold. "The Puritans and the Reform of Prose Style," *ELH*, XIX (1952), 229–248.

Frere, W. H., and C. E. Douglas, eds. *Puritan Manifestoes*. London, 1954.

Fulke, William. *A Brief and Plain Declaration Concerning . . . Discipline and Reformation*. London, 1584.

Fuller, Thomas. *The Church History of Britain*. Oxford, 1845. 6 vols.

Gardiner, Samuel R. *History of England from the Accession of James I to the Outbreak of the Civil War, 1603–1642*. London, 1883. 10 vols.

George, Charles H. "A Social Interpretation of English Puritanism," *Journal of Modern History*, XXV (1953), 327–342.

_____ and Katharine. *The Protestant Mind of the English Reformation*. Princeton, 1961.

Gorham, George C. *Gleanings of a Few Scattered Ears during the Period of the Reformation*. London, 1857.

Hallam, Henry. *The Constitutional History of England from the Accession of Henry VII to the Death of George II*. Boston, 1861. 3 vols.

Haller, William. *The Rise of Puritanism*. New York, 1938.

_____. *The Elect Nation: The Meaning and Relevance of Foxe's "Book of Martyrs."* New York, 1964.

Hart, A. Tindall. *The Country Clergy in Elizabethan and Stuart Times, 1558–1660*. London, 1958.

Henson, H. Hensley. *Puritanism in England*. London, 1912.

Herr, Alan F. *The Elizabethan Sermon*. Philadelphia, 1940.

Hill, Christopher. *Economic Problems of the Church from Archbishop Whitgift to the Long Parliament*. Oxford, 1956.

_____. *Society and Puritanism in Pre-Revolutionary England*. New York, 1964.

Hingham, Florence. *Catholic and Reformed: A Study of the Anglican Church, 1559–1662.* London, 1962.

Hulme, Harold. "Charles I and the Constitution," in *Conflict in Stuart England*, ed. W. A. Aiken and H. B. Henning. London, 1960.

Hutton, William H. *The English Church from the Accession of Charles I to the Death of Anne (1625–1714).* London, 1903.

Jordan, Wilbur K. *The Development of Religious Toleration in England.* Vols. 1–2. Cambridge, Mass., 1932–1936.

Kennedy, W. P. M. *Elizabethan Episcopal Administration.* London, 1924. 3 vols.

Klein, Arthur Jay. *Intolerance in the Reign of Elizabeth, Queen of England.* London, 1917.

Knappen, M. M. *Tudor Puritan Diaries.* Chicago, 1939.

——————, ed. *Two Puritan Diaries.* Chicago, 1933.

Lamont, William M. *Marginal Prynne, 1600–1669.* London, 1963.

Laud, William. *The Second Volume of the Remains.* London, 1700.

Lewis, C. S. *English Literature in the Sixteenth Century.* Oxford, 1954.

McGinn, Donald. *The Admonition Controversy.* New Brunswick, N.J., 1949.

Maclure, Millar. *The Paul's Cross Sermons, 1534–1642.* Toronto, 1958.

Marchant, Ronald A. *The Puritans and the Church Courts in the Diocese of York, 1560–1642.* London, 1960.

Miller, Perry. *The New England Mind: The Seventeenth Century.* New York, 1939.

——————. *Orthodoxy in Massachusetts, 1630–1650.* Cambridge, Mass., 1933.

Mitchell, Williams M. *The Rise of the Revolutionary Party in the English House of Commons, 1603–1629.* New York, 1957.

Mozley, J. F. *John Foxe and His Book.* London, 1940.

Neale, John E. *Elizabeth I and Her Parliaments, 1558–1601.* London, 1953–1957. 2 vols.

——————. *Queen Elizabeth.* New York, 1934.

New, John F. H. *Anglican and Puritan: The Basis of Their Opposition, 1558–1640.* Stanford, 1964.

New Schaff-Herzog Encyclopedia of Religious Knowledge. New York, 1908–1912. 12 vols.

Notestein, Wallace. *The English People on the Eve of Colonization, 1603–1630.* New York, 1954.

——————, and Frances H. Rellf, eds. *Commons Debates for 1629.* Research Publications of the University of Minnesota. Minneapolis, 1921.

Parker, Matthew. *Correspondence*, ed. John Bruce and T. T. Perowne. Cambridge, 1853.

Pearl, Valerie. *London and the Outbreak of the Puritan Revolution.* Oxford, 1961.

Pearson, A. F. Scott. *Thomas Cartwright and Elizabethan Puritanism, 1535–1603.* Cambridge, 1925.

Peel, Albert, ed. *Essays Congregational and Catholic.* London, *ca.* 1931.

————————. "A Puritan Survey of the Church in Staffordshire in 1604," *English Historical Review,* XXVI (1911), 338–352.

————————, ed. *Tracts Ascribed to Richard Bancroft.* Cambridge, 1953.

Perkins, William. "The Art of Prophecying," in his *Works,* II, 643–673. London, 1613.

Pollard, A. F. *The History of England from the Accession of Edward VI to the Death of Elizabeth.* London, 1910.

Porter, H. C. *Reformation and Reaction in Tudor Cambridge.* Cambridge, 1958.

Powicke, F. M. *The Reformation in England.* London, 1941.

Preston, John. *Riches of Mercy to Men in Misery.* London, 1658.

Procter, Francis, and W. H. Frere. *A New History of the Book of Common Prayer.* London, 1911.

Read, Conyers. *Lord Burghley and Queen Elizabeth.* New York, 1960.

————————. *Mr. Secretary Cecil and Queen Elizabeth.* New York, 1955.

Richardson, Caroline F. *English Preaching and Preachers, 1640–1670.* London, 1928.

Ridley, Jasper G. *Nicholas Ridley.* London, 1957.

Robinson, Hastings, ed. *Original Letters Relative to the English Reformation* (First Portion). Cambridge, 1846.

————————, ed. *The Zurich Letters.* 2nd ed. Cambridge, 1846.

Rosenberg, Eleanor. *Leicester, Patron of Letters.* New York, 1955.

Rupp, E. G. *Studies in the Making of the English Protestant Tradition.* Cambridge, 1949.

Scott, Walter, ed. *A Collection of Scarce and Valuable Tracts* [Somers Tracts]. Vol. 1. 2nd ed. London, 1809.

Shaw, William A. "Elizabethan Presbyterianism," *English Historical Review,* III (1888), 665–667.

Strype, John. *The Life and Acts of . . . John Whitgift.* London, 1718.

————————. *The Life and Acts of Matthew Parker.* Oxford, 1821. 3 vols.

Tanner, J. R. *English Constitutional Conflicts of the Seventeenth Century, 1603–1689.* Cambridge, 1948.

Trevor-Roper, Hugh R. *Archbishop Laud.* 2nd ed. Hamden, Conn., 1962.

_____. "James I and His Bishops," *History Today*, V (1953), 571–581.

_____. *Historical Essays*. London, 1955.

_____. "Scotland and the Puritan Revolution," in *Historical Essays, 1600–1750*, ed. H. E. Bell and R. L. Ollard. New York, 1963.

Usher, Roland. *The Presbyterian Movement in the Reign of Queen Elizabeth as Illustrated by the Minute Book of the Dedham Classis, 1587–1589*. London, 1905.

_____. *The Reconstruction of the English Church*. New York, 1910. 2 vols.

_____. *The Rise and Fall of the High Commission*. Oxford, 1913.

Walzer, Michael. *The Revolution of the Saints*. Cambridge, Mass., 1965.

Wedgwood, C. V. *The King's Peace, 1637–1641*. London, 1955.

Willson, David H. *James the First and Sixth*. London, 1956.

White, F. O. *Lives of the Elizabethan Bishops*. London, 1898.

Whitgift, John. *The Works*, ed. John Ayre. Cambridge, 1851–1853. 3 vols.

Part Two: Individual Authors

I have not listed the writings of the authors represented in this book, though in its preparation these works were quite as important as those listed. But the former, or at least most of them, are listed under the authors' names in Pollard and Redgrave's *Short-Title Catalogue, 1475–1640* (London, 1926) and Donald Wing's *Short-Title Catalogue, 1641–1700* (New York, 1945–51). The works immediately below were used in preparing more than one introduction. Titles listed in Part I are omitted.

Bancroft, Richard. *Daungerous Positions and Proceedings*. London, 1593.

Beesley, Alfred. *The History of Banbury*. London, ca. 1842.

Bradford, John. *Writings*, ed. Aubrey Townsend. Cambridge, 1848–1853. 2 vols.

Brook, Benjamin. *The Lives of the Puritans*. London, 1813. 3 vols.

Clarke, Samuel. *A Generall Martyrologie*. London, 1651.

_____. *The Marrow of Ecclesiastical History*. 3rd ed. London, 1675.

Cooper, Charles Henry and Thompson. *Athenae Cantabrigienses*. Cambridge, 1858–1861. 2 vols.

Daiches, David. *The King James Version of the Bible*. Chicago, 1941.

Davids, T. W. *Annals of Evangelical Nonconformity in the County of Essex*. London, 1863.

Foster, John. *Alumni Oxonienses, 1500–1714*. Oxford, 1891. 4 vols.

Fuller, Thomas. *The Worthies of England*, ed. John Freeman. London, 1952.

Hill, Christoper. *Puritanism and Revolution*. London, 1958.

Hooper, John. *Early Writings*, ed. Samuel Carr. Cambridge, 1843.

Kirby, Ethyn Williams. *William Prynne*. Cambridge, Mass., 1931.

Knappen, M. M. "Richard Greenham and the Practical Puritans under Queen Elizabeth." Unpublished Ph.D. dissertation, Cornell University, 1933.

Mullinger, J. Bass. *The University of Cambridge from . . . 1535 to the Accession of Charles I*. Cambridge, 1884.

Neale, Daniel. *History of the Puritans*. London, 1822. 5 vols.

A Parte of a Register. Middleburgh, 1593.

Peel, Albert, ed. *The Notebook of John Penry*. London, 1944.

——————————, ed. *The Second Parte of a Register*. Cambridge, 1915. 2 vols.

Peil, John. *Biographical Register of Christ's College*. Cambridge, 1910–1913. 2 vols.

Stephen, Leslie, and Sidney Lee. *The Dictionary of National Biography*. Oxford, 1917. 21 vols.

Strype, John. *Annals of the Reformation*. Oxford, 1820–24. 4 vols.

Venn, John and S. A. *Alumni Cantabrigienses*. Cambridge, 1922–27. 4 vols.

Wood, Anthony à. *Athenae Oxonienses*, ed. Philip Bliss. London, 1815. 4 vols.

John Bastwick

A Brief Relation of certain special and most material passages . . . at the censure of . . . Dr. Bastwick. N. p., 1637.

Rushworth, John. *Historical Collections*. London, 1721–22. 8 vols.

Thomas Cartwright

Dowden, John. *Outlines of the History of the Theological Literature of the Church of England*. London, 1897.

Geisendorf, Paul-F. *Théodore de Bèze*. Geneva, 1949.

Pearson, A. F. Scott. *Church & State: Political Aspects of Sixteenth-Century Puritanism*. Cambridge, 1928.

Peel, Albert, and L. H. Carlson, eds. *Cartwrightiana*. London, 1951.

Laurence Chaderton

Howell, Wilbur Samuel. *Logic and Rhetoric in England, 1500–1700*. Princeton, 1956.

Shuckburgh, E. S. *Laurence Chaderton, D.D., Translated from a Latin Memoir of Dr. Dillingham*. Cambridge, 1881.

Smith, G. Gregory, ed. *Elizabethan Critical Essays*. Oxford, 1904. 2 vols.

Arthur Dent

Kocher, Paul. *Science and Religion in Elizabethan England*. San Marino, 1953.

Wright, Louis B. *Middle Class Culture in Elizabethan England*. Chapel Hill, 1935.

Edward Dering

Bayley, John. *The History and Antiquities of the Tower of London*. 2nd ed. London, 1850.

Bell, Doyne C. *Notices of the Historic Persons Buried in the Chapel of St. Peter ad Vincula, in the Tower of London*. London, 1877.

Calendar of the Manuscripts . . . Preserved at Hatfield House. Historical Manuscripts Commission Report, Pt. 2. London, 1888.

Hume, Martin A. S. *The Great Lord Burghley*. London, 1898.

Murdin, William, ed. *A Collection of State Papers Relating to Affairs in the Reign of Queen Elizabeth*. London, 1759.

Pollen, John H. *The English Catholics in the Reign of Queen Elizabeth*. London, 1920.

Sandys, Edwin. *Sermons*, ed. John Ayre. Cambridge, 1841.

Thomas Gataker

Ashe, Simeon. *Grey Hayres Crowned with Grace*. London, 1655.

Echard, Laurence. *The History of England*. 3rd ed. London, 1720. 2 vols.

Frye, Roland M. "The Teachings of Classical Puritanism on Conjugal Love," *Studies in the Renaissance*, II (1955), 148–159.

Gataker, Thomas. *A Discourse Apologeticall*. London, 1654.

——————————. *Opera Critica*, ed. Herman Witsius. Utrecht, 1698.

Hallam, Henry. *Introduction to the Literature of Europe in the Fifteenth, Sixteenth, and Seventeenth Centuries*. London, 1882. 4 vols.

Haller, William and Malleville. "The Puritan Art of Love," *Huntington Library Quarterly*, V (1941), 235–272.

Hole, Christina. *The English Housewife in the Seventeenth Century*. London, 1953.

Reid, Thomas. *Memoirs of the Lives and Writings of Eminent Divines Who Convened in the Famous Assembly at Westminster*. Paisley, 1811–1815, 2 vols.

Spilsbury, William H. *Lincoln's Inn: Its Ancient and Modern Buildings*. London, 1850.

Anthony Gilby

A Brief Discourse of the Troubles Begun at Frankfort. London, 1846.

Collinson, Patrick. "The Authorship of *A Brieff Discourse off Trouble Begonne at Franckford,*" *Journal of Ecclesiastical History,* IX (1958), 188–208.

Garrett, Christina. *The Marian Exiles.* Cambridge, 1938.

Richard Greenham

Baxter, Richard. *A Christian Directory.* London, 1673.

"Richard Greenham," *Notes and Queries,* ser. 6, VII (1888), 366; ser. 6, VIII (1888), 55.

Samuel Hieron

Brushfield, T. N. *The Literature of Devonshire up to the Year 1640.* Privately printed, 1893.

Dredge, John I. "A Few Sheaves of Devon Bibliography," *Devonshire Association Transactions,* XXIV (1892), 476–526.

Harris, S. G. "Samuel Hieron: A Devonshire Vicar in the Reigns of Elizabeth and James I," *Devonshire Association Transactions,* XXIV (1892), 77–85.

Tawney, R. H. *Religion and the Rise of Capitalism.* London, 1948.

White, Helen C. *English Devotional Literature [Prose], 1600–1640.* University of Wisconsin Studies in Language and Literature. Madison, 1931.

Wilkins, John. *Ecclesiastes.* London, 1646.

Thomas Hooker

Archibald, Warren S. *Thomas Hooker.* New Haven, 1933.

Emerson, Everett H. "Thomas Hooker and the Reformed Theology." Unpublished Ph.D. dissertation, Louisiana State University, 1955.

––––––––––––. "Thomas Hooker: The Puritan as Theologian," *Anglican Theological Review,* XLIX (1967), 190–203.

Mather, Cotton. *Magnalia Christi Americana.* London, 1702.

Miller, Perry. "Thomas Hooker and the Democracy of Early Connecticut," *New England Quarterly,* IV (1931), 663–712.

Rossiter, Clinton. "Thomas Hooker," *New England Quarterly,* XXV (1952), 439–488.

Walker, George L. *Thomas Hooker.* New York, 1891.

John Hooper

Foxe, John. *Acts and Monuments,* ed. Josiah Pratt. London, 1870. 8 vols.

Gairdner, James. "Bishop Hooper's Visitation of Gloucester," *English Historical Review,* XIX (1904), 98–121.

Hooper, John. *Later Writings,* ed. Charles Nevinson. Cambridge, 1852.

Hughes, Philip. *The Reformation in England.* Vol 2. London, 1953.

Price, F. Douglas. "Gloucester Diocese under Bishop Hooper, 1551–3," *Transactions of the Bristol and Gloucestershire Archaeological Society,* LX (1938), 51–151.

Smyth, C. H. *Cranmer & the Reformation under Edward VI.* Cambridge, 1926.

Tytler, Patrick F. *England under the Reigns of Edward VI and Mary . . . Illustrated in a Series of Original Letters.* London, 1839. 2 vols.

West, W. Morris S. "John Hooper and the Origins of Puritanism," *Baptist Quarterly,* XV (1954), 346–368; XVI (1955), 22–46, 67–88.

John Milton

Barker, Arthur. *Milton and the Puritan Dilemma.* Toronto, 1942.

Darbishire, Helen, ed. *The Early Lives of Milton.* London, 1932.

Diekhoff, John S., ed. *Milton on Himself.* New York, 1939.

Haller, William. *Liberty and Reformation in the Puritan Revolution.* New York, 1955.

Hanford, James Holly. *John Milton, Englishman.* New York, 1949.

Hunter, William B. "Milton's Arianism Reconsidered," *Harvard Theological Review,* LII (1959), 9–35.

Milton, John. *Complete Prose Works,* ed. Don M. Wolfe. Vol. I. New Haven, 1953.

————————. *Of Reformation,* ed. E. H. Emerson, in *The Prose of John Milton,* ed. J. Max Patrick and others. New York, 1967.

————————. *The Complete English Poetry,* ed. John T. Shawcross. New York, 1963.

————————. *The Prose Works,* ed. J. A. St. John. London, 1909.

Saillens, Emile. *John Milton.* New York, 1964.

William Perkins

Baarsel, Jan Jacobus van. *William Perkins.* 's Gravenhage, 1912.

Bishop, William. *A Reformation of a Catholike Deformed: M. W. Perkins.* N.p., 1604.

Colville, Frederick L. *The Worthies of Warwickshire . . . 1500–1800.* Warwick, *ca.* 1870.

Fuller, Thomas. *The Holy State and the Profane State,* ed. M. G. Walten. New York, 1938. 2 vols.

Fuller, Thomas. *Abel Redivivus: or, The Dead Yet Speaking; The Lives and Deaths of the Moderne Divines.* London, 1651.

Heylyn, Peter. *Aerius Redivivus: or, The History of the Presbyterians.* Oxford, 1670.

Lupton, Donald, trans. *The History of the Moderne Protestant Divines.* London, 1637.

McNeill, John T. "Casuistry in the Puritan Age," *Religion in Life,* XII (1943), 76–89.

Peil, John. *Christ's College.* London, 1900.

Ritschl, Otto. *Die reformierte Theologie des 16. und 17. Jahrhunderts.* Vol. 3. Göttingen, 1926.

Sisson, Rosemary. "William Perkins, Apologist for the Elizabethan Church of England," *Modern Language Review,* XLVII (1952), 495–502.

Wood, Thomas. *English Casuistical Divinity in the Seventeenth Century.* London, 1952.

Wright, Louis B. "William Perkins: Elizabethan Apostle of 'Practical Divinity'," *Huntington Library Quarterly,* III (1940), 171–196.

John Preston

Ball, Thomas. *The Life of . . . Preston,* ed. E. W. Harcourt. London, 1885.

Maclear, James Fulton. "Puritan Relations with Buckingham," *Huntington Library Quarterly,* XXI (1958), 111–132.

Morgan, Irvonwy. *Prince Charles's Puritan Chaplain.* London, 1957.

Henry Smith

Lievsay, John L. " 'Silver-tongued Smith,' Paragon of Elizabethan Preachers," *Huntington Library Quarterly,* XI (1947/48), 13–36.

Mallet, Charles E. *A History of the University of Oxford.* Vol. I. London, 1924.

Nashe, Thomas. *Pierce Penilesse, His Supplication to the Devil (1592),* ed. G. B. Harrison. London, 1924.

Simpson, W. Sparrow. *Chapters in the History of Old S. Paul's.* London, 1881.

Smith, Henry. *Works,* ed. Thomas Smith. Edinburgh, 1866, 1867. 2 vols.

Strype, John. *Historical Collections of the Life and Acts of John Aylmer.* Oxford, 1821.

White, Helen C. *Social Criticism in Popular Religious Literature in the Sixteenth Century.* New York, 1944.

Richard Stock

Fletcher, Harris F. *The Intellectual Development of John Milton.* Vol. I. Urbana, Ill., 1958.

Gataker, Thomas. *Abrahams Decease . . . Delivered at the Funeral of . . . Richard Stock.* London, 1627.

Masson, David. *The Life of John Milton.* Vol. I. Cambridge, 1859.

Job Throckmorton

Bonnard, G. *La Controverse de Martin Marprelate, 1588–1590*. Geneva, 1916.

Coolidge, John S. "Martin Marprelate, Marvell, and *Decorum Personnae* as a Satirical Theme," *PMLA*, LXXIV (1959), 526–532.

Holden, William P. *Anti-Puritan Satire, 1572–1642*. New Haven, 1954.

Kemp, Thomas, ed. *The Black Book of Warwick*. Warwick, 1898.

McGinn, Donald J. *John Penry and the Marprelate Controversy*. New Brunswick, New Jersey, 1966.

Pierce, William. *An Historical Introduction to the Marprelate Tracts*. London, 1908.

—————————. *John Penry*. London, 1923.

—————————, ed. *The Marprelate Tracts, 1588, 1589*. London, 1911.

Salzman, L. F., ed. *The Victoria History of the County of Warwick*. Vol. II. London, 1945.

"A Short Confference between Mr. Dod and Mr. Throgmorton, upon his death bed, comfortable for all poore afflicted soules." Unpublished MS, Folger Shakespeare Library.

Sutcliffe, Matthew. *An Answer Unto M. Iob Throckmorton*. London, 1595.

Sutherland, James. *English Satire*. Cambridge, 1958.

Wilson, J. Dover. "The Marprelate Controversy," *Cambridge History of English Literature*, ed. A. W. Ward and A. R. Waller. Vol. III. 1908.

Walter Travers

Hooker, Richard. *The Answer . . . to a Supplication*. Oxford, 1612.

Knox, S. J. *Walter Travers: Paragon of Elizabethan Puritanism*. London, 1962.

Maxwell, Constantia. *A History of Trinity College, Dublin, 1591–1892*. Dublin, 1946.

Sisson, C. J. *The Judicious Marriage of Mr. Hooker and the Birth of the "Laws of Ecclesiastical Polity."* Cambridge, 1940.

Urwick, William. *The Early History of Trinity College, Dublin, 1591–1660*. London, 1892.

Walton, Isaac. "The Life of Mr. Richard Hooker," in *The Works of . . . Hooker*. Vol. 1. Oxford, 1850.

John Udall

Arber, Edward, ed. *"The Epistle" by Martin Marprelate*. London, 1880.

—————————. *An Introductory Sketch to the Martin Marprelate Controversy, 1588–1590*. London, 1879.

Calderwood, David. *The History of the Kirk of Scotland*, ed. Thomas

Thomson. Edinburgh, 1844. 8 vols.

Emerson, Everett H. "John Udall and the Puritan Sermon," *Quarterly Journal of Speech*, XLIV (1958), 282–284.

Howell, Thomas B., ed. *Corbett's Complete Collection of State Trials*. Vol. I. London, 1816.

Le Neve, John. *Fasti Ecclesiae Anglicanae*, ed. T. D. Hardy. Oxford, 1854. 3 vols.

Luders, A., T. D. Tomlins, et al., eds. *The Statutes of the Realm*. London, 1810–1828. 11 vols.

Mullett, Charles F. *The Bubonic Plague and England*. Lexington, Ky., 1956.

A New Discovery of Old Pontificall Practices . . . Evinced by their Tyrannicall Persecution of . . . Mr. John Udall. London, 1643.

Udall, John. *The State of the Church of England*, ed. Edward Arber. London, 1879.

————. *A Demonstration of . . . Discipline . . .*, ed. Edward Arber. London, 1888.

William Whately

Fripp, Edgar I. *Shakespeare, Man and Artist*. London, 1938. 2 vols.

Laud, William. *The History of the Troubles and Triall of William Laud*. London, 1695.

Salzman, L. F. *The Victoria History of the County of . . . Warwick*. Vol. III. London, 1945.

Scudder, Henry. "Life of William Whately," in William Whately, *Prototypes*. London, 1640.

Worthington, John. "Life of Mede," in Joseph Mede, *Works*. 4th ed. London, 1677.

Index

Note: main entries are in italic type; these are not analyzed. Selections are indicated by bold-face type.

Abbott, George, archbishop: successor to Bancroft, 34; lax administrator, 39; a conservative, 42

Acts of Supremacy and Uniformity, 10

Adam and Eve, Whately's view of, 262–278

Admonition controversy, 16–18; Whitgift's role, 67; Gilby's possible role, 94–95

Advertisements, Parker's, 12–13

Alvey, Richard, 80–81

Ames, William: High Calvinist, 37; on sermon form, 45; a Ramist, 102; student of Perkins, 155; a casuist, 157; association with Hooker, 219–220

Andrews, Lancelot, bishop, 202; developer of school of piety, 25; preacher and liberal, 27; interests of his school, 35; elaborate sermon style, 45; enemy of Preston, 238

Aristotle, 57, 103, 237

Arminianism: development of, 37–38; opposed by Prynne, 42; taught by Montague, 241–242

Arundel, Thomas, 47

Articles of 1583, 22

Aylmer, John, bishop: forced to accept Charke, 21; issued warrant for Cartwright's arrest, 70

Bale, John, 4

Ball, John, 236

Bancroft, Richard, bishop and archbishop, 30–33, 219; pluralist, 19; exposed presbyterianism, 25, 84, 158; at Hampton Court Conference, 29; opponent of Puritans, 34; friend of Chaderton, 103; effective administrator, 181

Baptism, 122; sign of the cross in, 9, 10, 28, 179; private, 17, 30; by midwives, 20; Greenham's teachings on, 146

Barrett, William: questioned predestination, 27, 35

Barrow, Henry, 25

Bastwick, John, *251–254;* pilloried, 42; witty style, 283; **255–258**

Baxter, Richard: recommended Greenham's works, 147; a casuist, 157

Bayly, Lewis, 179

Baynes, Paul, viii

Beza, Theodore, 168; Cartwright's admirer, 66; friend of Travers, 79

Bilney, Thomas, 3, 4, 93

Bilson, Thomas, bishop, 29

Bishops' Wars, 43

Blench, J. W., 46

Bois, John, 199

Book of Common Prayer: first and second, 5, 7; Genevan, 6, 134; Elizabethan, 7, 25; rubrics of, 14; discussed at Hampton Court Conference, 29–30; subscription to, 22, 23, 32, 68; used by Cartwright, 71; not used at Antwerp, 80; opposed by Gilby at Frankfort, 93; not used at Emmanuel College, 103; suspension for failure to use, 119, 122; Hieron's approval of, 179; not used by lecturers, 220

Book of Discipline: subscribed to by Cartwright, 70, 71; edited by Travers, 79, 83, 85

Book of Sports, 35

Bourgeois values, vii; identified with Puritanism in early seventeenth century, 33, 35; defended by Prynne, 42; defended by Perkins, 157; in Gataker's sermons, 200–201

Bownd, Nicholas, 26–27, 147

Bradford, John, 144

Bradshaw, William: defender of congregationalism, 32; friend of Gataker, 199; subject of biography by Gataker, 200

Bridges, John: author of *Defense,* 83; replied to Fulke, 134; attacked by Martin Marprelate, 134–135, 142–143; commended by bishops for book, 137–138

Browne, Robert: separatist, 70; studied with Greenham, 144

Bucer, Martin: taught at Cambridge, 4; objected to vestments, 5; opposed Hooper on vestments, 49; author, 87, 159